5/2000

Race in the
Mind of America

Race in the Mind of America

Breaking the Vicious Circle between Blacks and Whites

Paul L. Wachtel

Routledge
New York and London

Published in 1999 by
Routledge
29 West 35th Street
New York, NY 10001

Published in Great Britain by Routledge
11 New Fetter Lane
London EC4P 4EE

Printed in the United States of America on acid-free paper.

10 9 8 7 6 5 4 3 2 1

Library of Congress Cataloging-in-Publication Data
Wachtel, Paul L., 1940–
Race in the mind of America : breaking the vicious circle between
Blacks and Whites / by Paul Wachtel.
p.   cm.
ISBN 0-415-92000-0.
1. Racism—United States—Psychological aspects. 2. United
States—Race relations—Psychological aspects. I. Title.
E185.615.W25   1999
305.8'00973—dc21   98-25715
                      CIP

Contents

Part Three
The Seamless Web of Problems and Solutions

Preface

The deeper currents of our thoughts and feelings often reveal themselves in unexpected ways. This book draws on a very wide range of sources to explore the psychological underpinnings of our continuing racial divisions—interviews, casual conversations, newspaper accounts, opinion surveys, psychological experiments, psychoanalytic inquiry, explorations of historical debates and policy disputes, interpretations of public and private rhetoric. But perhaps the most striking observation accrued almost by accident, in the course of responding, hundreds of times over the five or six years of working on this book, to the seemingly innocent question, "What are you working on these days?"

In many ways, the conversations in which this question arose varied enormously. But they had one striking thing in common. Virtually every person, black or white, who heard what I was working on said some version of, *"You're very courageous to be writing such a book."*

This extraordinary consistency tells us something of crucial importance about the underlying feelings and attitudes about race in America that is not captured by polls, surveys, or statistics. Several recent influential books have emphasized how far we have come in race relations. They point both to a substantial narrowing of the gap between blacks and whites in income, education, and the like over the last few decades and to polling data that suggest that attitudes have softened and even that interracial friendships are becoming more and more common. These findings are heartening, and they do represent one facet—indeed, an important facet—of our complex social reality. But what does it tell us about the deeper reaches of our experience of race and about the possibility of genuine dialogue when (in spontaneous utterances rather than in considered responses to formal surveys) it is so consistently viewed as requiring "courage" to speak one's mind about the topic?

It is my aim in this book to understand the foundations of this anxiety and discomfort, to explore how we perpetuate these feelings, and to consider the prospects for transcending them. I am writing about race relations from a relatively unusual vantage point. I am a psychologist, a specialist in the dynamics of individual personality and in the factors that promote or impede change in troubling life patterns. The problem of race in America is a problem of a different scale. It is usually addressed from the vantage point of history, sociology, economics, or other disciplines more inclined toward the study of groups and social forces than of individuals.

There is, however, no contradiction or disjunction in my psychological emphasis. The psychological perspective I employ is one in which the social and historical contexts for our actions are considered far more than in the kinds of psychology with which many readers may be familiar. In an earlier book, *The Poverty of Affluence*, I undertook a psychological analysis of the consumer way of life and of the unacknowledged psychological side effects of economic growth. In that analysis, I similarly applied a psychological perspective to matters usually considered from an economic or sociological vantage point. There as here, my aim was to illuminate large-scale social forces by illuminating the conflicted experiences of individual human beings, and simultaneously to further the understanding of individual experience by placing it in a larger context.

Attempts to bring psychological perspectives to bear on the analysis of social issues often end up being highly reductionistic. Attitudes and behaviors that are products of an enormously complex mix that includes economic interests, class attitudes, religious beliefs, and ethnic, national, and occupational identities are reduced to the impact of early experiences with mother or to responses on an inventory of personality or attitudes. In the account presented here, psychoanalytic concepts will certainly figure prominently, as will insights from other areas of psychological research. But it will be apparent that the psychological formulations are complementary to, and indeed only have meaning within, an understanding of the larger social and historical context. It is a naive and simplistic psychology that divorces itself from the play of large-scale social and historical influences.

But if psychological interpretations must not dominate or ignore more socially and historically oriented analyses, neither must they be subordinated to such analyses. The forces that shape our attitudes and actions in the social arena operate not only in events and institutions of large social and historical sweep, but also in the nitty-gritty details of everyday living. It is in large measure the experiences and interactions of concrete individuals that are the point of activation of the larger social forces, and that in turn feed back to maintain or to change those forces. Attention to the details of these countless individual transactions is not a retreat to atomistic individualism but rather a perspective which highlights the "glue" that holds together the complex structure of social, economic, and political forces that are the context for our lives.

The ways we select and organize the countless impressions that impinge upon our senses; the ways we distort or hold rigidly to a view in order to ward off anxiety or maintain our self-esteem; the attachments and identifications that can lead us, often without awareness, to act against our immediate material interests in pursuit of deeper, if unrecognized, yearnings—these and other psychological processes must be understood and their implications plumbed if we are to make progress in overcoming the attitudes and ingrained patterns that divide us.

What most distinguishes the approach I take here is its grounding in an elaborated theory of the role of vicious circles in human predicaments, and in years of studying the configurations and dynamics of such circles. I have been repeatedly struck by the regularity with which people's psychological difficulties take the form of patterns in which the very efforts we make to feel better or change a troubling feature of our lives end up *preventing* change and *perpetuating* our misery. Much of my work as a psychologist has centered on charting and articulating these patterns and examining the possibilities for extricating ourselves from them.

A great many people offered assistance of various sorts in the course of my work on this book. Early in my efforts at formulating the ideas expressed here, I met with the minority student group in our clinical psychology Ph.D. program to share my thoughts with them and get their feedback. That meeting was extremely valuable to me, and further exchanges with several students in the group—especially Norma Cofresi, Rob Jones, Debbie Kennedy, and David Rodriguez—helped sharpen my thinking and facilitated my understanding of what it is like to be the object of racism.

Debbie Kennedy and Adette Williams assisted me in running interracial dialogue groups that helped to stimulate and clarify many of the ideas in this book. Darryl Henderson several times co-taught with me a course on the psychology of racial and ethnic stereotypes that was a similar source of ideas and examples for this book. The course included a good deal of students' exploring their own experiences, conflicts, and anxieties and examining each others' stereotypes of the different ethnic groups in the class. Darryl contributed creatively to that endeavor and introduced a number of experiential exercises that facilitated and deepened the exploration.

Several students served as research assistants at various points in the work. I wish to thank Shari Davis, Justine Fitzgerald, and Julia Weston for their help in gathering needed materials and information. Lee Peterson offered particularly needed assistance at a crucial culminating point in the work, as well as a friendship that I continue to value.

Two individuals played a particularly prominent role in helping to make this project a success. In the early stages of the work, Diane Ungar served as much more than just a research assistant. Diane not only gathered materials, offered ideas, and carefully read some of the early chapters, but her enthusiasm and insights were important in sustaining the effort through the formative stages of the work. After Diane left City College to attend a doctoral program elsewhere, Annette DeMichele began working with me on the project and quickly became indispensible. Annette had an almost uncanny understanding both of the ideas I was groping toward expressing and of my style of writing. She read virtually every draft of every chapter, offering feedback so tuned-in to the rhythms of my prose and so perceptive and trenchant that it felt like she had an EEG machine directly hooked up to the idea and articulation centers of my brain.

A number of friends and colleagues provided valuable and much needed feedback on various chapters. I am very grateful in this regard to Elisha Fisch, A. J. Franklin, Charles Gerson, Mary Joan Gerson, Cynthia Grace, Rob Jones, Steve Rosenheck, David Rudenstine, Seymour Sarason, Marcia Sheinberg, Myron Sheinberg, Zina Steinberg, and Robin Waite.

My agent, Jill Grinberg, offered warm encouragement and support that were much appreciated. My editor at Routledge, Heidi Freund, combined a friendly smile and a tough-minded sense of what the book needed that helped me to make the book more keenly focused.

Finally, my wife, Ellen, was there for me in so many ways I can scarcely enumerate them. In acknowledgement sections of my previous books, I have referred to her contagious zest for living that kept me from being one more author who had to apologize to his family for absenting himself; Ellen ensured that I would enjoy her and my family too much to lock myself up obsessively in my study. Perhaps because our children are now grown and out of the house, perhaps because this has been a particularly difficult and complex project, this time around I *have* found myself working nights and weekends more often than I would like, so I finally do have occasion to thank her not only for keeping life fun (which she has continued to do) but for tolerating my being more preoccupied and absent than usual. Now that this book is finished, I am looking forward to getting back out of my study and resuming my natural rhythms, of which she is such a central part.

1

Introduction

The Ironic Dynamics of Race

Blacks and whites in America are partners in a complex and fateful dance. It is a dance that can boast little grace and brings little pleasure, but it is performed with such perverse and practiced regularity that it is, by now, almost impossible to say who leads and who follows. Mostly without awareness, we each issue the cues that lead our partners across the racial divide to perform their roles and in turn to transmit to us the cues that again elicit ours. In reproducing the same tragic *pas de deux* over and over, we are caught in a vicious circle of vast proportions. A crucial element in that circle is our very failure to recognize that it *is* a circle, that we are *all* implicated in perpetuating it.

The visions that blacks and whites hold of each other are befogged with stereotypes, and the explanations offered for the persisting inequalities and racial tensions that plague us are soaked in "either-or" and "us-them" thinking. In one prevalent view, we are a racist society in which African Americans are systematically prevented from succeeding and even those who seemingly have made it continue to encounter prejudice, suspicion, and a host of obstacles to their full and free participation in the life of our society. In another, that first view is seen as an "excuse," as a crippling attitude that prevents African Americans from taking advantage of the many opportunities that have become available in recent decades. In this view, it is largely their own behavior and attitudes that now prevent blacks from advancing as successive waves of poor and disadvantaged immigrant groups have done throughout our history.

To be sure, there are moderate and nuanced versions of both positions, which at least potentially open the door to greater understanding and cooperation. Many who see continuing racism as the chief obstacle to black advancement do acknowledge the progress we have made in recent decades. They dissent from those who view our society as "irredeemably" racist and who can see whites only as oppressors, but nonetheless feel a barely contained rage at what they experience as almost daily affronts to their dignity and at the inability of most whites to appreciate their pain or acknowledge the degree to which racism, in subtle and not so subtle forms, persists in our society.

Correspondingly, many who take the position that blacks' own behavior and attitudes are now the chief obstacle to their advancement acknowledge that racism and discrimination have been facts of life for most of the history of this country and even that racism endures in a variety of forms today. Unlike those who, in a harsher and more benighted variant of their position, characterize blacks and other minorities as simply lazy, complaining, or lacking in responsibility or other so-called middle-class virtues, they recognize the difficulties blacks still face. At the same time, they feel great frustration and irritation at what they experience as an enormous hypersensitivity by blacks that perceives slights where none are intended, as well as a readiness to blame virtually every failure or frustration they encounter on racism. White holders of this view, moreover, resent the resentment that *they* encounter, the ready assumption that they are oppressors and blacks are victims.

There are, of course, still other understandings of the unequal status of blacks and whites that do not fit readily into either of the two broad positions I have described, even in their more subtle or moderate versions. Moreover, counter to stereotype, there are whites who hold to the view that our society is fundamentally racist and blacks who believe that excessive claims of racism are being used as a crippling excuse. But by and large, with many variations, these two broad perspectives capture a vast portion of the political and moral landscape in our country, and they do largely tend to correlate with the race of the perceiver. The stark truth is that to a great degree blacks and whites in America see *each other* as the problem, and blame each other for the tensions and divisions that so stubbornly persist.

In this book I aim to offer an alternative to this dead-end approach. Examining in detail how blacks and whites have responded to each other and to the inequalities that continue to divide us, I will show how the vicious circles in which we are caught have emerged and tightened—and what is required for us to begin to extricate ourselves from them.

My analysis draws very largely on psychological research and theory and on my experience as a practicing psychotherapist, researcher, and teacher and supervisor of doctoral students in clinical psychology. Based on this experience and perspective, the book highlights aspects of our dilemma that are largely absent from the sociological and political accounts that are more common in this area. I am centrally concerned with the ways people's interpretations of events are mediated by residues of earlier experiences and by the need to protect self-esteem; with the selective perceptions, misperceptions, and self-deceptions that arise as a consequence; with issues of identity and threats to identity; with the deeper sources of rage, guilt, prejudice, and self-doubt and with their parallel roots in everyday experience; with the pervasive role of conflict in our psychological makeup and with the ways in which blacks and whites alike tend to *overlook* that conflict (in themselves and in the other) in the polarized and simplifying rhetoric that presently dominates our discourse on race.

Put differently, I am concerned with how we have constructed our worldviews about race, how the world *looks* to us and how we *feel* about the events we experience or hear about on the nightly news. A key element in breaking the entangling patterns I will examine in this book lies in reconstructing our dialogue, changing the ways we think about our problems and each other and the ways we talk to each other. Our dialogue—such as it has been—has been accusatory and linear: *Who is the cause of our problems? You are.* I aim to point us toward a different kind of discourse, one that recognizes the circularity of our problems and frames our task as extricating ourselves from an impasse to which all sides have by now contributed.

I am not, however, attempting to offer myself as a "therapist" to our troubled society. I am, after all, one of the patients in the asylum. An important thread in contemporary social criticism involves critique of the overly "therapeutic" orientation of our society and the naively reductionistic nature of psychological analyses of social issues. Although psychological understanding is central to what I believe is fresh and useful about the analysis offered here, I hope it will be apparent that the psychology that grounds this analysis is not a psychology divorced from the realities of race, class, history, or politics. Psychological accounts that ignore the powerful impact of large-scale social forces are not only needlessly chauvinistic; they are poor psychology.

I will draw upon psychoanalytic insights in my account, as well as on research in social, cognitive, and developmental psychology. But the reader will not find our complex social reality reduced to Oedipal preoccupations, anal complexes, or responses to personality inventories. Most centrally, I will emphasize four closely related themes throughout the book:

- First, the ubiquitous and largely unappreciated role of vicious circles in our racial impasse.
- Second, the critical role played in those circles by the impact of years of injustice on African Americans' confidence, attitudes, and opportunities to develop educational and occupational skills, and the difficulties both blacks and whites have had in finding constructive ways to acknowledge and address that impact.
- Third, the ways in which defensive operations by both whites and blacks, arising from the need to ward off guilt, shame, or other threatening feelings, have made it difficult for us to recognize the roles we reciprocally play in maintaining these circular patterns and have impeded our efforts to come to grips with the complex sources of our persisting inequalities.
- Fourth, the *ironic* nature of much of what we confront, the ways in which our difficulties are marked by unwittingly self-fulfilling prophecies and by efforts to prevent or ward off untoward developments and experiences that end up bringing about precisely the consequence we hope to avert.

There are concrete policy recommendations that flow from the account I offer in this book, and some of them are spelled out in Part Three. But the primary focus of the analysis offered here is to explicate the substructures of thought and feeling that have silently shaped the way we have approached our racial divisions thus far and to point us toward an understanding that can elicit more creative and effective initiatives in the future.

Moving beyond Deadlock: Understanding the Tangle in Which We Are Caught

The first step in developing a more productive approach to the gulf that exists between us is to recognize that we will not overcome our difficulties by the victory of one side's views over the other. Neither side is going to convince the other that they are wrong or that their perceptions are invalid. Rather, we must begin by understanding how the world looks through each lens and by acknowledging the core elements of validity in each view.

Such an effort to understand the experiential basis of each side's position should not be confused with a bland ecumenicism, a shallow avoidance of conflict by piously declaring that each side's views must be respected. *Of course*, no one group of people is likely to hold a monopoly on truth or insight; but such a platitude, no matter how widely acknowledged, is likely to have little impact on the attitudes that really direct people's behavior and organize their lives. Rather, what we require is a *dynamic* understanding of why these differing views continue to be compelling to different segments of our society. That dynamic understanding, I believe, can be achieved by attending to the pervasive influence of vicious circles in human affairs. The opposing views about our racial impasse described at the beginning of this chapter are part of a larger pattern in which, in countless ways, blacks and whites seem to "confirm" each other's fears and resentments—and in which each side is largely oblivious to its role in the perpetuation of the pattern and sees our persisting difficulties preponderantly in terms of the actions of the other.

I have spent most of my professional life studying such patterns and how to break them. In exploring the many ways in which vicious circles operate to perpetuate human misery, I have been struck not only by how regularly these ironic patterns can be discerned by the attentive observer, but also by how difficult it can be for those caught in the circle to appreciate its structure. The general idea of the vicious circle is a regular part of our vocabulary, but it is rare for the participants in such a circle to really see and understand what they are caught in.

The tendency to fix blame seems quite regularly to lead us to be satisfied with partial explanations that offer some cathartic relief but contribute little to real resolution of our difficulties. In attempting to apply the analysis of vicious circles to the persisting tensions between the races in our country, I hope to provide a point of departure for transcending the adversarial accounts that are themselves a part of the problem they seek to explain.

Vicious Circles in the Psychological Dynamics of Individuals

Vicious circles operate in many ways and at many levels in human affairs, but they are often insufficiently appreciated, even by professional students of human behavior. The problematic patterns that bring people to psychotherapists, for example, are often attributed to very early experiences, which are repressed and then exert a continuing influence on adult life as an unassimilated piece of childhood buried in the psyche. Early in the history of psychoanalysis, these hypothesized fragments from childhood were understood as repressed memories of actual traumatic events, later as unacceptable wishes or fantasies, and now frequently as "primitive" or "archaic" images of the self in relation to fantasized others.[1] But the basic explanatory structure at all three stages is very similar. Something from childhood is directly preserved, and exerts a continuing influence of the past upon the present.[2]

In contrast, a vicious circle account of how early experiences shape our later life points to a myriad of daily events that, in an almost infinite series of actions and reactions, keep aspects of our thoughts or behavior looking much the same as they did when we were small. In such accounts, it is not really the original experience or psychic formation that causes today's problems, but its heirs; and it is not the *direct* impact of the early experience that is crucial but the ironic *further* reactions that are likely to follow.[3]

Thus, if a child learns rather early that expressions of anger or disagreement are dangerous or unacceptable, she may repress the anger and institute a "reaction-formation," an exaggerated opposite attitude that keeps the threatening anger far from consciousness. Years later, her dreams, fantasies, and occasionally anomalous behav-

ior may reveal that behind her unusually meek and overly cooperative behavior lies a struggle with anger so intense and unmodulated
that it can seem to merit the labels "primitive" or "infantile." But the
anger against which she struggles is *not* anger from childhood. It is
anger that is, ironically, generated by the very efforts she makes to
ban anger altogether from her experience.

This happens because her fear of anger or of being seen as taking advantage of others leads her to be *excessively* nice, to the point
where she fails to get her fair share in interactions. She is so agree-
able that what *she* wants is continually shunted aside, and the result
ultimately is considerable frustration and smoldering resentment.
But since angry feelings are unacceptable to her, this new anger
must *also* be buried, and so still further defensive behavior is necessary. In turn, these new efforts to be so nice that nothing angry
shows lead to still further frustrations and still further buildup of
anger. In effect, the anger is generated by the very effort to defend
against it, and the anger defended against today is the product of
trying to ward off the anger similarly generated yesterday.

One may represent such a circular pattern visually as follows:

There are, of course, many further complexities in the process
that maintains the person's fear of anger and the continual fueling
of anger that ironically results.[4] But in their basic outline, such circular patterns may be seen with regard to the entire range of feelings and motivations that human beings can experience. They may
arise as well in the ways that African Americans attempt to cope

with the stress of pervasive stereotyping.[5] The impact of stereotyping and myths about intellectual inferiority can lead to withdrawal from intellectual pursuits, which in turn leads to failure to develop the skills that would contradict the stereotype. Here again, we may represent that circular pattern graphically:

Vicious Circles on the Interpersonal Level: The Question of "Punctuation"

A second type of vicious circle occurs in the interactions between two or more individuals. Consider, for example, a frequently observed relationship pattern in which, to use a terminology common among couples therapists, one participant is a "pursuer" and one is a "distancer."* The pursuer keeps trying to pull a response from the distancer, keeps inquiring into what he is feeling or complaining that he is too unrelated and uninvolved. From her point of view she does so *because* he is so distant; if only he would be a bit more forthcoming, she would forebear. But from the distancer's experience, he holds back to preserve his privacy and integrity from the relentless intrusiveness of the pursuer; he would be more communicative and emotionally available if only she would be a bit less

---

* In the illustration I am offering here, the pursuer is female and the distancer is male. Such a pattern can, of course, be reversed in gender, with the man as the pursuer and the woman as the distancer, and it can also be apparent in relationships between people of the same sex. It is most often reported, however, in the form depicted here.

engulfing and demanding. From the viewpoint of the vicious circle, it is most of all the pattern *between* them that is at issue. The question of who "really" is responsible for the pattern is fruitless. What must be understood is the circle itself, how each brings out in the other precisely the behavior he or she wishes would stop.

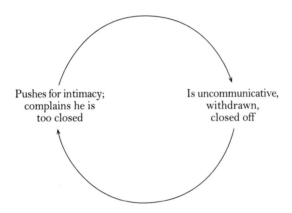

Pushes for intimacy; complains he is too closed

Is uncommunicative, withdrawn, closed off

After such circular patterns have operated for any period of time, it becomes almost impossible to establish where the sequence begins and where it ends. The pattern has taken on a life of its own, and one can as readily take the pursuer's behavior or the distancer's as the starting point for analysis. Each is likely to contend that his or her behavior is a reaction to the provocation of the other's behavior, and the vying to establish where the sequence begins and where it ends constitutes much of the struggle in which the pair is engaged. Family therapists refer to the question of where the pattern started as one of "punctuation."

In grammar, punctuation is used to indicate where a sequence begins and ends. A capital letter, for example, may indicate a beginning and a period an end. In the metaphorical extension of the concept to the analysis of circular patterns between people, much the same is implied: *What is the starting point for the sequence and what is the end?* Punctuation of interpersonal sequences tends to be rather subjective and arbitrary; each participant implicitly punctuates the sequence in a way that justifies his or her own behavior, usually by viewing the sequence as having begun with the offensive behavior of the other.

Vicious Circles in the Sphere of Race:
The Question of Responsibility

Something similar happens in the vicious circles that constitute the interactions between blacks and whites in our society. Here too, both sides tend to hold to a linear view in which they are simply reacting to the behavior or perceived provocation of the other. Yet here too, as I will show throughout this book, the pattern has taken on a life of its own, such that the punctuation of the sequence is by now often arbitrary and self-justifying and serves to obscure the active role of the party doing the punctuating.

The question may arise, however, whether an account that emphasizes vicious circles, by showing how *both* sides contribute to the impasse, obscures crucial differences between the roles of whites and blacks. Do history and moral accountability melt away in a specious crucible in which all bear equal responsibility?

It is thus important to remind ourselves that when it comes to the pattern between blacks and whites in America, there is a stark and clear starting point: blacks were brought here in chains and enslaved. Virtually all of the patterns described in this book, including those in which the pattern has by now indeed assumed a life of its own, can be traced back to an actual origin in which there were unambiguously innocent and guilty parties. I do agree strongly that whites living today cannot be held responsible for the events of prior centuries; the concept of collective responsibility, especially collective racial responsibility for sins committed before one was born, has been the source of some of the most terrible atrocities in human history and cannot be the foundation for constructing a more just society. Nonetheless, in applying the analysis of vicious circles to our contemporary racial difficulties, we will not get far unless we acknowledge that *these* circles virtually reek of their origins.

Slavery, moreover, is not the only brutally direct point of origin for the circular patterns in which contemporary race relations are ensnared. Officially sanctioned segregation in a huge swath of Southern states is an obvious further example. But equally causal, and often scarcely less disguised, was a degree of discrimination throughout the entire nation that made it virtually impossible for blacks to enter society's mainstream. More subtle, but a powerful source nonetheless of the painfully impacted circumstances we face today, was the way in which the accelerating European immigration that coincided with the decades after the abolition of slavery created a need in new Americans to distinguish sharply and invidiously between blacks and whites. Even the lowliest European immigrant, though often despised and mistreated by other whites whose families had been here longer, could experience at least a modicum of status simply by virtue of having white skin in a society that had reserved its lowest depths for those of a different hue. As the eminent black psychologist Kenneth Clark put it, "the blacks were always there: down below. . . . Being white in America made [immigrants and lower class whites] feel equal to all other whites, *as long as the black man was down below*."[6]

Finally, from a more contemporary vantage point, there is still another asymmetry of responsibility, notwithstanding the circular nature of the patterns we confront. This asymmetry is particularly crucial to understand, both because it provides a potential point of leverage for change and because it is so readily swept under the rug. I have said that whites living today are not responsible for what was done to blacks by their forebears. But that does not mean that whites do not bear a special responsibility for the conditions that exist today. It is primarily whites who control the purse strings and the political levers that make our society run. A president is expected to take responsibility for what happens "on his watch," even for decisions not made directly by him but by those to whom he has delegated authority. By virtue of numbers and wealth, it is white America's "watch," and white America must accept the commensurate responsibility.

Stereotypes and Their Parasitic Connection to Reality

There has existed for some time a highly problematic social compact in which people of good will have been constrained in discussing the behavior and attitudes of those who have been disadvantaged in our society for fear of being accused of "blaming the victim." As a consequence, understanding of how the disadvantaged's own behavior contributes to the circles in which they are caught has been hampered, and the vacuum has been filled by those whose inclination truly is to blame. In some simplistic accounts of our contemporary racial impasse, such as Dinesh D'Souza's *The End of Racism,*[7] the part of the process that includes African Americans' own behavior becomes virtually the entire story, and discrimination against blacks is portrayed as "rational." The injustices that generated, *and still maintain,* the problematic behaviors are blithely swept aside.

It will be readily apparent to the reader that my views are radically different from D'Souza's. If we are to ground our efforts at change in a full and realistic assessment of the difficulties we confront, and yet do so without becoming complicitous in the mentality of blame, we will need both frankness and empathy. On the one hand, we must be prepared to acknowledge that fears of black street criminals or perceptions of high rates of teenage pregancy and welfare dependency among blacks have some foundation in fact. Such behaviors *are* in fact disproportionately evident among the black residents of our inner cities[8], and while it is crucial that we understand the *reasons* why this is the case, it is a grave error simply to dismiss white reactions to these behaviors as racist. As selective and complexly motivated as those white reactions might be, and however much they too are a crucial part of the vicious circle in which we are caught, they are also reactions to a reality. They are likely to diminish if that reality diminishes or to persist to the degree that it persists.

However, if achieving greater progress toward solution of our social problems requires that we feel freer to acknowledge the harsh and troubling realities of inner-city life, this brings with it a greater responsibility to be clear about the stereotypic ways of perceiving that channel and distort our judgments. Stereotypes tend to be maintained not by completely ignoring reality or making something up out of whole cloth, but by forms of selective perception that fixate on partial truths in such a way that the fuller truth is obscured. The capacity to hold together in consciousness elements of reality that are in tension with one another—and to recognize when, despite the superficial appearance of contradiction, they are in fact different facets of a more complex and encompassing truth—is among the most priceless components of intelligence. The adversarial mindset that so pervasively characterizes both blacks' and whites' discussions of racial issues tends to sacrifice this more subtle and capacious intelligence for the narrower aim of attempting to win an argument by compiling and organizing the evidence tendentiously.

Mastering our troubles requires more of us. It requires us to transcend the simple antinomies of "black" or "white" perspectives, of liberal or conservative viewpoints, and to address instead the variegated reality that confounds the seductively single-minded truths of those who prefer debate to dialogue and advocacy to analysis. We must be able, for example, to acknowledge the substantially higher rates of street crime among blacks[9] *and* to be clear that the large majority of blacks are *not* criminals but hardworking (and, all too often, underpaid) taxpayers and citizens. Similarly, although attempts to distract us from the overrepresentation of blacks on welfare by citing the fact that millions of welfare clients are white are specious—more whites are on welfare because there are so many more whites in the country, but the rate of participation in programs like Aid to Families with Dependent Children (AFDC) is almost *five times higher* for blacks than for whites[10]—what is crucial is that we see clearly *both* that blacks are overrepresented in these categories *and* that crime or welfare dependency are by no means exclusive to blacks but are amply evident in the white population as well.

In truth, the evidence indicates clearly that the crucial element in generating a wide range of behaviors that are stereotypically associated with blacks is not race but poverty. In white neighborhoods characterized by low income, the crime rate is quite comparable to the rate in poor black neighborhoods, and it is considerably higher in poor white neighborhoods than in black neighborhoods where income is more substantial.[11]

Blacks rightly complain that much contemporary discussion of American society, even when it is sympathetic, treats *them* as the problem. The behaviors of whites that contribute to our "social problems" tend to be airbrushed out. Addressing whites' role in what many perceive to be an accelerating breakdown in the social covenant means not only being clear that whites too commit crimes and go on welfare, but also attending to those antisocial behaviors that are *more* prevalent among whites. It is well known and widely acknowledged, for example, that whites commit more white collar crimes—a differential attributed by almost all observers to the fact that whites tend to have more opportunity to commit this sort of crime.[12] Less widely known is that whites have a higher rate of arrests and convictions for drunk driving, a crime that accounts for considerably more loss of innocent life each year than muggings, but tends to be viewed with considerably less alarm in our cataloguing of social ills.[13] It is also, we may note, an antisocial act that signifies impulsiveness of a sort that if exhibited by blacks would surely be gravely overinterpreted.

Even more germane to this book's focus on vicious circles are those white behaviors that are a direct link in the circles I will trace. These include refusing to sell or rent homes to blacks or to hire them for responsible positions, making "innocent" jokes and comments that perpetuate stereotypes, joining country clubs that discriminate, or engaging in a host of other behaviors that are central to the "race problem" in this country. White participation further includes the failure of moral imagination that leads many whites to forget how unlikely it would have been that they or their children would have succeeded under the circumstances in which many African Americans grow up.

Here too, however, we must guard against stereotypes and overgeneralizations. It is as crucial to be attentive to the complexities and variations in white behavior as in black. In interracial dialogue groups I have conducted, participants were asked, among other questions, what stereotypes of their group seemed to them most prevalent and most wrong. Black participants often referred to images of blacks as criminals, as lazy, and as stupid. Whites consistently referred to images of whites as racist.

I will discuss in the next chapter the frequently voiced claim that in a society such as ours every white must be assumed to be racist, as well as the complexities and confusions in the way the words "racist" and "racism" have come to be used. But quite apart from that discussion, it should be clear that white attitudes and behavior toward blacks vary enormously from individual to individual and that error is introduced when whites are perceived through the distorting lens of a stereotype, just as it is when blacks are similarly misperceived.

Even more, perhaps, it is essential to recognize that most people are *in conflict* regarding the highly charged and multifaceted issues associated with race in our society. Competing inclinations and attitudes vie with each other and are evoked and shaped by a myriad of experiences. Fears, frustrations, ideals, images of justice and fairness, naked and disguised self-interest, rationalizations, group pressures, media messages, identifications with one's own group and with one's children, changing trends and political climates, images of one's better self, and a host of other constituting elements combine in a way that, even when yielding a manifestly stable equilibrium, is nonetheless a potentially volatile composite. The underlying forces whose resultant seems so stable may in fact be in such delicate balance that, as with a plate that comes crashing to the ground after hanging on the wall for years, a slight shift in the forces which have been silently groaning in opposition can yield a dramatic change in the overall picture. Much opportunity is lost if this dynamic tension, which so often underlies apparently stable and implacable attitudes, is not recognized or acknowledged. When the element of conflict is overlooked or denied, when, for example, whites are simply written off as racist, the prospects for change are obscured by a miasma of pessimism that impedes effective action and becomes a self-fulfilling prophecy.

The Essential Indivisibility of Psyche, Society, and History

Much of this book will be about the conflicting feelings and attitudes that complicate the task of resolving our nation's persisting racial divisions. I will be exploring the psychological sources of racial prejudice and examining the differing implications of conceiving of those prejudices as the product of fundamental and deeply rooted needs or as deriving from the ways that human cognition, in the process of simplifying the vast array of stimuli we encounter at every moment, introduces distortions that in certain circumstances can become institutionalized and toxic. I will consider as well how the impact of false stereotypic expectations can end up eliciting behaviors and emotional reactions from their target that seem to "confirm" those false expectations.

Beyond this, I will consider the complex psychological impact on African Americans of the injustices and affronts they have encountered on these shores. My concerns will include both the resourcefulness and creativity with which African Americans have at times transformed duress into strength, and the more painfully ironic ways that adaptations that have been necessary and useful in coping with privations and discrimination have at times contributed

to the dynamics that *keep* African Americans outside of the American
mainstream. I will also (in Part Three) examine a number of specific
realms (such as crime, housing, jobs, and schooling) in which vicious
circles complicate the problems we face, and I will consider how
understanding of these circular patterns and their complex interconnections can guide us in formulating more effective strategies for
resolving our racial divisions and conflicts.

But before addressing the intersecting social and psychological
dynamics that are the central concern of this book, it will be necessary to confront a number of tendencies that have created obstacles
to their untrammeled exploration and have contributed to the perception, noted in the Preface, that it requires "courage" even to take
up the topic. Part One of this book is therefore largely devoted to
creating the space for the formulations and analyses that follow in
Parts Two and Three. A formulation that emphasizes the role we *all*
play in perpetuating the vicious circles that entrap us is likely to
encounter powerful countervailing presuppositions from both the
right and the left. Part One therefore addresses some of the key
impediments to open dialogue and real listening. These include,
from different directions, the accusation that discussion of certain
topics is racist or constitutes blaming the victim, the intellectually
suspect and socially poisonous arguments of Richard Herrnstein and
Charles Murray in *The Bell Curve*, and the difficulties encountered
in finding a language for discussing the harm that injustice has
wrought in many African American communities.

While this book is primarily addressed to the contemporary conflicts and passions that maintain us in a state of tense division, I will
consider as well (especially in some of the early chapters) the *origins*
of our constricted dialogue in a number of debates and reactions that
dominated a crucial turning point in the civil rights struggle in the
1960s and 1970s. In so doing, I have in a sense followed the course
pursued by many psychotherapists—understanding the inhibitions
and lacunae of the present by examining the state of affairs at a point
before repression (in the psychological sense) rendered invisible some
of the psychological forces at play beneath the surface.

There is a long history behind the dilemmas we face today, and
one of the crucial issues of contention is just what role that history
plays in the problems we currently face. Here again, adversarial,

either-or positions are seductive, but will not get us very far. In truth, we are both the objects and the subjects of history, both its victims and its propogators. In matters concerning race, each of us, black or white, is the unfortunate inheritor of shameful acts and terrible suffering inflicted by people who lived long before we were born. Each of us bears a burden that, at least in part, we do not deserve. But most of us, in the way we take on that burden, become at least somewhat complicitous in perpetuating it and in bequeathing it in turn to still another generation. Centuries of slavery, segregation, and racial oppression and violence form the quicksand foundation of our present way of life. And myriad daily choices and actions—by *both* blacks and whites—contribute to our being drawn into the mire.

We cannot escape our history, but we must not submit to it. Without an appreciation of the cumulative and reverberating impact of the injustices and injuries inflicted over the centuries, any analysis of race relations in this country will be shallow and evasive. Yet it is essential as well to recognize how our contemporary difficulties have been shaped by the changes, both positive and negative, of the past few decades and by the ways blacks and whites have responded to those changes. We ignore our history at our peril. We ignore our own behavior at perhaps even greater risk.

Who is Qualified to Write about Race?

This introductory chapter would be incomplete without addressing a subject that is in certain respects a matter of personal justification but which is essential to address for reasons that are emblematic of the very issues this book is about. The question will undoubtedly arise in the minds of some readers—it has already been broached to me on a number of occasions: What is a white person doing writing a book on race?

Most often, the import of the question really turns out to be: What is a white person doing writing a book about *blacks?* At one level, the question can be answered by pointing out that this is *not* a book about blacks; it is a book about *blacks and whites*, about the tangles the two get into in relation to each other.[14] In that sense, I am as much a part of what I am writing about as a black author would be, and am both qualified and constrained by that fact to the same degree.

But I do not wish to rest with this argument alone. The idea that one can only understand one's own group is prevalent today, and it is an idea I believe to be both specious and destructive. First, just what *is* one's own group? Does a particular black author have special insight into all blacks? Only, if she is a woman, into black *women?* Middle-class black women? Middle-class black women who grew up in a poor single-parent household?

Similarly, what is the group about which I am granted a license to write with authority? All whites? White men? Urban white men? Urban white male intellectuals? Should I be presumed to have a better intuitive grasp of the experience of a white cowboy in Wyoming or a white pipe fitter in Alaska than of the experiences of my black colleagues at City College, who share so much more of my lifestyle and values?

Certainly in the aggregate I have greater access to white experience (whatever such a global term might mean) than to black. But I have had numerous opportunities to build experiential bridges over the gulf that is so widely believed to exist: I have taught for more than twenty years at a college that has a very large minority enrollment and in a doctoral program that is widely recognized for its efforts to recruit minority students and, however imperfectly, to address minority concerns. In my years at City College I have had considerably more opportunity than most white people to work with black and Latino students and colleagues and thereby both to understand their concerns and know their talents. Moreover, I teach and supervise in a psychological clinic where the patients tend to be black and Latino as well. I thus have had the opportunity to hear the more *intimate* stories of minority group members to a degree unusual for a white person.

More recently, as part of the research for this book, I have taught courses on issues of race to undergraduates and graduate students in which self-study and open discussion of feelings and attitudes about this topic was a primary medium of exploration, and I have run a variety of interracial dialogue groups that further probed the passions and beliefs that underlie the interactions between the races in our society. I will draw upon these experiences and observations throughout this book.

A Final Note: Why Black and White?

The account of vicious circles in this book has obvious relevance to ethnic conflicts in many parts of the world. It is particularly pertinent to the situation facing other minorities in the United States, especially the Latino minority that faces many of the same circumstances and is trapped in many of the same vicious circles. But the psychological dynamics I will discuss here must be understood not only in terms of the psychological processes that perpetuate the circle but also in the context of the social and historical influences that set them in motion and that continue to exert a powerful influence upon them. In the case of relations between blacks and whites in America, the continuing ramifications of our history of slavery and legally sanctioned segregation create unique dynamics that are not quite paralleled by other groups in this country. Identifications, traditions, and shared meanings arise out of specific historical circumstances. The difficulties are substantial even for generalizing about the black experience in the face of the enormous diversity within the black community. To attempt to extend the generalization still further to other groups who have encountered discrimination in America or to ethnic conflicts in other parts of the world would place a burden upon the analysis that is difficult to assess.

I have thus chosen to devote this book specifically to the dynamics between blacks and whites in America. Nonetheless, it is my hope that the analysis presented here will be helpful in efforts to break the cycle of despair in these other communities as well.

PART ONE

Impediments to Dialogue: Why We Talk past Each Other

2

Talking about Racism

How Our Dialogue Gets Short-Circuited

Among the elements perpetuating the vicious circles that are the focus of this book, perhaps the least understood is the way we talk to each other about matters related to race. Outright insults and directly hostile comments are, of course, obvious contributors to the perpetuation of our divisions. But less readily understood is the impact of what we do *not* say, the ways in which communication is blocked or inhibited. In different ways, both sides are afraid they will say something that confirms the stereotype the other holds of them. As a consequence, conversations between blacks and whites are often stilted and restrained.

In another of the many ironies we shall encounter, evasions that arise from the sense of estrangement and unease end up exacerbating the very feeling of unbridgeable difference from which they arise. Absence of frankness, bred of discomfort, breeds further discomfort. And on a policy level, our ability to develop concrete programs that could get at the roots of our difficulties and interrupt the repetition of the circle is hindered by an absence of candid exchange that places subtle restrictions even on what we are able to think.

In this chapter, my focus will be on how our ability to speak straightforwardly and productively about race is affected by the shifting ways we have come to use the labels *racism* and *racist*. In the rest of Part One, I will examine a number of other ways in which our dialogue has been short-circuited, to the detriment of our ability to understand and address the circular patterns in which we are caught.

Racism: A Term with a Host of Meanings

Consider the following scenarios—some tragic and dramatic, some mundane, but all sadly recognizable features of the racial landscape in America:

- A KKK mob burns a cross on the lawn of a black family that has moved into a formerly white neighborhood.
- A white person crosses the street to avoid encountering several black teenagers walking toward him.
- A black couple looking for an apartment is told that it is rented, but a white couple sent by a civil rights group to test for discrimination is shown the apartment an hour later and told it is available.
- A white person says he supports fair housing laws because he believes it is unfair and unjust to discriminate on the basis of race, but confesses that he himself would be afraid to live in a neighborhood that was not mostly white.
- A professor claims he has data proving that blacks are inferior in intelligence.
- A sports commentator comments that blacks are more naturally gifted as athletes.
- A white resident in an expensive co-op makes a friendly comment to a black woman riding in the elevator with her, but the comment makes it clear she has erroneously assumed that the black woman, who is in fact the editor of a leading magazine, is a maid.
- The owner of a jewelry store does not buzz in a well-dressed black man for fear he is a robber.
- Two middle-class whites discuss their annoyance when a black youth passes by with a boom box loudly blaring rap music, saying, "Kids like that have no consideration; they think they own the streets."
- An employer interviewed by a researcher says that he has

experienced repeatedly that blacks are more frequently late to work and tend to have an "attitude."

- A museum holds an exhibit of leading contemporary artists and none of the artists chosen are black.
- A literature survey course on the greatest works of world literature from Homer to the present has no black authors on the reading list.
- A candidate for office states that this country was founded as a white Christian nation and that is how it should remain.
- A high school institutes a writing requirement for graduation that requires mastery of standard English.
- A test is given for a civil service job and whites score higher on the test than blacks.
- A search committee for a faculty job at a prestigious university refuses to modify its criteria in considering a black applicant who has published few papers in leading professional journals.
- A black woman shopping in a department store that has had many robberies is watched more closely by the store detective than are the white women around her.
- A black child attends a school that has large classes, few books or study aids, and not nearly enough desks and chairs to go around.
- A teacher in that school says she is no longer as idealistic as she was when she began and that no matter how hard she tries, the kids don't seem to learn.
- A study reveals that garbage pickups in poor black neighborhoods are less frequent than in middle-class white neighborhoods.
- An activist for global environmental preservation advocates increasing efforts at promoting birth control in third world countries, where population increase is greatest.

These scenarios differ in a multitude of ways, but they have one significant thing in common: All have been labeled as instances of racism.

Do they all embody racism? Some of them seem to me clearly to merit the use of that term, but whether they all do is a virtually impossible question to answer. The platinum meter rod that lies in the International Bureau of Weights and Measures and defines for all of us just what a meter is has no real equivalent in the realm of language; no one owns a platinum dictionary that is the final arbiter of what the word racism should refer to. A word with such powerful emotional connotations, that is used to describe events and attitudes so close to the heart of our society's most basic afflictions, is bound to be a source of contention. "Looking it up in the dictionary" is utterly beside the point when a central issue is who gets to write the dictionary, who defines the terms of the debate. (Several of the black participants in our interracial dialogue groups contended that blacks cannot be racist "by definition" because the word racism means discrimination by the majority against an oppressed minority. Some of the whites, in turn, asked where they got that definition, and were convinced that most dictionaries did not define racism in that way—to which one black participant responded, "What color are the people who write the dictionaries?" This is at once a politically astute observation and an implicit acknowledgment that there is an element of arbitrariness that undermines *any* effort to assert in an absolute manner what racism "is.")[1]

But if we cannot really settle in any definitive or "objective" way what is and is not racism, we *can* ask what the *consequences* are of one or another way of using the term. Those consequences, I believe, point to the conclusion that we have seriously overused the words "racism" and "racist," to the detriment of the clarity and precision of our language and of our ability to overcome our racial divisions.

I make this suggestion not because I believe racism has disappeared in American life, nor out of a view that our racial problems have become less severe, therefore meriting our use of "milder" terms. Racism remains a central fact of our life together, and in certain respects our racial divisions have become more rather than less intractable in recent years. What I wish to introduce is not a "milder" vocabulary, not a list of euphemisms, but rather a more *precise* and *differentiated* vocabulary. My aim is not to sweep racism under the rug, but to understand more clearly the experiences and attitudes to which the term is usually applied.

The terms racism and racist have been so stretched and extended in contemporary dialogue on race and inequality that their usage has become a serious impediment to our efforts to come to grips with problems that are difficult enough to begin with. There

are many instances in which words like prejudice, bias, discrimination, stereotyping, ethnocentrism, insensitivity, inequality, injustice,
indifference, and even ignorance, denote far more accurately the
social and psychological reality of events now depicted almost
reflexively as "racist." Moreover, not only does the use of these alternative terms provide a sharper and more differentiated analytic tool
for understanding our society's dilemmas, it also enables us to avoid
falling into a number of costly pitfalls embedded in our current linguistic habits.

One key problem is that the words "racism" and "racist" tend to
be conversation stoppers. When "I disagree" or "You don't understand" or "You don't know the facts" or even "You're wrong" becomes
"You're racist," real dialogue ceases. And it ceases regardless of
whether what is evoked is an angry retort or a deferential and ultimately insincere genuflection. When whites walk on eggshells in
their interactions with blacks, fearing that to express their views in
all their complexity would leave them open to the accusation of being
racists, all that results is a covering over of real issues and feelings
that are essential to address if any progress in race relations is to be
made. In this respect, blacks may actually not appreciate how guilty
many whites feel about the inequalities that exist in our society (even
if that guilt is frequently repressed or insufficiently a source of remedial action). The use of a term that feels to blacks merely descriptive,
simply an account of what they encounter every day of their lives,
can create in whites a defensive attitude that stifles honest communication. And while there may be short-term advantage to blacks in
being able to intimidate whites in this way, and a kind of poetic justice in being able to turn the tables in certain respects, there is, as I
shall elaborate below, a high cost ultimately to be paid for whatever
satisfaction is thereby achieved.

Moreover, overextension of the terms "racism" and "racist"
actually can serve to obscure rather than make clearer the degree of
racial injustice that pervades our society. "Racism" is a strong word,
and part of the rationale for its use is that it takes a forceful message
to break through strong denial: euphemisms permit continuing evasion. But volume is not the only determinant of what gets heard.
After a while one habituates to—or "tunes out"—even the loudest
noise if it is unvarying. Indeed, at times a silence that replaces a
steady noise is a more attention-getting stimulus than the noise

itself. A varied vocabulary is not just an aesthetic virtue; it also counters the tendency to tune out. Conveying the message in a language about which the intended hearer is set to be defensive is likely to have less impact than doing so in a language that is straightforward and pulls no punches, but is not needlessly provocative.

In a 1992 panel discussion on the *MacNeil-Lehrer NewsHour*, black journalist Joseph Boyce lamented the fact that

> at one time the last thing anyone wanted to be called was a racist, whether they were or not. It was a mark to be avoided. And today I don't think people really care that much, some of them, you know. They'll say, "Yeah, I'm a racist, so what, so what are you going to do about it?"[2]

This is indeed a regrettable state of affairs, but I believe that one reason for it is that the word racist has been bandied about so much that for some people it has lost its impact, lost its power to shock, to evoke guilt or revulsion. A term that once referred to the most deplorable and shameful of traits and actions has been extended to include virtually universal human characteristics and to include within its purview practically everyone in our society.

It should *not* be easy and common to say with equanimity "Yes, I'm a racist, so what?" But if we are told in essence that *every* white person is a racist,[3] then it *becomes* a matter to which a ho-hum response becomes possible. Racism *is* a strong word (or at least it *was* a strong word), and it should remain one. It should *not* be a word whose power habituates. We are much the worse off when people can acknowledge racism with impunity, as a simple, familiar fact of life rather than a terrible aberration.

Bull Connor or Joe Next Door?

The phenomenon painfully noted by Boyce was certainly not intended or expected by those whose rhetoric first created the expansion of the word's usage. In large measure the expansion developed as a response to the changing challenges of the civil rights movement as it moved from the South to the North. As long as the South persisted in a particularly explicit and ugly form of racial segregation and disparagement of blacks, the subtler, but often no less persistent or destructive segregation of the North was effectively shrouded. Especially combined with the earlier close association of the South with outright slavery, this pattern of difference between North and South enabled the rest of the country to externalize its own quite considerable racial prejudices by holding to a fantasy of the "bad" South and the "good" North. When the most egregious features of racial discrimination in the South gave way in the 1960s, it became increasingly apparent that the North differed much less from the South than it had thought. Workers for change were confronted with a set of prejudices and institutional constraints that were more diffi- cult to confront than those of the South precisely because they were more subtle, disguised, and unacknowledged.

In response to this, and in an effort to communicate to whites in the North that "you're not as different as you think from the Southerners you have been smugly criticizing," writers and activists began increasingly to employ a term that had once stood in the national imagination for such violent acts as lynchings or the vicious use of police dogs by Birmingham police chief Bull Connor. Their aim was to break through the numbing denial, to confront North- erners with the need for changes as radical in their own way as the opening of schools, lunch counters, and other public facilities to blacks in the South. But in the process, a term that had largely pointed toward the most serious and heinous offenses against human dignity began, in effect, to be watered down to stand for more com- mon human foibles. As a consequence, subtle but powerful changes in connotation were set in motion: On the one hand, the special emo- tional impact of the word "racism" was diminished; if it is not a term referring to violence and the extremes of inhumanity, but rather to what the folks down the block do, then it's not really so bad. On the other hand, if the Bull Connors of the world are no different really from you or I or Joe next door, then an unfortunate covert link of solidarity is subtly fostered between flawed but decent people and people who deserve nothing but contempt.

The Paradoxes of Guilt

It may seem inconsistent to point out that "racist" is such a strong word that it stops meaningful dialogue and invokes defensiveness in whites, and simultaneously to contend that its overuse has desensitized us to the real horror the term should connote and enabled people to accept with equanimity the description of them as racist. The inconsistency, however, is more apparent than real. At the simplest level, we may note that different responses to the term can be manifested by different people; some may be intimidated or defensive while others are inured and desensitized. Moreover, even for the same person, the accusation of racism may sometimes be experienced as an intimidating conversation-stopper and sometimes as a tiresome harangue that has little real impact whatever formal obeisance may or may not be paid. Whether one or the other response is evoked will depend on many factors: who is making the accusation; how it is presented; with what mood or set the accused enters the encounter; the number of people present and the ratio of blacks and whites among them; and a host of other aspects of context and personality.

Moreover, the two seemingly antithetical reactions can often be but two sides of the same response. Both the defiant embrace of the term referred to by Boyce ("Yeah, I'm racist. So what?") and the reaction of boredom or disinterest that mutes the impact of a message that needs to be heard ("Here we go again! More rhetoric!") can be defensive responses to having been made to feel guilty. In these instances, it is *because* the impact of the accusation is so strong that its conscious acknowledgment is so minimal.

Guilt is a complex emotion and does not always produce the response we might wish or expect. Sometimes, to be sure, it leads to efforts to right the wrong one has done. But very often, especially if guilt threatens to be overwhelming, the response to guilt can be paradoxical: still *further* insensitivity to those we have harmed, and anger at them for confronting us with our inadequacies and iniquities. Conveying the bad news is a subtle art. Whether in a marriage or friendship or in a larger social context, it is far from universal that when we succeed in making the person we think has wronged us feel guilty we end up pleased with the results.

Salutary responses to feelings of guilt are most likely to occur when there is something productive and reparative the individual can do to relieve the guilt. Global and overextended depictions of white racism block this healthy and useful response. If whites are left feeling they are going to be seen as racist no matter what they do—"if I'm not an overt racist, I'm a covert one"—then the response is likely to be one of "why bother?" or some other defensive reaction. Ritualistic acknowledgments of "racism" may be offered, but they will be *in place of* effective action to heal our social wounds rather than a harbinger of such actions.

"Institutional Racism"

Different problems are introduced by another way in which the use of the term racism has been expanded over the years. Increasingly, discourse on racism has stressed its *institutional* nature rather than simply the attitudes of individuals, and the concept of "institutional racism" has become a central feature of contemporary dialogue on issues of race.

As James M. Jones, a leading African American writer on racism and prejudice, has delineated the distinction, "The critical aspect of institutional racism that distinguished it from prejudice and from individual racism was the notion that institutions can produce racist consequences *whether they do so intentionally or not.*"[4] Robert Miles, a British sociologist who has written a comprehensive examination of the manifold ways in which the concept of racism is employed in contemporary discourse, offers a closely related definition of how the term is used—"all processes which, *intentionally or not,* result in the continued exclusion of a subordinated group."[5] In contrast with Jones, however, Miles sees serious difficulties with the concept. Although he views racism as indeed a central problem in contemporary society and regards the dissection of racism as a crucial task for social analysis, he decries the "conceptual inflation" that leads the term racism to be overused and overextended and its original sharp meaning to be significantly blurred. As the concept of racism is extended into the terminology of *institutional* racism, the role of the motivations and attitudes of actual human beings becomes increasingly confused, and a highly abstract and impersonal conception becomes mischievously merged with one of the most emotionally charged words in our vocabulary.

The original use of the term institutional racism by Stokely Carmichael and Charles Hamilton in their influential book, *Black Power,*[6] was not as divorced from intentionality. They did depict two different kinds of racism—individual and institutional—and they noted how the latter, *seemingly* impersonal, can allow "respectable" individuals to dissociate themselves from the acts of those with the poor taste to be overtly racist, while continuing to benefit from the ways in which our institutions maintain the inequalities between blacks and whites. But Carmichael and Hamilton's conception of institutional racism does not eliminate motivation or intention. They state quite explicitly that

> Institutional racism relies on the active and pervasive operation of anti-black attitudes and practices. A sense of superior group position prevails: whites are "better" than blacks; therefore blacks should be subordinated to whites. This is a racist attitude and it permeates the society, on both the individual and institutional level, covertly and overtly.[7]

I believe that Carmichael and Hamilton accurately identified an attitude that continues to prevail in America to a disturbing degree, and I agree as well that it merits the description as racist. But as the idea of institutional racism evolved over the years, it has increasingly come to be evoked whenever differences between the races are found, *regardless* of whether there is any evidence of racist intent. The outcome itself is taken as proof that racism *must* underlie the differences.[8]

It is indeed crucially important to understand how our institutional arrangements maintain inequalities and place continuing burdens on a people who already have a long history of oppression. But the labeling of these processes as institutional "racism" has muddled as much as it clarifies. The confusion arises because a term replete with connotations of intention is used to denote a process *outside* of specific intentions, a process almost mechanical in its impersonality and inexorability. To the white who says, "That's *not* how I feel; that's not what I want," the proponent of the concept of institutional racism can say, "You're misunderstanding what I'm saying. I'm not saying *you* want this to happen, I'm saying that the whole society is set up in such a way that certain outcomes inevitably result, and those outcomes are consistently to the detriment of people of color in comparison to whites."

This distinction is logically coherent (and, in my view, it is rooted in a largely accurate perception of how our society works). But it is couched in terms that fail to take into account how real people think and react. As a consequence, it injects into our public discourse a terminology that is misleading and inflammatory. No matter what disclaimers may be offered by the speaker, it is extremely difficult for whites (or blacks for that matter, though with a different set of reactions likely) to hear the term institutional *racism* without other, more sinister connotations of the word racism seeping in.

As a consequence, the concept of "institutional racism" can contribute to obscuring the very phenomenon it was designed to highlight. Because the terms "racism" and "racist" are likely to evoke in the hearer connotations of motivated rather than impersonal and systemic outcomes, whites who do not recognize racist *intent* in the operations of our dominant institutions or in the outcomes they yield are likely as a consequence to find claims of "institutional racism" implausible. In the process, they are enabled to avoid coming to grips with how the workings of our society do disadvantage blacks and other minorities even when there is no specific intention that that be the outcome.

As obvious as it ought to be that our social arrangements have a predictably differential overall impact on blacks and whites, it is easy not to see it, *and one need not be a racist not to.* For our society's customary way of thinking leads us to look away from predictable group differences and to emphasize instead individual choice and responsibility. This tendency is not limited to our perceptions with regard to minorities. It obscures as much about the differences in income and access among whites as it does about blacks. Part of the system we live under is that we are systematically trained not to see the system. That is, we are taught to understand the differences in income and influence that result from the way we organize our society as solely the result of individual choices and individual merit; and we are taught *not* to notice the statistical probabilities that make the bright child of a truck driver or a manual laborer less likely to go to college than the child of a doctor or lawyer.

Instead, we are trained to notice the *exceptions.* Since there are some children of truck drivers and manual laborers who do go to college—indeed, a sizable enough group to be noticeable—we affirm that we are a "land of opportunity," and essentially ignore the fact that we can predict with virtual statistical certainty the differential life courses of the children of the two groups.[9]

In similar fashion, we may use the existence of a growing black middle class to obscure the reality that blacks remain greatly overrepresented among those who receive the least of our society's rewards. Here again, the exceptions obscure the rule. The roots of the confusion lie in the fact that the effects of institutional arrangements are statistical rather than universal. That is, it is not the case that *no* blacks are able to succeed in our society or that all whites do better than the average black. Rather, what is predictable is that, all in all, the status and station of blacks is likely to be lower than that of whites; or, put differently, that the circumstances most blacks encounter from birth on are likely to make it harder for them to succeed than are the circumstances most whites encounter. Since there are fairly numerous exceptions—blacks who make it anyhow, through noteworthy talent, drive, or persistence—it is easy to overlook the way the cards are stacked against this happening. Instead, the very fact that *some* blacks have made it leads many whites to conclude that those who haven't simply do not try hard enough, are not sufficiently meritorious, or in some other way "deserve" the deprivation they endure.

If we are to transcend this superficial and censorious way of understanding the disparities that haunt our society, we will indeed have to make clearer the *institutional* aspects of what has been called institutional racism. The rhetoric of institutional racism can impede such understanding, leading people to focus on personal attitudes in a way that obscures precisely the institutional dimension. What results are responses such as, "This talk about institutional racism is nonsense. It's just an excuse. I'm not a racist. I judge people as individuals. I don't care if they are black, white, green, or purple. If they work hard and follow the rules, I respect them, and if they expect special favors, I say 'life's hard for me too.'"

I've certainly had enough psychoanalytic training to know that such a response *might* be covering over "unconscious racism." But I've also had enough psychoanalytic training to know that such an automatic assumption is a misuse of psychoanalysis. What is more obvious and definite is that such a response reflects highly *individualistic* assumptions that obscure the way social conditions influence people's behavior and aspirations. When people believe that everyone makes his or her own fate, and ignore the role of circumstance, they are unlikely to be sympathetic to those who do not make it, regardless of race.

This is not to imply that racial feelings play no part in our society's readiness to accept institutional arrangements that leave so many people of color disadvantaged. Rather, the question is whether "racism" is the best way of understanding those racial feelings. I turn now to an alternative conceptualization that I believe is both more accurate and more likely to contribute to the sense of recognition that is an essential precursor of change.

"Otherness" and Indifference

A more useful way, I suggest, to conceptualize the broad commonality among the diverse experiences typically labeled as "racist" is to focus our attention on the sense of "otherness" that is central to these experiences. "Otherness" is not as sexy a word as racism. It is unlikely to come into widespread use as a catch-all term, and indeed, that is one of its great advantages. It points us toward an understanding of the underlying foundations of these various problematic features of our life as a society without co-opting the differentiations.

There are subtle differences among the words that depict the attitudes increasingly lumped together under the global rubric of racism. Some whites, for example, may be able to hear and consider a claim that they have been *prejudiced* in some situation or other but will reject (or only give superficial lip service to) the claim that they were being racist. What is the difference? Prejudice implies jumping to a quick, and even unfair, conclusion, but for many people it does not imply hostility and brutality as does racism.* While it is not pleasant to acknowledge the former, it is still a far cry from being guilty of the latter.

In similar fashion, for a white to be confronted with having been *insensitive* in some remark he might have made can be a quite different experience from having the remark described as racist. Once again, although both are likely to be painful to acknowledge, the first characterization is much more likely to get through than the second.

What is perhaps most important of all for whites to acknowledge and understand is *indifference*. A great deal of what is often characterized as racism can be more precisely and usefully described

---

* James M. Jones, for example, in a prominent textbook on racism and prejudice, depicts racism as something "far more sinister and deep" than prejudice (Jones, *Racism and Prejudice*, p. 196).

as indifference. Perhaps no other feature of white attitudes, and of the underlying attitudinal structure of white society as a whole, is as cumulatively responsible for the pain and privation experienced by our nation's black minority at this point in our history as is indifference. At the same time, perhaps no feature is as misunderstood or overlooked.

"Otherness" is at work in all of the destructive ways in which people of different groups interact. Prejudices, biases, stereotypes, and the like would have no objects were not some people experienced as "other". But "otherness" is perhaps especially germane to the role of indifference, which in a sense can be viewed as a pure culture of otherness. That is, in prejudice, stereotyping, ethnocentrism, and other such obviously problematic features of how groups of human beings interact, something is *added* to otherness. There is something more active in these behaviors and attitudes that makes them a bit more able to be detected. Indifference, in contrast, is a *quiet* toxin. It severs the sinews and nerves of society without announcing itself. Its effects are devastating, but its tracks are hidden in the overall attitude of "each man for himself" that is so prominent a part of our society's ethos.

Further obscuring the central role of indifference in our social problems is that highly immediate and visible tragedy can transcend the sense of otherness. Few white Americans would fail to rescue a black child trapped in a well or a black man pinned under the wreckage of a building collapse. At such moments the sense of human solidarity takes center stage, not the sense of differentness. And indeed, this is one of the reasons that most white Americans do not really believe in their heart of hearts that they are racist.

But when it comes to the slow bleeding that daily drains the spirit and hope from life in our nation's inner cities, indifference shows itself in full measure. We tolerate the misery in the midst of our affluent society because of the strong sense of "them" that attaches to the miserable, the sense that "they" are not like "us," that they are different. And so most whites, who are aware of little feeling of outright hostility, who believe in fair play and equal opportunity, see little that has to do with them in the painful realities of our inner cities. In both (ironically almost opposite) meanings of the phrase, what is happening there is "too bad." But for all too many whites, it is not perceived as their responsibility.

Of course, what I am describing comes very close in certain ways to what is often addressed under the rubric of institutional racism. Indifference, however, comes much closer to the unacknowledged core of truth in white America's guilty conscience. "Institutional racism" is unlikely to become a part of the phenomenological experience of white Americans; indifference can. It is indifference that whites can potentially recognize and acknowledge within themselves, and it is in combating indifference that the fulcrum of change may be most effectively placed.

Indifference and the sense of otherness are not experiences that are limited to issues of race. We may see them operating every time there is a plane crash abroad and the newscaster announces how many Americans are aboard. The likelihood, for any listener, that any American victim of the crash will be someone they actually know is exceedingly small; there are, after all, a quarter of a billion Americans. Yet this information is always supplied, for it defines whether the victim was "one of us," and, if truth be told, it defines to a significant degree whether we should *care*.[10]

This is precisely the issue that most burdens race relations in our society as well. The real meaning of race comes down largely to this: *Is this someone I should care about?* This is a terrible and shameful truth, and in its full impact it will not be easy for white America to face. But it points much more precisely, I believe, to the true source of white guilt than does the label of racism. As a consequence, it has a better chance both of leading us to examine what is in our hearts and of generating the concrete social and economic changes that are essential for real justice and equality to be achieved.

Summary and Conclusion

Accusing a guilty man of the wrong crime is one of the greatest gifts one can bestow upon him. It fosters an orgy of self-righteous conviction of innocence, and conveniently diverts his attention from the offense of which he is truly guilty. In a similar fashion, the ubiquitous claim that racism is the cause of the grievous circumstances of life in our inner cities is, ironically, enabling white America to slough off its responsibility for the shameful neglect of the least privileged members of our society.

The real crime of which white America is now most guilty is not

racism. It is indifference. Understanding the difference between the
two is a crucial step in liberating ourselves from the sterile and
unproductive impasse that has characterized the dialogue on race
relations in recent years.

Distinguishing between racism and indifference is not a seman-
tic quibble. The constant invocation of racism, often in ever more
forced, abstract, and symbolic senses, can have the counterproductive effect of causing listeners to filter out potentially important
arguments because they sound repetitive, rhetorical, and, most
important, contrary to their experience. Racism is such a loaded
word, so tinged with associations to lynchings and unprintable racial
epithets, that many whites experience a sharp distinction between
their own attitudes and what they believe is implied by such a word.
As a consequence, accused of a crime of which their self-examina-
tion tells them they are innocent, they can go to bed with an undis-
turbed conscience.

But in fact there is little ground for a clear conscience in the
relations of white America to its black minority. Many whites who
can quite honestly claim that they hold no hatred for blacks, that
they do not wish them harm or disparage them as a group—in
short, that they are not "racist"—must acknowledge that it *is* true
that almost daily news reports of the terrors and privations of growing up in the inner city leave them with the feeling, "That's not my
problem." Such an attitude may be justified (or rationalized) by the
claim that "Maybe there once were obstacles to blacks getting into
college or getting good jobs, but times have changed. Now the
opportunities are there if they'll only apply themselves."

And although there is a certain amount of truth in such a view, it
fails not only to acknowledge the continuing discrimination that
does still exist, but even more importantly, it fails to take into
account how hard it is to *see* the new opportunities from the vantage
point of the typical block in our poorest neighborhoods. Boarded-up
buildings, drug pushers, gang members with guns, and the ubiquitous presence of unemployed men and women tend rather effectively
to block the view of the wider world of opportunity readily visible
from the suburbs. Few children, white or black, have the capacity to
see past such a compellingly bleak immediate reality.

To some in the black community, describing the predominant
white attitude as indifference rather than racism may seem like a

kind of plea-bargaining in which a lesser offense is acknowledged instead of the real crime. I disagree. For most white Americans the crime of which they are most guilty *is* indifference, *not* racism. Moreover, and even more important, indifference in the face of severe human suffering is not a minor offense.

Our society is deeply flawed by racial inequalities, but the unswerving emphasis on racism as the explanation has become part of the problem rather than part of the solution. It is time to retire the rhetoric of racism, not because white neglect has become benign, but because it is essential for the well-being of all of us, white *and* black, that that neglect be recognized and addressed.

3

Blaming the Victim?

Understanding the vicious circles in which we are caught requires attention to the ways in which all parties participate in their perpetuation. Clear understanding of the participation of whites, I have suggested, is impeded by an excessive focus on racism and outright discrimination, which diverts our attention from the more subtle, but perhaps more formidable and unyielding impact of indifference and the feeling that "those people are not my concern." Appreciation of the role of blacks is obscured in a different way. Here, the reality that the overall impact of our patterns of racial interaction is most palpably harmful to African Americans, combined with knowledge of the shameful history that initiated these patterns, can funnel our vision toward a view of African Americans as simple victims. In the process, the circular nature of the patterns between us may be obscured altogether.

We cannot begin to disrupt the vicious circles which bind us without attending to them in all their painful complexity. No aspect of those circles is more poignant and difficult to confront than the ways in which victimization itself has been cruelly transfigured, generating behaviors and attitudes that contribute to perpetuating the very conditions that are their source. In attending to how this happens, we must address the reproach that doing so entails blaming the victim.

While arising out of humane impulses and an understandable wish to defend those who have so often been disparaged and mistreated, oversensitivity to the rhetoric of "don't blame the victim," and overconcern for the potential misuse of frank examination of the troubling behavior in our inner cities, has at times painted advocates for society's less fortunate into a corner. The result, as Neil McLaughlin has noted in *Dissent*, has been that "liberal intellectuals, in an attempt to avoid blaming the victim, have suffered from a failure of nerve in dealing with poverty, crime, and social decay."[1]

When is Attention to Problems Blaming?

Concern that frank discussion of the more disquieting features of life in our inner-cities can be misused is by no means unwarranted. Influential voices have indeed seized upon the more problematic features of inner-city life as a rationalization for policies that perpetuate neglect and maintain inequality. The "pathology" is so deeply rooted, we are told, that it does not pay to invest in social programs to alleviate the difficulties; "throwing money at problems" is wasteful and ineffective because the poor do not really *want* to work or are so damaged that they *cannot.*

It is easy to understand why those committed to a more just and equal society would want to counter such tendentious characterizations. But frequently it has seemed that virtually *any* attention to the behavior and attitudes of blacks and other minorities—and especially to how these behaviors and attitudes may contribute to keeping them in their disadvantaged position—is labeled as victim-blaming. When this happens, our ability to understand and address our difficulties is seriously compromised, and the very aim of bringing the victimization to an end is impeded.

A key hallmark of arguments that are *rightly* described as blaming the victim is that (1) they so centrally emphasize and highlight the behavior of the disadvantaged themselves that they obscure thereby the role of the larger society in generating that behavior, and (2) they use their focus on the self-defeating behavior patterns of the aggrieved as an excuse for doing nothing to change things; the basic message is "these people can't be helped." It will be abundantly clear that the point of view of this book shares neither of these characteristics. I do, however, believe that without looking very closely at the problematic cultural and behavioral tendencies that have evolved in response to oppression, our efforts to combat that oppression are seriously hampered.

Poor schools, subpar housing, inadequate medical care, and grim job prospects are not all that our nation's disadvantaged face. They also face a culture of despair. In so many ways every day, they get messages that they cannot make it; and those messages are internalized and become self-fulfilling prophecies. By now it is virtually impossible to distinguish the chicken and the egg: year after year so many of them *don't* make it that each new cohort becomes convinced that they *can't*. As they live out that conviction, they become the foundation for similar conclusions on the part of their younger brothers and sisters.

Put most generally and most baldly, the truth is that the residents of our nation's inner cities are not oppressed only by something called "white society" or "mainstream society." They are oppressed as well *by each other*. The most obvious of these occurrences has to do with crime. One of the most terrible things about being poor in America is that the poor must frequently live vulnerably among a subset of their neighbors who, though arousing fear in the entire society, in fact do most of their damage close to home. The newspaper and magazine accounts in recent years detailing the impact on children of seeing their peers shot and killed, the stories of children planning their own funerals, are too numerous even to bother to document. Many, in the face of this, simply live out their lives as victims; some, partially out of self-defense, become victimizers themselves.

The larger social order and the conditions it permits to exist must bear the ultimate responsibility for this state of affairs. But the day-to-day victimization of the residents of our inner cities is often at the hands of their neighbors. Even litterers and scrawlers of graffiti add to the burden, augmenting the sense of living in a place that is grim and disregarded (and tempting each in turn to respond in kind, out of rage and self-contempt, and thus to keep the vicious circle going in still another way).

Perhaps most terrible of all is what amounts to peer pressure to fail. Defensiveness about "acting white," or about related accusations that they are "pretending" to be what they are not, that they are selling out, that they have become "oreos" (black on the outside, white on the inside), can play a significant role in the difficulties many black youths have in taking hold in school or gaining the skills needed to succeed in the mainstream economy. I have observed this phenomenon first hand or heard it reported numerous times in supervising clinical work with minority youths, in classroom discussions, and in the interracial dialogue groups I have run, and it has been an especially painful experience to confront. The psychological complexities of such attitudes are considerable, and they embody healthy defiance and affirmation of identity as well as defensive self-limitation and constricting mutual intimidation. I will have more to say about these complexities in later chapters. For now, I want simply to note that the way of life we have created in our poorest neighborhoods develops a dynamic whose painful ironies must be understood and confronted forthrightly if we are to generate effective strategies for promoting change.

More and Less Vicious Circles

This book is not the first analysis of our nation's racial impasse in terms of vicious circles. The Swedish Nobel Laureate Gunnar Myrdal very largely rooted his classic study of race relations, *An American Dilemma*, in a theory of vicious circles.[2] But ironically, although in principle the analysis of vicious circles is a mode of analysis especially suited to reconciling the competing perspectives that contend so fractiously in this realm, over the years such analyses have come to be themselves assimilated into the polarizing mindset that dominates our society's views of poverty and racial inequality.

Thus, some have depicted a "cycle of poverty" in which the characteristics of the poor themselves are virtually the only elements in the cycle, with the inequities and prejudices of the larger society playing scarcely any role,[3] while others have presented vicious circle accounts in which *all* the fault lies in the larger white society and the black poor appear *only* as victims. For example, Stokely Carmichael and Charles Hamilton, in their book *Black Power*, whose ideas had a fateful impact on the entire course of the civil rights movement, argued that the white power structure

> has perpetuated a vicious circle—the poverty cycle—in which the
> black communities are denied good jobs, and therefore stuck with

a low income and therefore unable to obtain a good education with which to obtain good jobs. . . . They cannot qualify for credit at most reputable places; they then resort to unethical merchants who take advantage of them by charging higher prices for inferior goods. They end up having less funds to buy in bulk, thus unable to reduce overall costs. They remain trapped.[4]

There is a great deal of truth in this description. There *are* vicious circles of this sort—Catch-22's—that keep people stuck. But note how in Carmichael and Hamilton's account no responsibility whatsoever falls to those in the black community. They are victims, pure and simple, unable in any way to determine their fate. The role of their own behavior, attitudes, and assumptions, the ways in which duress can lead people to make choices that end up contributing to further duress, the painful ironies that make the task of overcoming injustice so difficult and complex—all are completely left out of this narrative. Indeed, the authors are quite explicit about this:

> In the face of such realities, it becomes ludicrous to condemn black people for "not showing more initiative." Black people are not in a depressed condition because of some defect in their character. The colonial power structure clamped a boot of oppression on the neck of the black people and then, ironically, said "they are not ready for freedom."

To be sure, it *is* ludicrous to "condemn" black people for the oppressive circumstances in which so many of them live. But it is important to be clear that in Carmichael and Hamilton's analysis, vicious circles are something that *happen to* blacks, not something in which they participate. This is but the mirror image of the kind of "cycle of poverty" analyses that ultimately place *all* the responsibility on the black poor. Both are continuations of the rhetoric of polarization.[*]

---

* It should be clear that there have been many voices in the black community that, even while seeing the powerful role of oppression and injustice, have simultaneously stressed the role of African Americans' own responsibility and initiative in moving beyond our present circumstances. I cite the passage from Carmichael and Hamilton not as representative but, in the effort to clarify the varying ways that vicious circles can be conceptualized, as a particularly clearly stated version of one way that vicious circle accounts can be divisive and adversarial rather than balanced and comprehensive.

The vicious circles that are the central focus of this book are quite different in conceptualization. They are not limited to the behaviors of blacks alone or the depredations of white society alone. Rather, they point to the ways in which the behaviors and attitudes of whites and blacks *together* combine to maintain a repeated cyclical pattern of which both parties are scarcely aware, but from which they cannot extricate themselves. This conceptualization runs against the conservative grain that places responsibility entirely within the black community and sees little necessity for concrete programs to address our inequalities, and it runs against the liberal grain that regards attention to problematic patterns among African Americans as blaming the victim.

The Roots of Restricted Dialogue: The Controversy over the Moynihan Report

The circles I am describing are not completely round. They lack the symmetry that would make it equally easy to discuss the role of participants on each side of our racial divide. Far more pain and far more injustice are endured by African Americans than by whites, and the result is that it is more difficult for people of goodwill to address comfortably the ways in which African Americans' own behavior is woven into the tragic pattern.

Concern about the sensitivities of those who have already been hurt considerably by years of injustice is understandable and appropriate. But lamentably, this concern has yielded one more of the ironies that beset us in this realm. When those concerned about the sensitivities of African Americans have been hesitant to address issues that can cause pain or be misused, the result has not been that those issues have been kept out of the realm of public discourse. It has been, rather, that those issues have become political fodder for those much less concerned about either those sensitivities or the frequently difficult and unjust circumstances in which many African Americans live.

Issues of crime, welfare, single-parenthood, drug use, and a cultural orientation in some inner-city neighborhoods that glorifies violence or derides working hard in school as "acting white" all need to be examined in much more complex ways than they have tended to be by those who set the tone of public debate. The role of white indifference and the continuing inequities encountered by black children from the day they are born need to be integrated into our discussion of these issues. But the introduction of these crucial dimensions will be neither persuasive nor an accurate guide to policy if they are injected as a way of diverting our attention from painful realities. Years of injustice and neglect have created genuine and serious problems in many sectors of the African American community, and if people of goodwill do not address those problems frankly, they will become the unchallenged preserve of moralistic and racially divisive commentators, who are all too ready to exploit the everyday realities that progressive thinkers attempt to fudge.

In attempting to create space for more frank and productive discussion of our racial impasse, and for the kind of vicious circle analysis I believe is the most useful path toward its resolution, I wish now to turn to the roots of what I believe is a continuing and counterproductive evasion of hard but essential issues. My focus will be on an episode that was a watershed in the recent history of our society's discourse on race—the controversy over the document that came to be called the Moynihan Report. The impact of that controversy was to create powerful taboos that to this day have restricted and misdirected progressive approaches to addressing our racial divisions and inequalities. To understand the anxieties that continue to constrain our perceptions and impede appreciation of the circular nature of our nation's racial dynamics, it is useful to return to the point at which the restrictions on our dialogue were introduced. As in any attempt to resuscitate a buried conversation, understanding is best achieved by examining the poles of the conflict when they were most raw and intense, before the barriers of repression blurred our vision and truncated our thinking. Santayana and Freud converge in the lesson that those who ignore the past are condemned to repeat it.

In 1965, Daniel Patrick Moynihan, then an assistant secretary of Labor in the Johnson Administration, wrote a document officially titled "The Negro Family: The Case for National Action." Almost universally referred to as the Moynihan Report after its principal author, it was the center of a controversy that shaped and constrained our nation's dialogue on matters of race and poverty for decades.

The Report was not originally written for public consumption. It was intended for a small readership of key officials who might influence or implement programs addressing the persisting inequalities between blacks and whites.[5] Before long, however, it became not only widely known and publicly released; it became a *cause célèbre*. While some defended the Report as a savvy and prescient piece of social science analysis and as a sincere effort to come to grips with the sources of our continuing inequalities, others accused Moynihan of subtle racism and of providing a screen to cover the nation's retreat from any real commitment to social justice and equality. Though the phrase had not yet become a central feature of our social rhetoric, in essence they accused Moynihan of blaming the victim.

At the heart of Moynihan's account was the view that centuries of slavery, racism, oppression, and discrimination had led to the development of a family structure in the black community that impeded assimilation into the middle class and perpetuated some of the most problematic features of inner-city life. In essence, Moynihan was offering a vicious circle explanation of our nation's failure to overcome its past: forces had by now been set into motion that made it difficult for blacks to grab hold of the new opportunities introduced by the civil rights revolution, and that turn of events, among other factors, threatened to perpetuate the disadvantaged status of blacks in our society for years to come.

Although the vicious circle analysis offered in this book differs in a number of significant ways from Moynihan's, the negative reaction to Moynihan's analysis was so extraordinarily sweeping and intense, and the impact on the permissible boundaries of our dialogue was so profound, that an analysis such as I am presenting in this book must confront quite directly the import of that reaction.

It may be difficult for many contemporary readers to envisage how extreme and passionate the opposition to Moynihan's analysis actually was. Consider, for example, the response to the Report by James Farmer, the national director of CORE (the Congress of Racial Equality), who asserted that the Report "contains a great number of statistical facts, misread, . . . misinterpreted and warped into a series of conclusions that could make Robert Shelton [the Grand Dragon of the Ku Klux Klan] into a holy prophet." Farmer stated as well that "this report, when studied carefully, emerges in my mind as *the most serious threat to the ultimate freedom of American Negroes to appear in print in recent memory*."[6]

Equally overwrought was the posture, reported as the consensus view of a meeting of radical civil rights activists, that "the Moynihan Report was establishing that the Negro family has degenerated to the point where it could be truthfully said that the American Negro was in fact . . . somewhat less than human."[7]

To be sure, not all civil rights leaders responded in such fashion. Whitney Young, the executive director of the Urban League, stated bluntly that, "The Negro, if he fails to recognize his deprivation or acts as though it doesn't exist, is guilty of stupid chauvinism. And the white person who ignores this reality or acts as though it doesn't exist is guilty of dishonesty."[8]

Martin Luther King saw potential problems and dangers in the Moynihan thesis, but he could recognize as well the ways in which it called attention to issues that were by no means antithetical to the quest for racial equality. In his view,

> As public awareness [of the breakdown of the Negro family] increases, there will be dangers and opportunities. The opportunity will be to see it as a social catastrophe and meet it as other disasters are met with an adequacy of resources. The danger will be that problems will be attributed to innate Negro weaknesses and used to justify, neglect and rationalize oppression.[9]

Even James Farmer, writing just a year after essentially equating Moynihan with the Grand Dragon of the KKK, stated that,

> There have been great gains in job opportunities and educational opportunities for Negroes over the last few years and with organizations like CORE demanding justice, these opportunities will continue to expand. *But we can no longer evade the knowledge that most Negroes will not be helped by equal opportunity.* These are staggering problems for which the traditional CORE program of antidiscrimination is ill-equipped.[10]

These are words that, except for their focus on CORE, could have come right out of the Moynihan Report.

Perhaps most emblematic of the response to the Report, and a disturbing portent of the constraints that have impeded fruitful dialogue on our nation's problems and made their solution so much more difficult, was a declaration by approximately one hundred leaders of civic, religious, and civil rights groups at a meeting organized by Benjamin Payton. Referring to a scheduled White House con-

ference on civil rights (a conference whose initiative came largely
through Moynihan's efforts), they stated that, "It is our position
that the question of 'family stability' be *stricken entirely from the
agenda.*"[11]

Such demands were, unfortunately, all too successful. For many
years, and to some degree even today, the issues that Moynihan
raised *were* largely stricken from the agenda. They became a taboo
topic among those aligned with the aims of the civil rights movement, and especially among liberal whites, who felt particularly vulnerable to the implicit, and sometimes not so implicit, charge that
even to consider the topic was to traffic in racism. The criticisms of
the Report were so intense and often so personal that few writers
were willing to bear the heat. Those who might have explored ideas
with even a passing resemblance to Moynihan's, thought better of
it. As a consequence, the development of effective strategies to combat persisting inequalities has been severely hampered, as ideology
and wishful thinking replaced hardheaded examination of the terrible fallout of centuries of injustice.

The absence of a liberal perspective on the problems Moynihan
was addressing, however, did not mean that they disappeared entirely from public discourse. They became instead the property of
the right, whose influence in national affairs was strengthened
because they seemed to the majority of Americans to be speaking
about reality when liberals would not. And, not surprisingly, in their
hands the implications of observations such as Moynihan's were
indeed often presented as justification for abandoning social programs and moralistically blaming the victims of social inequality.
The fears of blacks and of whites on the left that discussion of the
issues Moynihan raised would inevitably lead to victim-blaming and
social reaction became one more in the long list of self-fulfilling
prophecies that make our lives more difficult than they need to be:
by ceding the topic to the right, they prevented a progressive perspective on the problem from emerging, and thereby found "confirmed" their fears that discussion of it could come to no good.

Weaknesses in the Report

To be sure, there were many elements in Moynihan's account that
understandably caused unease. Particularly prominent among the

more reasoned criticisms was the contention that Moyhihan generalized too broadly, that his discussion of "the Negro family" (in the
terminology of the day) failed to recognize the enormous diversity
among black Americans.[12] Added to this was a concern about his
emphasis on pathology. The Report seemed to many to find little of
strength or value in the families he was describing. Consequently,
many of the Report's critics focused on its omission or misunderstanding of the role played by extended family ties in the black community or of the greater readiness to offer sustenance not only to
family members but to neighbors, friends, and even relative strangers.
Omitting these aspects of black family life, many critics suggested,
played into the hands of racist elements, conveying an impression to
readers that the difficulties blacks were having in our society were a
result not of injustice or discrimination but of there being something
wrong with the way black people were brought up.

Central to the Report's perceived potential for misuse and to its
failure to consider the sensitivities of those who had already borne
the brunt of our society's inequalities was its language. As depicted
by Lee Rainwater and William Yancy, in an authoritative review of
the controversy over the Report, much of the reason for Moynihan's
unusually frank and pungent language was his effort to get the
attention of a slothful establishment that would be resistant to new
initiatives and protective of existing programs and strategies simply because they existed. As Moynihan himself put it, describing his
decision to write the Report, his aim was to "explain some of the
issues of unemployment and housing in terms that would be new
enough and shocking enough that [the officials who read it] would
say, 'Well, we can't let this sort of thing go on. We've got to do
something about it.'"[13]

If the Report had remained solely a document to stimulate
thought—and, importantly, action—on the part of foot-dragging
officials, Moynihan's strategy might have appeared in retrospect as
effective and perhaps even wise. But viewed as a public document,
many features of it seem needlessly provocative and very poorly
chosen. Thus, he states that among poorly educated working-class
blacks "the fabric of conventional social relationships has all but dis-
integrated."[14] He refers to "deep-seated structural distortions" in
the life of black Americans.[15] And in a phrase repeated several times
in the Report, he describes the problems in the black community

and the difficulties he addresses in the black family as a "tangle of pathology."

Ironically, this last phrase did not originate with Moynihan but with the distinguished and highly respected black social scientist Kenneth Clark, who said about the response to Moynihan's report, "It's a kind of wolf pack operating in a very undignified way. If Pat [Moynihan] is a racist, I am. He highlights the total pattern of segregation and discrimination. Is a doctor responsible for a disease simply because he diagnoses it?"[16] Nonetheless, in the context of the Moynihan Report and the climate in which it was received, the phrase became a particularly problematic lightning rod.

A number of other features of the Report further contributed to its unproductive reception. Its focus on illegitimacy, for example, was understandably perceived by many in the black community as an attack on the *morality* of blacks. Although ostensibly Moynihan was simply presenting "data," the prevalence of racist myths about the prodigious and "primitive" sexuality of blacks, and the history in our nation of lynchings of black men who had the misfortune to run up against white fantasies about their sexual appetites, made the topic one whose emotional load should have been anticipated.

Overemphasizing the Family

Perhaps most substantively problematic—and of continuing relevance to contemporary efforts to address racial inequality—was Moynihan's central emphasis on the family and on female-headed households. In arguing for family dysfunction as "the fundamental source of the weakness of the Negro community at the present time," Moynihan maintained that, "The role of the family in shaping character and ability is so pervasive as to be easily overlooked. The family is the basic social unit [and socializing unit] of American life. . . . By and large, adult conduct in society is learned as a child." Elaborating on this idea, he cited what he called a "fundamental insight of psychoanalytic theory . . . that the child learns a way of looking at life in his early years through which all later experience is viewed and which profoundly shapes his adult conduct."[17]

But the possibilities for change are obscured if we fail to understand just *how* the past is perpetuated in the present. In the account offered by Moynihan (and by many psychoanalytic writers), the adult environment appears almost as an irrelevancy, simply the context within which the inevitable will manifest itself. This is most disturbingly evident in Moynihan's contention that, "At this point, the present tangle of pathology is capable of perpetuating itself *without assistance from the white world.*"[18]

To be sure, people caught in a cycle of poverty often act in ways that prevent them from seeing or grasping opportunities that others find readily available. I will discuss this dimension of our impasse extensively throughout this book. But to assume that the world in which they live—however skewed by the consequences of their own behavior and perceptions—is entirely of their own making is to introduce a profound distortion. There is *enormous* "assistance from the white world" in maintaining the patterns Moynihan describes as a tangle of pathology.

Moreover, even granting that early experiences do play a pivotal role in creating the patterns of behavior that are then tragically repeated throughout life,[19] much is missed by equating "early experience" with "family." As profoundly influential as the family is in shaping who we become, it is but one of a *set* of influences that gives form to our view of the world. The behavior patterns that so disturbingly impair many of our nation's poor are not set in stone during the first year or two of life. They are much more powerfully influenced by the years when the *peer group* exerts an increasingly influential pull.[20]

Indeed, even the family patterns Moynihan emphasizes may be understood as having their most significant impact via abdication—that is, precisely through increasing still further the already powerful influence of peers on the developing child's norms and habits. When the influence of peers is not modulated by the (hopefully) more mature and nuanced values of parents, children—of *any* class or ethnic group—may develop their view of life within a youth subculture in which the development of salutary habits and perspectives is significantly impaired.

A primary function of the family in a society such as ours is to protect children from excessive influence by a peer culture which—*as a function of age, not class or ethnicity*—tends to be impulse ridden, short-sighted, and short on empathic appreciation of the needs and points of view of others.[21] If the dangers of peer influence are even greater in the inner city, that is because parents are often over-

whelmed by the circumstances under which they live, thus potentially ceding more influence to the peer group,[22] and because the particular behavior patterns toward which peer pressures push youngsters are shaped by the realities in which they live. Neither the
family nor the peer group are autonomous agents of socialization,
unaffected by the circumstances they encounter in the world at large
or by the media messages that bathe us daily.

Racist Screed or Blueprint for a Progressive Agenda?

Given the the insensitivities and problematic formulations I have
just described, there was certainly a basis for criticism of the Moynihan Report. But what makes the episode such a poignant and illus-
trative object lesson is that, far from being the reactionary, even
racist, document that it was so widely perceived to be, for all its
flaws the Report was in large measure a blueprint for progressive
social action, indeed a design for intervention in our inequalities that
has continuing relevance to this day. In contrast to the view of some
critics that Moynihan acknowledged the guilt of American society
only *in the past*, but that his essential message was to absolve whites
in the present of such responsibility,[23] we may note that Moynihan
stated quite explicitly that "the racist virus in the American blood-
stream still afflicts us."[24] Moreover, the Report placed the blame for
persisting segregation in housing and schooling on policies directly
promoted and financed by the federal government, specifically citing "the construction . . . of the vast white, middle- and lower-middle-class suburbs around all of the Nation's cities."[25]

   In accounting for the processes of family dysfunction on which
the Report focused, he stated that the "fundamental, overwhelming
fact" is the continuing disastrous level of unemployment experienced by black men. A fair reading of the Report would leave the
reader quite clear that programs aimed at enabling blacks to attain
comparable levels of employment and income to whites—*not* an attitude that things are so bad in the black family that it is not possible
to attempt this—was its guiding presumption. It should not be overlooked that the very title of the Report included the phrase, "The
Case for National Action," which is also the title of the concluding
chapter.[26]

   Moynihan objected vigorously to the notion that things were so

bad that nothing could be done.[27] Rather, the aim of the Report was
to show that we need to do *more* than just pass civil rights laws and
pretend that now the playing field is level. The Report stated
unequivocally that, "It is not enough that all individuals start out on
even terms, if the members of one group almost invariably end up
well to the fore, and those of another far to the rear. . . . The principal challenge of the next phase of the Negro revolution is to make
certain that equality of results will now follow. If we do not, there
will be no social peace in the United States for generations."[28] Or, as
Moynihan put it in his redrafting of the ideas for President Johnson's influential Howard University speech, "We seek not just freedom but opportunity—not just legal equity but human ability—not
just equality as a right and a theory but *equality as a fact and a
result.*"[29] Thus, far from rationalizing inequality, the thrust of the
Report can be seen as one of the key documents laying the foundation for affirmative action.

In a memorandum to the president summarizing the Report and
elaborating on its policy implications, Moynihan not only vigorously
advocated a jobs program to assure jobs for all able-bodied black
men, but stated quite explicitly that "housing programs should be
initiated that provide decent family housing and, in particular, that
the housing in suburbs must be planned so that families could escape
the ghetto."[30] This emphasis on eliminating segregation in housing
by assuring that blacks were not excluded from the suburbs was not
only ahead of the curve at the time of the Report but, sadly, remains
largely an unfulfilled dream even today. (See Chapter 11 for more on
this topic.)

I highlight these features of the Moynihan Report to make clear
the degree to which the serious problems that have emerged out of
our history of racial oppression—problems that greatly complicate
the tasks we face as a nation but that must be confronted if we are
finally to transcend that history—became a taboo topic to address.
To be sure, there were errors and ambiguities in the Report, and
debate about them was not only appropriate but essential. But
the degree of defensiveness, demagoguery, and vitriolic attack it
elicited—as if it were a racist screed designed simply to keep blacks
in their place—is a measure of how difficult it has become to maintain
honest and productive dialogue on matters of race in our society.

In recent years, concern about the status of the black family has reemerged in public discourse, not only among whites but among many blacks as well. Expressions of apprehension about the high proportion of black children being raised in poor single-parent families have resurfaced because, far from being an exaggeration and a distortion, the data Moynihan cited have turned out to be only the tip of a frightening and rapidly growing iceberg. Where Moynihan saw as a powerful danger signal that a quarter of black children were being raised in single-parent homes, now more than *half* of black children are being raised in such households.[31] And concerns about this trend have been evident across the full spectrum of political positions and among blacks as well as whites.

To be sure, the critics of the Moynihan Report (as well as more recent critics of "victim blaming") are absolutely right that many of the same trends evident in black families can be found in white families as well. The proportion of children raised in single-parent households, for example, has risen precipitously in virtually all groups in our society. But the stresses on single-parent families are most severe among the poor, and because poverty assails blacks at a far higher rate than whites, and because the black poor are becoming increasingly isolated not only from the rest of society but even from other blacks,[32] it is not an exaggeration to refer to their plight as constituting a crisis. Moynihan may have phrased his thesis carelessly, overgeneralizing and overemphasizing race, but the calamity he pointed to is there for all to see. It is only a segment of the black community that fits his description, but it is a sizable segment and one whose suffering and its ramifications have a powerful impact on our entire society.

4

The Debate
over Culture

The debate over the Moynihan Report was part of a larger controversy regarding the causes of black poverty and the persisting disparities in income between blacks and whites. Whereas Moynihan
focused on the family as the context within which poverty is replicated from generation to generation, others have pointed more
broadly to the influence of culture. The family, after all, is immersed
in a cultural framework that very largely shapes the form it takes
and the values it represents.

Culture exerts its influence not only indirectly, through its
impact on the family, but in more direct ways as well. Cultural systems and cultural values, once established, are maintained by the
way each person observes what "everyone else" in the neighborhood
does, and by the way each, in acting similarly, further contributes to
perpetuating the sense of "this is what everybody does." This shared
sense of appropriate behavior and appropriate aims, recreated over
and over by the reciprocal impact of each person on the other, is an
example *par excellence* of the circularity in human behavior that is at
the heart of this book.

At times, especially under conditions of privation, the cultural
patterns that evolve and persist in this fashion take on a troublingly
ironic cast. Shared values, habits, and perceptions that facilitate cop-

ing with harsh circumstances and limited opportunities can contribute to *maintaining* those circumstances or to preventing people
from leaving the restricted world to which they have adapted. Ironic
patterns of this sort are among the most painful of the vicious circles
to which this book is addressed.

The dimensions of these ironic patterns—which can be both
cultural and individual—are manifold. People who perceive little
hope of their efforts bringing just deserts can begin to live for the
moment, thereby impeding their prospects of developing the background and skills to take advantage of new circumstances if the
opportunity structure changes. Children who perceive little prospect
that hard work in school will bring rewards can begin to turn away
from and even disparage efforts at academic achievement. Patterns of
male-female interaction and child-rearing that arise from limited
economic opportunities for both men and women can become institutionalized and begin to be simply what is expected. General expectations that "white society has no place for us," deriving from a reality in which that perception reflected a clear and brutal truth, can
lead to behavior and attitudes that become a self-fulfilling prophecy
even as the depth of unexamined racist attitudes in the white community begins to diminish.

Many of these and similar patterns have been described by various authors as characterizing a "culture of poverty," a pattern of
behaviors and cultural values that arises from difficult circumstances
but then begins to be at least partially self-perpetuating. As we shall
see, the idea of a culture of poverty has been used in rather disparate
ways. Some have focused on the ironies it points to in order to
address more effectively the deprivations and inequities encountered
by people who are mired in multigenerational poverty. Others have
employed these ideas in ways that entail little more than disparagement and a rationale for doing little or nothing to help. In the eyes of
many advocates and activists, however, explanations of persisting
disadvantage in terms that include characteristics of the disadvantaged themselves are *almost always* inaccurate and demeaning, and
serve so readily to divert attention from inequities that are built into
the society at large that they are, at best, highly suspect. Sociologist
Douglas Glasgow, for example, author of an important study of the
black underclass, argues that even when well intentioned, theories

of cultural deprivation, as well as theories that stress the skills deficits that result from substandard education, distract attention from the need to create jobs and combat racism. Such theories, he suggests, "reinforce whites' belief in the inherent inadequacy of Blacks" and "subtly justify for whites their continued receipt of preferential treatment: Since youthful Blacks are considered to have failed to achieve upward mobility because of their own incapacity, they can without social guilt be legitimately banished to the wasteland of the ghetto."[1]

The Culture of Poverty and the Issue of Race

The position taken by Glasgow and numerous other commentators[2] presents a substantial obstacle to the kind of vicious-circle analysis that is the central concern of this book. If indeed attention to cultural adaptations, to habits and attitudes, or to the impact on people's skills and motivations of being deprived and excluded is nothing more than blaming the victim or placing the onus upon the oppressed instead of the oppressor, then there is little constructive place for the kind of analysis I have to offer. It is therefore essential to confront these objections in order to clear ground for the more complex picture I wish to portray.

The culture of poverty is not the only concept that has been employed to point to patterns of assumptions, values, and behavior on the part of the poor or disadvantaged that contribute to maintaining our inequalities and divisions. I shall have occasion in this book to consider various characterizations of black, African American, or Afrocentric cultures, inner-city or ghetto culture, the cultures of what University of California anthropologist John Ogbu has called voluntary and involuntary minorities, and the "culture of segregation" described by sociologists Douglas Massey and Nancy Denton.[3] These conceptualizations, as well as a number of others I will address, partially overlap but are not equivalent. My focus in this chapter is primarily on the culture of poverty because this is the concept that has been most thoroughly and hotly debated. In the course of examining this debate, I hope to clarify further why I believe that, properly pursued, a vicious-circle analysis, although it includes the behavior of the disadvantaged in its understanding of how disadvantage is perpetuated, is not a regressive defense of injustice or the status quo.

The relevance of the culture of poverty debate to the topic of this book should be obvious. A disproportionately high percentage of African Americans are poor, and understanding the sources of poverty, especially poverty that seems to be "multigenerational," is one of the key issues that any analysis of the dynamics and significance of race in America must confront. But in pursuing the implications of this concept, there is a danger of reinforcing stereotypes that already frequently distort the way African Americans are perceived. Anthropologist Hylan Lewis, a strong critic of the culture of poverty concept, argues that, "The idea of a culture of poverty is a . . . *political* fact," and adds that, "There are times when it seems chillingly like the idea of race."[4]

It is therefore essential to emphasize that *the majority of the poor are not black, and the majority of blacks are not poor.* Many of the ways in which blacks are confronted with the persisting effects of prejudice and discrimination have relatively little to do with poverty. Even blacks who have attained very high levels of professional and economic success encounter almost daily a host of affronts and indignities that even rather poor whites do not experience.[5] The issues that confront the black middle class will not be central to the discussion in this chapter; they will be taken up later in the book. But it should be borne in mind that in exploring the controversies surrounding the behavior and circumstances of the black poor, we are addressing here only a segment of the black community, and only a portion of the impact of our history of slavery and discrimination and of the vicious circles that history has engendered.

Far from being specific to African Americans, the patterns that have been described as constituting a culture of poverty have been observed in all parts of the world and in segments of many different racial and ethnic groups. The noted anthropologist Oscar Lewis, who more than anyone was responsible for developing and articulating the concept of a culture of poverty, based his ideas on observations of slum families in Mexico, Puerto Rico, and elsewhere. Central to Lewis's work was the conclusion, based both on his own research and the data of other social scientists, that "certain persistent patterned associations of traits" were characteristic of families mired in poverty throughout the world.[6]

The Culture of Poverty and Its Critics

Lewis did not view the culture of poverty solely negatively. He stated quite explicitly, "It is not only a matter of economic deprivation, of disorganization, or of the absence of something. It is also something positive and provides some rewards without which the poor could hardly carry on." But he emphasized that the same cultural adaptations that enabled the people he studied to cope and find a measure of meaning in their difficult lives also contributed to their inability to break out of the trap of poverty and deprivation:

> Once the culture of poverty has come into existence it tends to perpetuate itself. By the time slum children are six or seven they have usually absorbed the basic attitudes and values of their subculture. Thereafter they are psychologically unready to take full advantage of changing conditions or improving opportunities that may develop in their lifetime.[7]

It is perhaps this paragraph that best captures what troubled the critics of the culture of poverty concept, who saw it as providing a potential rationale for abandoning the poor or as contributing to their disparagement. Some of the critics recognized that this was far from Lewis's intent, but as with the Moynihan Report, the debate became at times intensely personal, as if good and evil were clashing rather than different ways of understanding how to help people out of a predicament. William Ryan, for example, author of *Blaming the Victim*, acerbically stated that the ultimate effect of cultural explanations

> is always to distract attention from the basic causes and to leave the primary social injustice untouched. And, most telling, the proposed remedy for the problem is, of course, to work on the victim himself. . . . They want to change his attitudes, alter his values, fill up his cultural deficits, energize his apathetic soul, cure his character defects, train him and polish him and woo him from his savage ways.[8]

In both the academic world and the larger world of civil rights activism, an either-or style of thinking prevailed, in which attention to the impact of cultural and psychological adaptations and the ways they could become ironically self-defeating and self-perpetuating was seen as antithetical to concern about racism and structural barriers in the society at large. Those who wished not to be viewed as insensitive to the impact of discrimination or social injustice learned to avoid discussion of cultural patterns and their impact on people's skills, motivations, and attitudes. As summarized by social historian Michael Katz, a progressive who is by no means a proponent of cultural understandings of poverty, "With an outraged civil rights movement behind them, the critics [of the culture of poverty concept] drove cultural questions out of poverty research."[9] The result, he points out, was to leave an important gap in the conceptual framework used to approach poverty and disadvantage, and the breach was filled by advocates of policies that the opponents of the culture of poverty concept could scarcely have desired.[10]

Thus we have here one more of the self-fulfilling prophecies that maintain the circular patterns with which this book is concerned. As William Julius Wilson has pointed out, the declining influence of liberalism has owed much to the reluctance of liberals "to discuss openly or, in some instances, even to acknowledge the sharp increase in social pathologies in ghetto communities."[11] Grounded in the adversarial assumptions and either-or way of thinking this book is devoted to challenging, activists and intellectuals eager to defend the black poor ended up creating the very danger they feared. Rather than offering a left or liberal alternative to the kinds of cultural explanations that were viewed—with considerable justification in many instances—as one-sided and censorious, the left in essence declared the whole topic of culture out of bounds, regarding it as either inherently unfair and accusatory or necessarily a line of inquiry that would be put to socially regressive uses. The ironic— but not really surprising—result was that, with the field of inquiry left open to the right as their exclusive preserve, the topic took on a right-wing spin. In effect, inquiry into the implications of the cultural and behavioral patterns of the poor—patterns that could as readily have been studied for insights into the oppressive consequences of social and economic inequality and for clues as to how to make efforts at change more effective—*became* a right-wing idea; and thus the fears on the left that the topic was dangerous and its discussion nefarious were "confirmed."

Misuse of the Culture of Poverty Concept

I do not mean to suggest that concerns about the ways in which cultural concepts could be used were ungrounded. Accounts which depicted the alleged cultural characteristics of the poor as almost exclusively responsible for their poverty, and in which inequalities generated by the policies, institutions, and distribution of wealth and power in the larger society played virtually no role, were certainly prevelant. Consider, for example, the contentions of Edward Banfield in *The Unheavenly City Revisited,* one of the most influential books on poverty and urban problems of our era. Banfield was a powerful influence on the social policy thinking of the Reagan and Bush administrations and, before that, was chairman of the President's Task Force on Urban Affairs under Richard Nixon. When a revised edition of the book appeared after twenty-two printings, the publishers included a special note stating that "it remains one of the most widely read and widely debated of all books on contemporary American urban problems."

Banfield anchors his argument around a conception of class that rejects income, occupation, schooling, or status as defining criteria, emphasizing instead "a distinct patterning of attitudes, values, and modes of behavior."[12] At the heart of this pattern for him, and offered as *the* crucial dimension for the purpose of social and policy analysis, is what he calls "psychological orientation toward the future."[13] As Banfield presents it,

> [T]he traits that constitute what is called lower-class culture or life style are consequences of the extreme present-orientation of that class. The lower-class person lives from moment to moment, he is either unable or unwilling to take account of the future or to control his impulses. Improvidence and irresponsibility are direct consequences of this failure to take the future into account.[14]

Judgmental terms like "improvident" or "irresponsible" are rare in social science writing, but they pervade Banfield's account. So thoroughly debased, so completely ruined, are these people in Banfield's view that there is little reason even to *try* to help them. Indeed, the humane thing is *not* to, for any well-intentioned efforts will likely as not only make things worse. Lower-class poverty, he asserts, is "inwardly" caused, and improvements in external circumstances are likely to affect it gradually if at all. Poverty of this type tends to be self-perpetuating. . . . In principle, it is possible to eliminate the poverty (material lack) of such a family, but only at great expense, since the capacity of the radically improvident to waste money is almost unlimited. Raising such a family's income would not necessarily improve its way of life, moreover, and could conceivably even make things worse.[15]

Banfield is particularly disdainful of efforts to address the problems of the disadvantaged via investing in better schooling. Such evidence as there is, he claims, "suggests that by the time he reaches school, the lower-class child's handicap is too firmly fixed to allow of its being significantly reduced by anything the school might do."[16] In terms that are breathtakingly sweeping, Banfield asserts that, "*no matter how* able, dedicated, and hardworking the teachers, *no matter how* ample the facilities of the school or how well-designed its curriculum, *no matter how* free the atmosphere of the school from racial or other prejudice, the performance of pupils at the lower end of the class-cultural scale will *always* fall short not only of that of pupils at the upper end of the scale, but also of what is necessary to make them educated workers."[17] This is, he suggests—and this time for once he is both accurate and understated—an "implication . . . that reformers find hard to accept."

Banfield states with apparent exasperation that despite his disclaimers to the contrary, when he refers to the "lower class," some readers will conclude that what he really means is blacks.[18] Perhaps we should believe him when he indicates that he feels a similar contempt for lower-class whites; Banfield may well be an equal opportunity bigot. But it does not take a rocket scientist to calculate the statistics that demonstrate that the burden of his "policies" falls disproportionately upon blacks and other minorities.

There is little in Banfield's theorizing about the lower classes (if one may dignify his fulminations with a term such as theorizing) that does not translate quite readily into "to hell with them." His depiction of the inner-city poor is so harshly moralistic, so thoroughly lacking in even a modicum of empathy, so filled with condemnation and arrogant assumption of superiority, and so extraordinarily simplistic and one-dimensional, that one might mistake it for a caricature of conservatism concocted by a paranoid leftist. Unfortunately, however, not only was he no fantasy, but he was both highly influential and merely the most egregious (or least subtle) of a substantially larger group of invidious interpreters of the meaning of cultural differences.

It is scarcely surprising that those concerned with furthering the cause of equality and social justice should be appalled by such arguments and eager to expose and contest their gross oversimplifications. It is understandable as well that arguments such as Banfield's would make one suspicious of cultural arguments generally. But the cost of such suspicion is very high. Understanding the circular patterns in which unrelenting poverty and discrimination can generate habits of thought and behavior that bring forth further deprivation and exclusion is essential if we are to intervene effectively to break the cycle. Without clear understanding of the painful ironies that confront us, any effort to create a better and more just society will flounder in a morass of good intentions and fatally inadequate execution.

Do the Poor Have Different Values?

Much of the debate over the existence of a culture of poverty comes down to the question of whether there is a subculture among the poor that differs from mainstream society not only in behavior and lifestyle but in fundamental attitudes and values. The claim of many of the critics of the culture of poverty concept is that the poor do not have different *values* from the rest of us, only a different likelihood of being able to *attain* or *express* those values. There may be a variety of ways in which their day-to-day behavior differs from that of more well-off members of society, but in this view it is an error to attribute those differences to a different value scheme or different habits of mind; they are simply adaptations to the circumstances the poor encounter, and, it is claimed, *they would change readily if the circumstances were to change.*

Much confusion has arisen from a misleadingly dichotomous way of framing the debate. It should be perfectly obvious that the only sensible answer to the question of whether those who are part of the culture of poverty share values with the rest of society or evidence a unique set of values and priorities is that *both* are true. Much like the relationship between a bay and an ocean, the currents within the culture of poverty are reflective of currents in the larger body, but have many features that reflect unique characteristics and dynamics. The culture of poverty is not a totally autonomous entity that is immune to the influence of the larger society; it reeks of that influence. But at the same time, it takes an almost willful myopia to overlook the powerfully important ways in which its way of life differs from that characteristic of most members of our society.

To be sure, differences in behavior do not in themselves imply differences in values. One can certainly imagine the critics of the culture of poverty concept responding, "*Of course*, life in the ghetto is different. How could it not be different given the degree of deprivation its residents experience? But the question remains whether that is a difference of values or merely a difference of circumstance."

There are indeed many indications that people trapped in poverty can nonetheless maintain a belief in the value of work, education, and other such "middle-class values," and that many of their "deviations" from such values are a result of frustration and the perception that opportunities to realize these values are blocked. Moreover, there is ample evidence that significant numbers of the poor *live* these values in their daily behavior. (Many of my own students are excellent examples of such persistence in the face of daunting external circumstances.) But it should also be abundantly clear that many of our nation's poor—whatever values they may express verbally—make daily choices that reflect a different set of governing priorities. If the concept of values is to have any utility at all in understanding human behavior, it is essential that we understand the difference between professed or nominal values and the values that actually guide everyday behavior. Asking people what they believe in may result in quite different impressions from those obtained by actually observing the choices and priorities evident in the way they lead their lives.

Which, then, are their "real" values? This is a question that is likely to lead to fruitless debate. All of us live by multiple and often *conflicting* values. The background values that the multigenerational poor share with the larger society and the frequently differing values that are reflected in the choices they make every day are *both* real. But when attempting to live by the broadly shared values of the society leads to continuing frustration and failure, the rather different values that have evolved as a way of coping with that frustration are likely to become increasingly salient.[19]

Open and Closed Systems

Whether the concept of a culture of poverty implies absolving the larger society and blaming the disadvantaged depends on what version of the idea one is discussing. An appropriately comprehensive version of the theory would make it clear that although there are ways in which the culture of poverty is a self-sustaining or self-perpetuating system, it is not a *closed* system. That is, its mode of operation is continually influenced by the larger system of which it is a part, and its capacity to perpetuate itself depends upon its relation to that larger system. It is a serious error to underestimate the powerful forces within the culture of poverty that repeatedly give shape to the lives of each generation that emerges within it; but it is an equally serious error to become so transfixed by the internal dynamics that one fails to notice—or intentionally ignores—the crucial role of the maintaining environment.

The culture of poverty *is* a largely self-perpetuating system. But it is an *open* system, not a closed one. If a powerful commitment from the larger society were to bring a significant infusion of money and opportunity to the inner city, the "self-perpetuating" quality of the culture of poverty would be seen to be *contingent* rather than absolute. When its sway *appears* absolute, it is because the external circumstances that sustain it have persisted.

Does this mean that if new jobs and opportunities were to confront the inner-city poor, their attitudes and expectations and their overt behavior would change instantly? Hardly. Any serious student of human behavior knows that change is rarely instant or rapid. We all tend to construe new experiences very largely in terms of what has come before. If new opportunities are made available to people who have been significantly deprived of such opportunities, the initial response is likely to be one of skepticism. The new initiatives are likely to be seen as insincere, condescending, illusory, lacking in real substance; in short, more of the same.

It is essentially this facet of our mental life that is emphasized when writers like Banfield contend that children born into lower-class cultures become unable to take advantage of new opportunities. And there is a certain amount of truth in the contention. But it is a half-truth, and like most half-truths it obscures more than it illuminates.

For good reason, we are not wired to conclude suddenly or easily that all the assumptions on which our lives are based must be jettisoned. But neither are we impervious to signs that something new is happening. Perception of difference is as fundamental to our thinking and our approach to the world as is the pull to interpret in terms of the familiar. And there are countless instances in the course of our lives in which the recognition of difference, of new possibility, wins the day. We would not have survived as a species if that were not the case.

The great Swiss student of psychological development Jean Piaget called these two tendencies, always in dynamic opposition and fusion in our psychological functioning, *assimilation* and *accommodation*, and we shall have occasion to consider them in more detail in Chapter 7. For our present purposes, what needs to be understood is that both of these seemingly contradictory tendencies are active in our every effort to apprehend the world. In considering whether the culture of poverty immunizes people against perceiving new opportunities when they become available—or whether a genuine change in the resources and possibilities the society makes available to those who had been disadvantaged will bring forth new attitudes and new behavior—the interaction between these two tendencies and their relative weight in any given circumstance is crucial. Expectations can be stubborn; the schemas through which we filter all perceptual input and construe all meaning can, to a considerable extent, refract and rework the messages we receive from the world in order to make them fit. But the tendency of these schemas to assimilate new input to old interpretations and expectations is neither omnipotent nor inexorable. *Accommodation* to the features of the new information that do not fit smoothly into the perceptual scheme we bring to bear is also an integral part of every perceptual act. If expectations are repeatedly disconfirmed, eventually those expectations begin to change.

What enormously complicates our perceptions of human affairs, however, and introduces the potential for extraordinary mischief, is that our expectations are not inert elements in the process. That is, our expectations would indeed change if repeatedly disconfirmed; but in certain circumstances the expectations themselves—or more precisely, the behaviors that result from those expectations—*prevent* the disconfirming events from occurring. In certain ways, this should be a familiar process. The notion of the self-fulfilling prophecy has entered our general vocabulary, and its rough outlines are grasped by almost everyone. But in fact the idea of the self-fulfilling prophecy is one that is easily misunderstood or misused, and a closer examination of its relevance in the present context is very much warranted.

Unexamined—or given a tendentious ideological spin—the notion of the self-fulfilling prophecy can easily lend itself to the simplistic view that the culture of poverty is perpetuated entirely from within. The politically motivated corollary is that there is virtually nothing we can do about it: "they" expect the world to be a certain way because their culture induces that expectation, and by hook or by crook they will see it that way and respond accordingly. Such a way of understanding the self-fulfilling prophecy conveniently leaves out the response of "us"—that is, of the larger society in which the culture of poverty is embedded.

Much closer to the truth is that the process whereby expectations of others are fulfilled is a *mutual* process in which, as it were, the expecter and the expected-of jointly participate. From everything we know about human behavior and human perception, we may assume that if input from the larger society indicating that things have really changed were to persist, the members of the culture of poverty would gradually begin to respond to that change. But everything we know about human psychology *also* indicates that this will take time and will require repeated confirmation that change is real; the poor are no less cautious about changing the views that have been at the heart of their survival than any of the rest of us. And herein lies the ironic heart of the impasse. For time may be just what the process of change does not have. If early initiatives directed toward providing greater opportunity to the disadvantaged do not encounter a receptive response, those initiatives may *not* persist. For the likelihood is high that society's mainstream will then conclude that "we have tried" and that "these efforts just don't work."[20] The result is that the race is lost—the wrong thing happens first. The middle class gives up before the poor can respond enough to keep the former's initiatives going, and each side concludes (for different reasons) that change was not really possible.

What is essential for us to understand is not the cliche that change takes time and requires patience (though of course it does). Rather it is that the process of change (or of failure in the effort at change) is a *dynamic* one. Expectations and responses from both sides not only determine the final outcome but, to a very significant degree, determine *each other*. The seeming failure of the hardcore poor to respond to social programs is not simply a matter of attitudes or lack of skills; it is equally a function of the equal and opposite skepticism of the mainstream. The suspicions of the poor lead them to respond in ways that confirm the suspicions of the better-off and vice versa. The self-fulfilling prophecies of the poor depend for their fulfillment on the self-fulfilling prophecies of the middle-class mainstream.

Acknowledging Harm and Staying the Course

Ultimately, understanding how and why the behavior patterns in the inner city are perpetuated requires that we transcend the overly narrow and simplistic ways in which the questions have been posed and the answers formulated. Writers on the right tend to see the behavior and the deprivation of the poor as "internally" caused. For Banfield, for example, the causes reside in cultural traits and values picked up so early in life that even by the time the child is ready to enter school they are virtually immutable. In the much publicized work of the authors of *The Bell Curve* (to be discussed in the next chapter), the answer, even more "internally," resides in the genes.[21] From the vantage point of these one-dimensional accounts, there is little reason to seek change by attempting to address inequities in the way we apportion opportunity and reward; through their lens such efforts are virtually doomed to failure.

But the answers offered from the left are often no less dichotomous and one-dimensional. In the eyes of the culture of poverty critics discussed in this chapter, instead of causality residing completely within the culture of the poor it resides completely in the external environment. Moreover, the consequences of the inequities to which they call our attention are portrayed as oddly limited: The prejudices and injustices embodied in our social order are seen as influencing those who have been marginalized only in rather concrete and material ways. They are deprived of money, jobs, decent housing, a decent education, proper medical care, a fair chance to show how far their talents can take them. Yet this deprivation has no impact on their hearts and minds, no effects on the assumptions they live by, the nature of their aspirations, their ability or readiness to persevere with the conviction that hard work and delay of gratification will bring future rewards. It does not produce a discouragement or alienation that would extend a single moment beyond the day when the concrete material deprivations were to be lifted. Give the poor a chance today—to be sure, a real chance, not a public relations exercise or a token effort—and they will promptly grab it, just like those who have spent their whole lives *expecting* to have a chance and preparing for that chance from first grade through graduate school. To suggest that anything different might be the case, that the deprivations and injustices they have experienced might have produced habits and assumptions that would make it difficult to grab hold in this way, is, according to this view, to engage in racist assumptions and victim blaming.

But notwithstanding the sometimes nefarious purposes to which the culture of poverty concept has been put, its implications for social policy are by no means limited to those asserted by Banfield and his ilk. Shorn of its specious connections to a brief for neglect, attention to the culture of poverty highlights two points that are crucial to any serious efforts to bring about change: First, our society's long-standing inequalities have in fact done *a lot* of damage to its victims. Therefore, we will have to commit *a lot* of resources to repair that damage. Second, change *will* be slow, *will* be impeded by long-standing habits that we have induced in those who have for so long been denied opportunity. Therefore, we must be prepared to stay the course rather than indulge in hopes of rapid and easy change that are bound to be dashed.

When opponents of the culture of poverty concept suggest that, "Resignation and fatalism may readily give way to individual aspiration or group confidence when there is a change in perceived opportunities,"[22] a false expectation is induced that undermines the persistence and determination required to achieve the difficult changes that we must seek. If we do not properly prepare the public for the complexities and difficulties we will face, if we sell people the idea that change will "readily" follow from the availability of new opportunities, this will inevitably yield disappointment and an unreadiness to follow through. Once more it will be all too easy to conclude that there is no point in "throwing money at problems."

Strengths and Ironies

Discussions of the culture of poverty (and analogous discussions of "black culture," "ghetto culture," "welfare culture," etc.) have been criticized for an ethnocentrism in which middle-class white culture is seen as the standard or even the ideal, and all departures from middle-class patterns are viewed as somehow inferior. Charles Valentine, for example, objects to "antipoverty programs designed to inculcate middle-class virtues into the children of the poor,"[23] and numerous writers have taken issue with formulations that view the low test scores of African Americans as indicative of cultural deprivation, contending that the scores do not reflect deprivation but difference.[24]

In many respects, the critique of ethnocentric bias in discussing the lifeways of the poor is well taken. Many of the adaptations that are evident in the cultural styles and habits of the poor enable them to cope with conditions that would likely overwhelm those schooled to deal with lives of relative ease and comfort. Moreover, the remarkable creativity that has survived, and perhaps even in certain ways been enhanced by, privation and isolation has led to abundant importing by the mainstream culture of musical, dance, and linguistic forms originating in the inner city, but not to corresponding respect for the sources of that creativity.

And yet, it is essential that in honoring the resourcefulness with which people cope with deplorable circumstances we not romanticize their plight. The conditions under which many of our nation's minority citizens live are brutalizing. They truncate human potential and place severe limits on people's opportunities to express—or even fully to recognize—their true capacities. This is precisely why we must fight so vigorously to change those conditions, and it ill behooves those working to change them to sentimentalize their impact. The heart of the matter is that the very adaptations that enable people to survive the harsh circumstances that generations of oppression and discrimination have yielded also make extricating themselves from those conditions or changing them very difficult. Much of this book is concerned with elaborating this irony and finding points of exit.

5

Ideology and IQ

Moving beyond the Bell Curve

The residues of injustice are not limited to the underclass or the culture of poverty. At *every* income level, differences are found between blacks and whites on a wide variety of tests assessing cognitive functioning and "IQ."[1] These observed differences have been a fertile breeding ground for views that are racist in the most fundamental meaning of the word—the idea that human beings can be divided into distinct races and that certain races are inherently inferior to others.[2]

Understanding fully the vicious circles that perpetuate our racial inequities requires us to come to grips with these differences in a more enlightened way. Under present circumstances, they are real, large, and replicable, and they account for a good deal of how our inequalities are maintained. At the same time, as I shall elaborate below, they are a clear product of those very inequalities, a sign or symptom of a society that has still not sufficiently overcome its history of severe injustice. To lose track of either half of this circular reality is to contribute to perpetuating still further the same lamentable state of affairs.

Addressing the meaning of these differences has become even more urgent since the appearance of Richard Herrnstein and Charles Murray's highly publicized book, *The Bell Curve: Intelligence and Class Structure in American Life*. Like Banfield's work, discussed in Chapter Four, Herrnstein and Murray's volume is ultimately a rationalization for doing nothing to assist those in need. Herrnstein and Murray, however, frame their argument much more explicitly in terms of race. Although they do indeed argue that poor whites too are inferior, they address racial differences *qua* racial differences in a way Banfield explicitly said he was not doing. More inches of their tome are devoted to intraracial comparisons, but it was their pronouncements on race that made the book headline news.

Herrnstein and Murray, moreover, go even further than Banfield in interiorizing the causes of poverty and deprivation. For Banfield, it is the *culture* of the lower class that renders them intractible to change. And although Banfield argues that the ill effects of lower-class culture are set very early, he implicitly acknowledges that the characteristics he depicts are not intrinsic. Herrnstein and Murray, in contrast, hinge their argument not around the concept of class but of intelligence. Class for them is but one more dependent variable, influential in a secondary way, but not the nub of the story. Moreover, they compound the accusation, as it were, by stressing a view of intelligence that is both unidimensional and highly determined by genetics.

Modern conceptions of intelligence increasingly emphasize that intelligence is multidimensional.[3] The image of intelligence emphasized by Herrnstein and Murray, in contrast, is one in which a single factor—"g," or "general intelligence"—is cast as the crucial determinant of human success. Moreover, not only are human beings in Herrnstein and Murray's scheme able to be assigned a single number that to an extraordinary degree determines their fate, but this magic number is in our very genes: It is our DNA, not society, that determines that some of us will accumulate vastly more wealth than others. Further, it is DNA, not racism or a history of slavery, segregation, and discrimination, that determines the significantly less ample life chances often experienced by blacks in our society.

Herrnstein and Murray's work differs from Banfield's in still another way: it is a much more *effective* attack upon the disadvantaged. Whereas Banfield wrote in such a blunderbuss fashion that it should have been obvious to virtually any reader that he had nothing but contempt for the people he described (and indeed, that his descriptions were little more than caricatures), Herrnstein and Murray are masters of the crocodile tear. Affecting great empathy and concern for the poor unfortunates who "for reasons that are not their fault"[4] simply have less gray matter than the "cognitive elite," they provide a socially acceptable covering for attitudes that once were relegated to dark corners and shameful whispers.

Moreover, they present an imposing—if selective and tendentiously interpreted—array of data, and they skillfully create the appearance of considering thoughtfully and thoroughly the arguments and findings of those who disagree with them. What they offer is in fact more like an adroit legal brief than a scientific argument—they highlight the facts that are consistent with the conclusion they wish to reach and brush over or attempt to cast doubt upon any findings that are inconvenient to their case. But their talent for making a brief look like objective science should not be underestimated.

Finding Inferiors

In considering the contentions of *The Bell Curve*, it is useful to begin with the following account by Claude Fischer and his colleagues in the sociology department at the University of California at Berkeley:

> Members of a minority, many of whom were brought to the country as slave labor, are at the bottom of the social ladder. They do the dirty work, when they have work. The rest of the society considers them violent and stupid and discriminates against them. Over the years, tension between minority and majority has occasionally broken out in deadly riots. In the past, minority children were compelled to go to segregated schools and did poorly academically. Even now, minority children drop out of school relatively early and often get into trouble with the law. Schools with many minority children are seen as problem ridden, so majority parents sometimes move out of the school district or send their children to private schools. And, as might be expected, the minority children do worse on standardized tests than majority children.[5]

The description is likely to sound familiar to an American reader. But Fischer and his colleagues are not in fact discussing blacks in America. They are discussing the Korean minority in

Japan, an ethnic group that in the U.S. is one of the "model minorities" to which blacks are compared invidiously, and one of the groups
The Bell Curve claims are at the very top of the IQ ladder. What differs is the circumstances under which Koreans arrived in the two
countries and the social position and social opportunities they have
encountered. Koreans came to the United States voluntarily and
with hope for a better future. In Japan, they have been a scorned
minority, first exploited as members of a brutally colonized nation
and then relegated to the position of a disdained lower caste.

Here again, the consequences of oppression are cruelly circular.
Those relegated to the lower reaches of society often do manifest
impairments and limitations that are the consequence of their sub-
jugation, and those inclined to defend social inequalities then cite
those limitations as an "explanation" for the group's lower status.
The tendency is not new. In the early part of this century, it was
Jews and immigrants from southern and eastern Europe who were
viewed as less intelligent. At that time, prominent social scientists
divided European immigrant "stock" into three types: Nordic,
Alpine, and Mediterranean. The latter two were deemed inherently
inferior, and "mongrelization" of the population by the polluting
effect of the latter two upon the first was deemed a real danger. Carl
Brigham, a leading psychometrician at the time of the First World
War, contended that his objective testing revealed that Jews "had an
average intelligence below those from all other countries except
Poland and Italy."[6]

As Thomas Sowell, who otherwise shares Charles Murray's
conservative political orientation, points out, the data "demonstrating" these European groups' inferiority was "as hard as any data
in *The Bell Curve*."[7] Sowell also notes that it was precisely in the
"abstract" items that European immigrants, such as Jews, showed
their inferiority at the beginning of the century.[8] Thus, Herrnstein
and Murray's claim that these items are culture-free and get at subjects' "real" intelligence, or that African Americans' poorer performance on these particular items makes a strong case for a genetic
rather than cultural or environmental basis for group differences,
requires quite creative accounting. Asians and Ashkenasi Jews, after
all, are the two IQ hero groups of *The Bell Curve*. Asians, however,
like Jews, once scored *below* native whites on IQ tests. For both
groups, things changed significantly as their social status did.

Indeed, throughout our nation's history there have been groups whom our more advantaged citizens have regarded as inherently inferior. Many whites who are tempted to give credence to *The Bell Curve*'s contentions might wish to reflect on how their own grandparents were perceived not that long ago and how they themselves would have been viewed in an earlier era when the taint of inferiority was seen as inherent in *their* group. Even the "Nordic" Swedes had their turn at being viewed as laughably inferior. A popular joke in the nineteenth century asked, "What is dumber than a dumb Irishman?" The answer: "A smart Swede."[9] What the joke implied about the intelligence of the Irish is of course also clear.

Herrnstein and Murray's vision of our current social landscape offers a replay of this familiar script, but to give it contemporary trappings they have given new roles to some of the old actors. Jews and Asians, cast as the dullards in older versions, now star as the elite of the cognitive elite. But Herrnstein and Murray retain the key theme that has played so well over the centuries: *The way things are is the way they have to be.* It's too bad that certain people or groups do so poorly, but that's God's doing, not ours. It's the genes He gave them, not the rules and social circumstances we've constructed that account for our inequalities.

What is the Role of Socioeconomic Status in Differences between Blacks and Whites?

It has long been known that IQ scores are significantly correlated with the socioeconomic status (SES) of the family in which one has grown up.[10] Since blacks are on average poorer and less socially advantaged than whites,[11] the difference in SES seems an obvious alternative to explaining IQ score differences in terms of genes— especially since the genetic explanation is not only hurtful and demeaning but entails a number of assumptions that are highly questionable and counter to contemporary understanding of population genetics and the relation between individual differences and group differences.

The authors of *The Bell Curve* acknowledge that the differences in overall IQ scores for blacks and whites diminish sharply when one controls for SES, but they attempt to counter this argument in several ways. First of all, they point out that controlling for SES reduces, but does not eliminate the differences between blacks and whites. Second, they argue that the differences in SES themselves reflect IQ differences: it is people of lesser intelligence, in their view, who *end up* with lower SES, and then pass their lower intelligence along to their progeny. Thus, controlling for SES may misleadingly wash out real differences in intelligence.

The appropriate way to consider whether blacks and whites differ in intelligence, according to Herrnstein and Murray, is to compare the two groups for those who have *the same* SES. Surely, they contend, that portion of the black population that is *not* economically disadvantaged ought to have the same IQs as whites if it is SES (rather than genes) that is causing the overall differences between the groups. But in fact, at *every* SES level, whites score higher than blacks on tests purporting to measure IQ.

What Herrnstein and Murray leave out in this argument is simply the entire nature of American society. They present their analysis as if SES meant the same thing for blacks as for whites. The evidence is overwhelming that this is not the case. In an enormous number of ways, the actual life circumstances of blacks and whites at the "same" SES are radically different.

Even at the most concrete material level, the data Herrnstein and Murray use to calculate SES—parents' education, occupations, and income—leave a hole large enough for a truck to drive through. For reasons very obviously rooted in the history that Herrnstein and Murray wish to minimize, blacks of a given income and occupation tend to have considerably less accumulated wealth than whites of the same income.[12] Thus, blacks of "the same" SES background in Herrnstein and Murray's analyses in fact come from homes in which economic circumstances are likely to be very substantially different. With less money in the bank, there is less to fall back on, hence both greater stress and more difficulty in supporting their children's pursuit of higher education.

But that is only the beginning. The environment a child encounters is determined not just by his or her family's own economic status but by the income level of the entire neighborhood. The consequence of persisting housing segregation[13] and of the gap in accumulated wealth noted above is that even as more blacks are entering the middle class than ever before in terms of income, the gap in living conditions remains considerably greater than these figures would suggest. Many middle-class blacks must live in neighborhoods where the overall income level is considerably lower than in the neighborhoods where whites live who share the same incomes and occupations. As a consequence, the educational opportunities and overall neighborhood environment of blacks and whites of the same "SES" are likely to differ quite substantially.

One study in Philadelphia, for example, found that, as a consequence of residential segregation and racial concentration, the children of affluent black families attended public schools in which the proportion of low-achieving students was *three times greater* than it was in the schools attended by comparably affluent white students.[14] Their money, simply put, does not buy the same kind of environment for them or their kids as a white person's money. Comparing blacks and whites whose families had equal "SES" thus spuriously equates environments that are vastly different.[15]

Stereotypes, Disidentification, and the Culture of Involuntary Minorities

Herrnstein and Murray are almost willfully blind to the social and psychological dimensions of the differences in the environments and experiences of blacks and whites. Daily encountering disparaging stereotypes and the disdain of one's fellow citizens has an impact that "controlling for SES" does not begin to capture. Stereotypes are not just vague abstractions in the minds of liberals or wispy "excuses" for poor performance. They are powerful—and demonstrable—social and psychological phenomena, whose consequences have been established convincingly by careful, systematic research.

Stanford psychologist Claude Steele has shown in a series of rigorous studies that having to cope with stereotypes can interfere with the functioning of even the most talented and advantaged African Americans.[16] In Steele's studies, white and African American students were presented with the same difficult test items. When the items were depicted as measures of intellectual ability, African American students did much worse than whites. When *the same items* were described as an experimental procedure that was *not* an evaluation of their abilities, African American students fully equalled the performance of whites.[17] The anxiety generated in the first condition—a condition much closer to that in which most intellectual evaluation is undertaken—masked the real ability of the African American subjects.

Anxiety, of course, can interfere with intellectual test performance for people of any ethnic group[18], and presumably affected some of the white subjects in the "evaluative" condition as well. But the *differential* impact on African Americans, Steele argues, reflects something over and above test anxiety per se—concern that they would confirm prevailing stereotypes about their entire group, a concern Steele calls "stereotype anxiety." Here once again a vicious circle is generated. Anxiety generated by the stereotype contributes to poorer performance, and the poorer performance in turn contributes to maintaining the stereotype.[19]

Steele's work has focused especially on those black students who are most identified with the academic realm, students one might say who are "survivors" who have persisted despite the implicit and explicit assaults on their legitimacy and self-esteem. That even these high-achieving young men and women are vulnerable to the effects of stereotype anxiety attests to the disruptive power of this phenomenon. An even larger number of African Americans, Steele points out, are discouraged long before they reach the level of achievement of the men and women in most of his studies. They "disidentify" with school rather early, and construct a life course organized around avoiding academic pursuits and challenges. As a consequence, measures of their intellectual performance that purport to gauge their inherited intellectual capacity are highly spurious.

In explicating the concept of disidentification, Steele notes that developing intellectually and performing well in academic settings requires one to *identify* with that domain, to put oneself on the line to some degree so that self-esteem itself in part depends on successful performance. In one important paper, Steele and co-author Joshua Aronson note that over time the effort to protect oneself against the pain and threat of stereotypes that are particularly directed toward African Americans' intellectual capacities—stereotypes, of course, that Herrnstein and Murray contribute to perpetuating and intensifying—can lead to turning away from the intellectual domain toward activities that are safer and farther from the eye of the storm. The self-concept itself is then redefined "such that school achievement is not a basis of self-evaluation nor a personal identity. This protects the person against the self-evaluative threat posed by the stereotypes, but may have the byproduct of diminishing interest, motivation, and ultimately achievement in the domain."[20] Recent research has demonstrated precisely such a phenomenon among African American children and youths.[21]

Such a pattern is not unique to African Americans. University of California anthropologist John Ogbu has studied the cultures and the intellectual performance of minority groups throughout the world, and has found impressive consistencies. Groups who have a caste-like lower status or who are incorporated into a society via slavery, conquest, or colonization develop very different patterns of adaptation than those who enter a society as voluntary immigrants. These differences produce quite different outcomes even when the economic circumstances of the family may be quite similar. Although voluntary immigrant groups also frequently encounter poverty and discrimination, the history and psychology of their engagement with the society leads them to see their hardships as temporary and capable of being overcome by hard work and education. Moreover, they are likely to compare their difficult circumstances not to those of the society's more privileged members but to what they would have encountered back home, in the society they decided to leave. Both these tendencies have positive implications for the confidence and motivation required to invest effort in education and push to learn the skills and habits that promote success, both occupationally and on "IQ" tests.

The groups Ogbu calls "involuntary minorities," in contrast, tend to compare their circumstances with those of the dominant group and to center their worldview on injustice and discrimination, which they view as "permanent and institutionalized."[22] Reflecting the suspicion which they feel toward a mainstream culture that has been experienced primarily as a source of oppression and disparagement, involuntary minority students manifest what Ogbu calls an "oppositional cultural frame of reference and identity." Unlike students from voluntary immigrant groups, involuntary minority students do not regard mastery of the mainstream's cultural and linguistic style as a legitimate aim to which concerted efforts should be directed. The language and behaviors required at school, viewed negatively or ambivalently, are experienced as a threat to the individual's and the group's identity. As a consequence, "involuntary minority students who adopt attitudes conducive to school success or who behave in a manner conducive to academic success are often accused by their peers of acting like their enemy. . . . Among U.S. blacks, such students may be accused of acting white or acting like Uncle Toms."[23]

All of these attitudes, of course, are likely to hinder performance on "IQ" tests and to render estimates of "innate" ability highly suspect. They reflect a cultural pattern that is by no means particular to African Americans. Ogbu found such attitudes and behavior patterns throughout the world wherever a group had been incorporated into a society by oppressive means, and he found as well the same kinds and sizes of performance decrements that Herrnstein and Murray are quick to attribute to genetics in African Americans. From the Maori of New Zealand, to the Burakumin of Japan (a group racially indistinguishable from other Japanese but isolated as a caste-like disparaged group), to the Untouchables in India, to Oriental Jews in Israel, the same fifteen-point gap in measured IQ is evident between the minority and the dominant group as between blacks and whites in America.[24] This is also, interestingly, precisely the gap between Protestants and Catholics in Northern Ireland.[25] And importantly, throughout the world, when these groups that appear so persistently "inferior" in their home society emigrate elsewhere, they do as well as members of their country's dominant group who have emigrated to the same place.[26]

In their 845-page volume, Herrnstein and Murray devote one paragraph to Ogbu's work, leave out most of the details I have just noted, and do not present a discussion of his arguments or data. The specific observations Ogbu and other scholars report raise serious questions about Herrnstein and Murray's readiness to explain group differences in genetic terms. The way Herrnstein and Murray treat those observations raises still other questions about the kind of argument they have constructed and about their self-assumed stance of distinterested scholar.

"IQ Tunnel Vision" and *The Bell Curve*'s Political Agenda

In general, *The Bell Curve* is constructed in such a way as to induce what might be called "IQ tunnel vision," a fixed, almost fetishized focus on IQ that obscures important facts and is likely to lead the unwitting reader to unwarranted conclusions. To begin with, the sheer weight of emphasis on IQ in the text—the repetitive demonstrations in page after similar page of correlations between IQ measures and socially important individual differences—is likely to divert readers not sophisticated in or comfortable with quantitative analyses from noticing that the very analyses presented in *The Bell Curve* indicate *how little* IQ accounts for the overall distribution of wealth and position in our society.

It is clearly Herrnstein and Murray's aim to portray IQ as the crucial element in alotting rewards and status in our society and to imply that our aversion to acknowledging this fact has led to a series of idealistic but terribly unrealistic efforts to abrogate nature and make everyone equal. But in fact, as Herrnstein and Murray themselves acknowledge,[27] IQ or "cognitive ability" accounts for only a small portion of the variation among people. Usually the variance accounted for is less than ten percent, and often it is less than five percent. Ninety-five percent of what determines wealth or poverty, crime or law-abiding behavior, family stability, welfare dependency, etc., is something *other* than cognitive ability.

The role of *genetically determined* differences in intelligence in determining social position—even accepting Herrnstein and Murray's highly skewed interpretations of the available data regarding the heritability of IQ scores[28]—is even smaller. Their own estimate is that a little over half of the variance in IQ scores is determined by inherited factors. Thus, whereas IQ scores that include the substantial influence of social and economic factors account for only five to ten percent of outcome or less, "genetic IQ" accounts for only half of *that*. In contrast, a recent study by economists David Cutler and Edward Glaeser of Harvard University and the National Bureau of Standards estimated, based on sophisticated data analysis, that a thirteen-percent reduction in our society's level of housing segregation would yield a *thirty-three-percent* reduction in the differences in economic and educational outcomes for blacks and whites.[29]

Also obscured by *The Bell Curve's* IQ tunnel vision is that far from being a direct measure of intellectual capacity or ability to function effectively in our society, the IQ score is a number that gains whatever validity or usefulness it might have from its correlations with other measures of how people function that are of more direct social significance. This is crucial to bear in mind because, as part of their effort to convey the impression that "social programs don't work," Herrnstein and Murray brush under the rug a host of demonstrable impacts on actual and important dimensions of social functioning, directing the reader's attention obsessively to whether these programs "increase IQ." Programs that increase the likelihood that participants will graduate from school, obtain a steady job with a decent income, or maintain a stable marriage and stay out of trouble with the law, but do not "raise IQs," point to the inadequacy of IQ measures, not to the inadequacy of the program. There are many programs that fit this description, and Herrnstein and Murray's fetishizing of IQ is very largely designed to persuade us not to spend money on them.[30]

Consider, for example, Herrnstein and Murray's discussion of the effects of Project Head Start and related programs. Herrnstein and Murray fault Head Start for not permanently raising children's IQ scores. (They do not address what it means that those scores—supposedly tapping a fundamental and genetically determined property of the individual—did change quite dramatically, even if for just a year or two.) But such programs do change a lot of other things that are more important—indeed, precisely the measures of social functioning that Herrnstein and Murray are so eager to show correlate with IQ.[31] Herrnstein and Murray's emphasis on IQ per se is designed to obscure this fact, so that money needn't be spent on such programs. But it is only because IQ correlates with such other measures that it is of any real interest socially.

Attempting to discredit Head Start from another angle, Herrnstein and Murray contend that Head Start programs do not in fact achieve these other desirable social goals either, that such changes are evident only in "far more intensive and expensive preschool interventions."[32] The results of these programs, they argue, "hardly justify investing billions of dollars in run-of-the-mill Head Start programs."[33] But there is an obvious alternative to run-of-the-mill programs—outstanding ones, funded generously and designed to succeed (rather than stripped down so as to prove that such programs fail). The issues—both moral and empirical—that Herrnstein and Murray sought to obscure were beautifully stated in a letter to the editor by Elizabeth Austin in response to a special issue of *The New Republic* devoted to discussion of *The Bell Curve*:

Murray states that the only preschool programs that have had a long-term effect on general intelligence are those that resort to "truly heroic efforts, putting children into full-time, year-round, highly enriched day care from within a few months of birth and keeping them there for the first five years of life. . . ." It should be noted that this "truly heroic" environment fits the description of the average white suburban preschooler's daily life.[34]

Heritability among Individuals Doesn't Mean
Group Differences Are Due to Genes

Even if one were to accept all the questionable contentions in *The Bell Curve* about both the crucial importance of IQ scores and the degree to which they are inherited, these arguments would *still* not constitute evidence that differences between blacks and whites on IQ tests reflect genetic differences between the groups. It is a fundamental understanding among geneticists that the heritability of a particular trait in any measured population tells us nothing about whether differences *between* populations on that trait are due to genetics. Here is another point that Herrnstein and Murray do acknowledge, but then largely ignore as they attempt to persuade the reader that there *is* a genetic basis for the differences in IQ scores between blacks and whites.

As Herrnstein and Murray themselves note, borrowing a common example for illustrating the point, genetically identical seeds planted in rich Iowa soil and in the Mojave Desert will generate very different results. And even though the crop yield in any single setting is powerfully a function of genetics, the difference between the two groups will be completely environmentally determined.[35]

Herrnstein and Murray acknowledge that "the environment for American blacks has been closer to the Mojave and the environment for American whites has been closer to Iowa."[36] But they find "implausible" the hypothesis that the environments of whites and blacks differ sufficiently to account for the observed group differences, contending that for this to be true "the *average* environment of blacks would have to be at the sixth percentile of the distribution of environments among whites."[37]

Part of the seeming implausibility of this explanation derives from the misleading air of precision that numbers misused can imply.

The term "average environment" implies that there is but a single dimension along which all environments could be laid out according to their score on a single key number. But how do we add together income, occupation, vulnerability to stereotypes, cultural attitudes, residential isolation, and a thousand other influences that ultimately affect the score a youngster receives on a test? Statistically, one can (more or less) obtain quantitative measures of each, convert them to "standard scores," and add them up; but how meaningful is such a number?

Almost *all* blacks encounter a kind of stereotyping that almost *no* whites do. Why then is the idea that *half* of the African American population encounters circumstances that only *six percent* of whites do so implausible? At about the time that the data from the National Longitudinal Survey of Youth (NLSY) were generated, data on which *The Bell Curve*'s analysis centers, residential segregation between blacks and whites was so great that, as Reynolds Farley noted in a summary of census data, "whites who have more than a college education are more residentially segregated from similarly well-educated blacks than they are from whites who have never completed a year of school."[38] Were not the environments of the black and white youths participating in the NLSY rather dramatically different? Infant mortality rates in black inner-city neighborhoods are higher than in Bangladesh, while white rates are among the lowest in the world. Why, apart from their urgency to reach the conclusion that blacks are genetically inferior, do Herrnstein and Murray find so implausible the idea that the environments of blacks and whites differ sufficiently to account for the differences in test scores?

Part of Herrnstein and Murray's skepticism, they claim, derives from their expectation that socioeconomic disadvantage "should most seriously handicap the children of blacks in the lower socioeconomic classes, who suffer from greater barriers to education and occupational advancement than do the children of blacks in the middle and upper classes." A socioeconomic explanation of the test score differences, they contend, should include the assumption that, "As blacks advance up the socioeconomic ladder, their children, less exposed to these environmental deficits, will do better and, by extension, close the gap with white children of their class."[39]

Having set up this straw man, Herrnstein and Murray then

knock it down by demonstrating that the differences in black and white IQ scores are greater as one moves up the socioeconomic scale. But that is exactly what they *should* have predicted if they had any understanding of (or any inclination to honestly address) the black experience. It is precisely at the higher end of the socioeconomic scale that the differences between the black and white experience are the greatest. To understand this, we need only consider some of the observations discussed above—for example, the differences in the neighborhoods available to middle-class whites and blacks or the studies of Claude Steele on the impact of stereotypes on the performance of talented black students. To be sure, there are substantial differences in the conditions confronted by poor whites and poor blacks as well. Because of the compounding effects of housing discrimination upon economic deprivation, poor blacks tend to live in more homogeneously poor neighborhoods than poor whites do. They also encounter stereotypes that are more severe and harder to shake. But the differential in black and white experience *increases* as income increases. Poor whites *share* many of the deprivations and even the disparagement that poor blacks confront. In contrast, middle-class and upper-middle-class whites are virtually free of stigma, whereas middle- and even upper-class blacks still encounter a great deal.

This point is easily missed because it can be confused with other phenomena—that a higher proportion of blacks than whites are poor, and that the stresses on the black poor are greater than on the black middle class. But Herrnstein and Murray are not comparing the impact on IQ of being black and poor with being black and middle class. There you *would* expect—and do find—that middle-class blacks do better. Rather, Herrnstein and Murray are comparing black poor with white poor and black middle class with white middle class. In *those* comparisons, the difference is greater at the upper end of the scale.

When "Science" is Steered by Politics

The real intent of *The Bell Curve* is to persuade us that there is no point in striving for greater equality. According to Herrnstein and Murray, we're already doing all we can: "[T]he more one knows about the evidence, the harder it is to be optimistic . . . it is hard to find new ways to use existing resources that are not already being done."[40] One must wonder: Have they ever been inside a ghetto school? Do they not see any differences between the schools in the inner city and those that tend to nurture their "cognitive elite"? Perhaps a small portion of the money from conservative foundations that have so generously supported Murray's work ought to go to buying him a copy of Jonathan Kozol's *Savage Inequalities*, or perhaps toward financing a field trip to an inner-city school that is doing "everything that can be done."

In their book, as in Murray's ubiquitous radio and television defenses of it, Herrnstein and Murray evince a stance of wounded innocence. They know they will be misinterpreted, but they just don't understand why people insist on seeing them as having any but the best intentions—the courageous pursuit of truth and the real interests of the poor souls whose lives would be so much better if they were not being tempted by those who insist on seeing them as equal. All Herrnstein and Murray want to do is to help them know their place and value their positions as janitors and domestics. Then we can all be one big happy family where everyone has a place.[41]

The Painful Issue of Deficits

Perhaps ultimately the most destructive consequence of works like *The Bell Curve* is that they exacerbate the bunker mentality of those who more genuinely have the interests of the disadvantaged at heart. In the face of insidious distortions, blatant—if unacknowledged— insults, and assaults on programs designed to overcome our inequalities, it is easy to understand why some civil rights advocates would be hesitant to acknowledge that the differences in average test scores between blacks and whites reflect any meaningful difference at all in preparedness to deal with educational or job challenges. But while the scurrilous interpretations of differences in test performance must be combatted with even greater vigor in the present climate, it is essential as well to examine and come to grips with the reality they also reflect.

Many of the arguments and findings I have cited in countering the "inferior genes" contention of Herrnstein and Murray point to experiences and circumstances that suppress African Americans' full development of their intellectual capacities. Stereotype anxieties, disidentification with school and academic pursuits, the development of an oppositional cultural frame of reference, concerns about "acting white," poorly funded schools in which there is little faith that students can really learn, neighborhoods marked by isolation and neglect, disparities in both income and wealth compared to whites, high rates of unemployment that provide relatively few role models, the temptations and threats of crime and drugs, the effects of poor prenatal care, maternal drug use, high rates of ambient lead in inner-city environments—the list of factors that place a special burden on African Americans goes on and on. It is no secret why Herrnstein and Murray downplay the impact of this palpably destructive array of social and material forces. But it is troubling to see advocates for African Americans, however different their motives, engaging in similar minimizing of how great can be the harm that such stresses and injustices produce.

To be sure, it is not difficult to understand why those—black *and* white—who are sensitive to the immense suffering that racism has inflicted would be hesitant to discuss the idea of deficits in occupational and educational skills. Not only have discussions of such deficits repeatedly been the foundation for arguments rationalizing inequality and inaction, but they are a potential source of still further pain for those who have already been hurt so considerably. Moreover, as historian Daryl Michael Scott powerfully describes, accounts of harm, even when well intended, are often experienced as condescending and disparaging:

> The history of the black psyche in social science imagery is the story of how liberal experts came to dominate the image of the African American . . . and how they came around to depicting the black psyche as damaged, directly and indirectly, by racial discrimination. It is also the story of how policymakers, manipulating the therapeutic ethos, sought to obtain black equality on humanitarian grounds by presenting blacks as damaged objects of pity rather than citizens whose rights had been violated.[42]

It is certainly not my aim to present African Americans as objects of pity. But I believe we cannot fully appreciate the extent to which their rights indeed have been violated unless we face squarely the damage that has in fact been done. There are many positive and

creative achievements that have come out of African Americans'
struggle against oppression, but there have been wounds too. The
last few chapters have attempted to establish a beachhead for a perspective that acknowledges the harm our society has done to African
Americans without using that harm as a rationale for perpetuating
the very conditions that created it. I have emphasized the ways in
which reactions to the very real victim blaming that has occurred
have driven black leaders and whites on the left to denial of the harm
itself. Among the many destructive consequences of Herrnstein and
Murray's book, one of the most worrisome is that it could again
derail efforts to come to grips with these difficult realities. For to any
person of goodwill, to have one's ideas mistaken for Herrnstein and
Murray's odious intellectual chicanery would be very disturbing.

But recognizing the fallacies and distortions in Herrnstein and
Murray's arguments does not mean that we can ignore the differences in performance they exploit, or attribute them solely to test
bias or cultural bias. Centuries of oppression have taken a toll, and
the skills and talents that may be observed in the classroom or the
workplace are, for many blacks, but a pale shadow of their true God-
given potential.

"Afrocentric" Explanations for the Differences in Test Scores

In recent years, the differences in test scores between blacks and
whites have increasingly been explained by a prominent subset of
black scholars as reflecting not deficits but difference—in particular, as reflecting an "African" or "Afrocentric" way of thinking that
is falsely scored as substandard by testing procedures which are not
universal but specific to European styles of thought. There are
numerous variations on this theme, some specifically emphasizing
modes of thought that were preserved from blacks' African past
despite the ravages of slavery, others seeming mostly metaphorical,
pointing not so much across the ocean as to the rural South and the
inner city, to the distinctive culture that African Americans created
out of hardship and oppression. In certain respects, such accounts
usefully point to the special strengths that evolved from the struggles of African Americans against injustice, and remind us that the
assumptions and ways of thinking that are dominant in the American middle class do not exhaust our species' repertoire of creativity

and problem-solving strategies. But the emphasis on Afrocentric values and modes of thought as simply an alternative and unappreciated set of strengths has also at times been a medium for denying that oppression has taken any toll at all on African Americans' ability to compete effectively for success and status in our society.

Among instances of the point of view I am here addressing, one of the most influential and powerfully argued can be found in an article by Janet Helms, a senior and well respected African American psychologist with substantial expertise in psychological assessment and the influence of culture.[43] Appearing in the *American Psychologist,* the flagship journal of the American Psychological Association and its most widely read publication, Helms's article rejects any explanation of differences in test scores between blacks and whites as reflecting deficits due to oppression or disadvantage. Rather, she contends, the differences in scores simply reflect the failure of the cognitive ability tests currently in use to assess the Afrocentric modes of thought that characterize black Americans.

Helms does not contest that differences between blacks and whites on cognitive ability tests show up with virtually unvarying consistency. She centers her inquiry on the *reasons* for these differences. Though she not surprisingly concurs with the views expressed in this chapter in rejecting a biological or genetic explanation for the differences in test scores, she is critical of the most common alternative explanatory approaches that have been offered, including approaches that form much of the core of the present chapter's critique of *The Bell Curve.* Grouping those alternatives under the rubric of "environmental" perspectives, Helms complains that environmental perspectives stress "the injurious effects of environmental factors on Blacks' performance" and hence that environmental perspectives share with genetic and biological accounts "the assumption that differences in Black-White test scores reflect deficits where Blacks are concerned." Moreover, she argues, when concepts such as *culturally deprived* or *culturally disadvantaged* are used to account for poor performance on cognitive ability tests, such an explanation implicitly assumes "that White-American culture defines the most intellectually rich environment."[44]

Helms advocates, as an alternative to both biological and environmental perspectives, what she calls a "culturalist" perspective. The values and modes of thought of black Americans, she contends, are misassessed if they are evaluated from a Eurocentric vantage point or by Eurocentric methods, because the thinking of African Americans is Afrocentric. Ironically, given that one of the characteristics of "Eurocentric" thought that she criticizes is "dualistic" and overly dichotomous thinking, Helms offers two pages of tables presenting sharply dichotomized distinctions between Eurocentric and Afrocentric thinking.

For Helms, as for an increasing number of "Afrocentric" thinkers, the idea that African Americans think in fundamentally different ways from European Americans, and that standardized tests reflect nothing more than "European" modes of thought, is a centerpiece in contesting the idea that lower test scores in any way reflect a problem or deficit that oppression and deprivation have wrought. Indeed, Helms suggests, the cultural orientation of African Americans is such that when they are confronted with multiple-choice tests, they are likely to choose "the more imaginative" response alternative,[45] and thus, when they choose "more intelligent or more creative answers" to these multiple-choice items, rather than "answers that the test constructors intended,"[46] they are unfairly penalized and misjudged as performing more poorly.

Such a conception may be reassuring in the short run, but the caricature pictures of "Eurocentric" and "Afrocentric" cultures ultimately consign blacks to an intellectual ghetto in which "rational thinking" and "the scientific method" are conceded to whites, while blacks show understanding of "the power of immaterial forces in everyday life."[47] Indeed, Helms ends up at several points in her article flirting with the idea that there is a separate "African g" distinct from "European g,"[48] a conception that Charles Murray would be only too happy to entertain. One can just imagine Murray's delight in explaining why computer companies looking to hire employees might prefer "rational linear thinking" to "organizing personal contact through moving."[49]

I am not in a position to evaluate the view, held by increasing numbers of African American intellectuals, that important features of African culture persisted in the lives of slaves, despite the efforts of slave owners to disperse members of different tribes and put together people who did not speak the same language. Nor can I bring any particular expertise in evaluating the even more controversial Afrocentrist claims that, for example, Greek culture was in essence stolen from cultural developments already achieved in black Africa, or that many of the inventions and discoveries attributed to Europeans were in fact a product of Africans.[50] But I am confident that higher scores on "Eurocentric" cognitive ability tests will predict success in the industrialized sector in Africa too, and that it is an urgent task of our own society to *create the conditions that enable African Americans to score well on those tests* rather than dismissing them as simply biased and irrelevant. In the latter direction lies continuing substantive neglect, masked by "compensation" that will, inevitably, be a vehicle for condescension and an absence of full and respectful acceptance.[*]

The point is not that the values and ways of thinking of the American middle class are invariably superior. I have written an entire previous book criticizing many of those values and assumptions.[51] But notwithstanding Helms's stereotype that individualism is European and communalism is African, I am deeply skeptical that the spirit of cooperation is distributed according to the outline of the continents. Nor, I must say, have I been struck that blacks are significantly more cooperative or spiritual than whites. In my experience, one encounters the full range of human possibilities in both groups.

We most assuredly should attempt to develop the diverse and multiple virtues of our entire population, including those that may, in a broad and general way, be emphasized more in some sectors of our overall society than in others. But the ready equation of black people with "African" thinking, reserving "European" thinking to whites, comes perilously close to endorsing the very distortions I have spent most of this chapter confronting. Charles Murray's mendacious claim is that social programs and remedial efforts won't help. It ill behooves those of us who reject what he stands for to counter with the claim that such an investment is not even needed.

---

[*] I will take up this theme further in Chapter 12 in discussing the complexities of affirmative action.

PART TWO

Prejudice, Vulnerability, and Identity: Psychological Foundations of Our Racial Impasse

6

Is Racism Inevitable?

Motivational Foundations of White Racial Attitudes

The powerfully disparaging attitudes with which many whites view blacks in our society are obviously a central element in the vicious circles that are the concern of this book. Many theories have evolved to explain these attitudes, and their implications for how to approach the task of extricating ourselves from those circles differ substantially. In this and the following chapter, I will examine a variety of ways of understanding the phenomena of racism and prejudice, both as they reflect a struggle with deeply seated needs and conflicts and as they derive from limitations in our cognitive capacity to come to grips with the complexity of our daily experiences with others.

In exploring attitudes and behaviors that are the continuing legacy of the saddest and least admirable aspects of our history, we shall again confront numerous ironies. We will see, for example, ways in which efforts to suppress feelings that are at odds with our better selves can at times increase the influence of such feelings.[1] We will also discover again how the consequences of holding prejudiced views can evoke, in those who are their target, behaviors that fallaciously seem to "confirm" those very views, thereby perpetuating further the vicious circle that ironically unites perceiver and perceived.

Origins: Rationalizations for Slave-Owning

We will probably never know precisely the psychological operations that enabled people who thought of themselves as good Christians to own slaves and countenance unspeakable cruelties. Most likely, however, they were but a variant of the rationalizations and self-deceptions that have been employed throughout history to justify actions that, if looked at with full and frank awareness, would make it difficult to sleep at night. Religious justifications were fashioned from selected and ambiguous passages of scripture; economic rationales were manufactured to persuade some that iron laws of human nature simply could not be abrogated; and notions of innate inferiority and lesser humanity were called forth to bolster the entire structure of rationalization. The result was that slave owners felt little need to justify their behavior in terms of the rules by which they ordinarily governed their interactions with other human beings. Since the slaves were thought of simply as "property," and sometimes as more like "animals" than people, the ethical obligations governing behavior toward other people were in effect psychologically annulled.

This bit of emotional legerdemain is chillingly captured in a passage from *Huckleberry Finn,* in which Huck makes up a story about an accident aboard a riverboat in order to explain his lateness to Aunt Sally:

> "It warn't the grounding—that didn't keep us back but a little. We blowed out a cylinder head."
> "Good gracious! Anybody hurt?"
> "No'm. Killed a nigger."
> "Well, it's lucky; because sometimes people do get hurt."[2]

Compounding the structure of rationalization still further, to the degree that the slaves *were* viewed with some recognition of their humanity, there was for many slaveholders even a sense that they were doing *good* for them. Bringing Christianity and civilization to "heathens" and "primitives" could be viewed as offering them something precious which could lead to their salvation and might eventually, when they had been sufficiently "improved" by their contact with our more advanced and enlightened culture, lead to their freedom as well.[*]

A different mode of psychological defense was called into play when the humanness of slaves was not explicitly denied, but their standing as *property* was experienced as a justification for treating them *as if* they were not human. Here we encounter what might be thought of as an obsessional focusing on categories. By looking narrowly only at the property dimension, slaveholders could effectively ignore that the slave was a person. That reality receded into the background, as the idea that the slaveholder had "legitimately" and "legally" bought him squeezed it out. As monstrous as it now seems to us, one can almost hear a note of indignation in the slave owner's subjective experience: "I paid for him fair and square. What about *my* rights?"

The psychological mechanisms whereby we rationalize the unacceptable and defend the indefensible—not only on a social scale but in ordinary daily living as well—often hinge on which contents get placed front and center in consciousness. Much of what we call defense mechanisms, when examined closely, entail not so much the either-or question of whether something is in consciousness or not, but the *placement* in consciousness. Most people can tolerate a good deal of inconsistency between their actions and their moral ideals if the inconsistencies, or the perceptions that point to the inconsistencies, are kept in the background of their consciousness. This especially is so if the considerations that justify one's behavior (such as "property rights") are placed in the forefront, so that a narrowed focus on them places the contradictions in relative darkness. "Yes, but" may be the most common defense mechanism of all

Psychological Mechanisms Underlying Contemporary White Racial Attitudes

The psychological operations underlying contemporary white racial attitudes are certainly not identical to the deceits that rationalized the owning of human beings as slaves. Although there are ways in

---

[*] The actual granting of freedom, of course, could not be hurried. The right of private property, after all, was a sacred one, and the civilizing process was rarely viewed as one that could be completed within the lifetimes of oneself or one's immediate heirs.

which the distortions and rationalizations that permitted slavery have in various ways continued to influence the ways whites view those with darker skin, the revulsion most contemporary whites feel toward the idea of slavery is strong and real. Any attempt to address their psychological makeup that places them on an even footing with people whose actions they fundamentally repudiate will fall on deaf ears. One can no more equate today's "whites" with the "whites" who several centuries before held slaves than one can legitimately equate today's Social Democratic Swedes with their marauding Viking ancestors who barbarously terrorized Europe centuries before.

Today, as in the days of slavery, the motives that lie behind prejudiced and disparaging attitudes toward blacks by whites are quite diverse. Now, as then, probably the most salient is the simple defense of privilege. Those who benefit from differential power, wealth, and opportunity have a stake in finding a way to justify that differential. Much of the time, the psychological efforts in this regard are not conscious, but they are no less consequential for that.

Most Americans are well aware of the injustices that were perpetrated upon blacks in our country for so many years, as well as of the continuing vast inequalities between the economic circumstances of blacks as a group compared to whites. Stereotypes and negative attitudes toward blacks help to justify those inequalities and keep potential guilt at bay.

"Liberal guilt" is a concept that has become a social cliche of contemporary America, but there is reason to believe that the hardened attitudes more typically associated with a conservative outlook may also be motivated to some degree by guilt, though guilt that is perhaps more deeply buried and fervently combatted. Most conservatives, after all, share in the general American value system in which equal opportunity is a central tenet. That children born in our neglected inner cities face vastly greater obstacles to achieving the American dream is difficult to deny, and the very extent of the inequalities, raising uncomfortable questions about just how fair the system really is, can be a powerful motivator for prejudicial views that justify those inequalities. Gordon Allport, one of the pioneers of American social psychology and one of the first psychologists to study prejudice in detail, concluded on the basis of his studies that stereotypes of minority groups are less a *cause* of prejudice and discrimination than a *consequence*. In Allport's account, stereotypes are seen as "primarily rationalizers" aimed at providing a measure of justification for discriminatory acts and for unfairness that is perceived, but denied.[3]

It is one of the great ironies of life in a sharply divided society that the negative stereotypes of oppressed groups may be sustained by the very guilt people feel about the unfairness of the disparaged group's circumstances. As noted in Chapter Two, guilt does not always bring out the best in us. Efforts to justify the behavior that has made us feel guilty, or anger at those who are the living symbol of our guilt, can lead to behavior that entails still further disparagement and hardship for the very people who have already been aggrieved. As far back as the first century A.D., Tacitus recognized that, "It is human nature to hate those we have injured."[4] Summarizing the findings of more modern social psychological research, Elliot Aronson concludes, "If we have done something cruel to a person or a group of people, we derogate that person or group in order to justify our cruelty. If we can convince ourselves that a group is unworthy, subhuman, stupid, or immoral, it helps *us* to keep from feeling immoral [if we treat them badly]."[5]

Further bolstering the tendency to denigrate those who have already undergone deprivation and discrimination is a phenomenon that has been intensively studied by psychologist Melvin Lerner and his colleagues at the University of Waterloo in Canada. Lerner's work was founded on the premise that for many people the "belief in a just world," a conviction that people get what they deserve, is a central pillar of their sense of well-being. From such a vantage point, when injustices occur there is a powerful motivation to restore the sense that justice prevails. Sometimes this can entail doing something to actually right the wrong—aiding the victim of injustice or punishing the wrongdoer. But there is much evidence that not infrequently the "solution" is to conclude that no injustice really occurred, and that those who might seem to be victims of injustice in fact deserved their fate.[6] Somewhat related tendencies have been studied by social psychologists in recent years under the rubrics of "system justification" and "false consciousness." Here again, inequities in the status quo are justified by purported characteristics of those who are disadvantaged.[7]

In a phenomenon that further complicates these tendencies and particularly clearly illustrates the operation of vicious circles, the discomfort that whites often feel in interacting with African Americans—discomfort that is at least in part a function of guilt or awareness of there being reason for resentment on the African American's part—can induce anxiety and discomfort in turn in the African American other, thus sparking a reverberating sequence that maintains the distance and mutual uneasiness.[8] As James M. Jones has summarized the process, "When a moderately low-prejudiced person interacts with a target who expects to be devalued, anxiety may exist on both sides. This mutual anxiety escalates miscommunication, and has a tendency to create a self-fulfilling prophecy whereby each 'confirms' his or her own negative expectation."[9]

It is possible, if one understands these processes sufficiently, to use that understanding to create opportunities for people with a wish for better relations to have a better chance at successfully modifying this frustratingly resilient pattern. In general, overcoming anxiety requires repeated immersion in the experiences we have fearfully avoided,[10] and anxieties with regard to contact with a minority or majority group are no exception. But, if the circumstances are not right, contact can *increase* mutual discomfort and mistrust rather than diminishing them. In general, when increasing contact is combined with direct efforts to examine and challenge stereotypes, and when there are shared goals and common interests, as well as greater equality of status, the chances of success are greater.[11] We will have occasion to look more closely at some of the ways that this unfortunate cycle can be broken in Part Three of this book.

Projection and Other "Actively Recruiting" Defenses

The psychological defense mechanisms discussed thus far are primarily "after the fact" reworkings of reality. That is, when they entail disparagement of blacks and other minorities, that disparagement is not the primary purpose, but is a secondary consequence of the need to justify privilege or ward off guilt or feelings of discomfort or implicit accusation. Such a distinction, to be sure, is of little use to those who are disparaged, whose suffering does not depend on the motives of the disparager. But its importance can be seen when we consider the still more ominous and malignant implications of a different kind of defense mechanism that can play a role in the process of stereotyping—projection.

As psychoanalysts use the term, projection is a psychological mechanism in which the individual deals with troubling aspects of himself by attributing them to others. Most typically this defense mechanism is conceptualized in relation to forbidden desires, but in fact it is not infrequently employed with other characteristics of the self as well. One may, for example, project onto another the sense that one is dirty, or damaged, or depraved. This is not so much a *wish* that is being shifted as a quality that one perceives (or fears exists) in oneself but finds intolerable.

Projection is far from an ideal defense. By projecting, one can blur one's sense of *who it is* that is angry or dependent or the possessor of other forbidden feelings or attributes, but one cannot escape the sense that such feelings are, one might say, in the air. It is much more comfortable to be unaware that there is even an issue than to sense it and then have to rearrange one's experiential world in order to avoid it. For the very scent of the forbidden experience brings with it some measure of distress. Moreover, in utilizing projection, one has to deal with the unpleasant fact that one is (at least as it is perceived) in the presence of someone who is angry, who is clingingly dependent, who is directing unwanted and perhaps depraved sexual feeings toward one, etc.

On the other hand, although far from an ideal situation, there are certain compensations in utilizing projection. If one attributes one's anger to another, for example, then one is warranted in being angry back. One's own anger now is justified, and a degree of cathartic relief can be attained.

In recent years, a closely related concept has gained increasing prominence—projective identification. In this latter operation, one similarly attributes a forbidden wish or disparaged quality of self to an other. But something more complicated happens as well. One continues to *identify* with the quality in the other. This has two components, which coexist in differing proportions in different instances. On the one hand, the identification permits one to gratify the forbidden wish by proxy (much as, in a less complicated or pathological way, one may gratify a wish to be swift, strong, and triumphant by identifying with an athlete on a TV screen, momentarily merging one's identity with his). On the other hand, in projective identification one also satisfies the need to *repudiate* the forbidden wish by repudiating the other. In such fashion one can bolster one's struggle against an impulse by actively fighting it in the other without ever acknowledging that one even *has* such an impulse oneself. Of course, one needs to find someone to attribute the wish *to* in order to oppose it (and secretly to gratify it). The discovery of an enemy or a disparaged or reproached other thus becomes an internally necessary operation.

Projection, then, is a more complex—and potentially more malign—defense than, say, rationalization, because it is not just an after-the-fact justification of behavior that, in effect, has already occurred. A key feature of projection, highly relevant to the issue of racial prejudice and discrimination, is that the individual who engages in projection is not merely justifying prejudicial behavior after the fact, but actively *seeking out* others to play a role in one's life as (most typically) the despised or devalued other.

To the degree that projection or projective identification is involved, the racist *needs* to have an "other" to disparage (and to fear). He may talk about wishing they were gone, and may even, like Hitler, try to totally eliminate those onto whom he has projected his conflicts and internal loathings. But were the job actually to be accomplished, his distress would probably increase rather than decrease, and he would soon need to find other objects for his projections. To be sure, the seeking out of a disparaged or frightening "other" can be done on an individual basis, and often is; people manage to find others to fit their projections quite regularly in everyday life. But socially shared stereotypes and prejudices provide an institutional foundation for projection; it is like having access to an inexpensive mass-produced product instead of having to go to the trouble to have one handmade.

One particularly interesting application of this perspective on projection and stereotyping is offered by psychoanalyst Neil Altman. Altman asks why it is that we hold so sharply to the dichotomized distinction between "black" and "white" when in fact our population is characterized by enormous variability along multiple dimensions. In part because slave owners frequently engaged in forced sexual relations with their slaves and in part because love relations developed between people of different races after slavery was abolished, the family trees of most people our society labels as "black" include significant representation of whites and other groups. Much of the reason for the dichotomous labeling is social and historical, a product of the notorious "one-drop" rule, in which any African ancestry at all made an individual unacceptable in white society. But Altman suggests an additional reason for this sharp split. We create sharply dichotomized racial categories, he suggests, "in the service of creating a focus for projection and introjection. The 'opposite' race creates a category of people who are 'not me' into which we can project unwanted psychic content."[12]

In a fascinating passage, Altman also suggests that, "The psyche, like a city or a society, has its 'bad neighborhoods,' populated by the aggressive, the dependent, the exploitative, the ruthless, the parts of ourselves that we define as bad or devalued. The psyche also has its idealized 'good neighborhoods,' which we try to protect and segregate."[13]

It should be obvious that whether racism and discrimination are the result of processes such as projection—or whether, as considered in the next chapter, they derive at least to some degree from cognitive and perceptual processes that are not necessarily "needed" by the individual to maintain his or her psychic equilibrium—has enormous implications. To the degree that projection is the primary source of prejudice, one must be rather pessimistic about the possibilities of overcoming or transcending it. If prejudice is truly built into people's most powerful and primitive need systems, if finding an "other" onto whom to project is an urgent inner imperative, it is difficult to envision reforms that could eliminate or even significantly mitigate such attitudes. If, on the other hand, a less need-driven conception of prejudice and racial intolerance is seen to have some foundation, there is more reason to hope for at least some possibility of change. (Importantly, there is also therefore more encouragement to *work* for such change. When one holds the view that racism is so deeply rooted in the psyche that it is virtually inevitable, still another vicious circle can be generated: believing that racism is inevitable makes it difficult to think in ways that can lead to its transcendence or to sustain the effort needed to accomplish the task. It is difficult, after all, to develop strategies to eliminate what one does not really believe *can* be eliminated. Thus, to the degree one holds such a view, one is likely to find that racist attitudes, especially their deeper and more subtle manifestations, are indeed unyielding, and thus to be "confirmed" again in the view that racism is, in the words of Derrick Bell, "permanent and indestructible.")[14]

"The Fantasy of Blackness"

Among those who have introduced theories of racism that view racist attitudes as tied to deeply seated needs, the contribution of psychoanalyst Joel Kovel has been especially prominent.[15] Focusing his analysis on what he calls the "Fantasy of Blackness," a mythical set of beliefs which equates blackness with badness and dirtiness, Kovel draws not only on Freud and his more direct followers but also on the work of Frantz Fanon. Fanon, writing as a psychiatrist, a revolutionary, and a person of color, offered a strikingly vivid, bitter, and powerful interpretation of the meanings blackness has had for European civilization:

> It would be astonishing, if the trouble were taken to bring them all together, to see the vast number of expressions that make the black man the equivalent of sin. In Europe, whether concretely or symbolically, the black man stands for the bad side of the character. As long as one cannot understand this fact, one is doomed to talk in circles about the "black problem." Blackness, darkness, shadow, shades, night, the labyrinths of the earth, abysmal depths, blacken someone's reputation; and, on the other side, the bright look of innocence, the white dove of peace, magical, heavenly light. A magnificent blond child—how much peace there is in that phrase, how much joy, above all how much hope! There is no comparison with a magnificent black child: literally, such a thing is unwonted. . . . In Europe, that is to say, in every civilized and civilizing country, the Negro is the symbol of sin. The archetype of the lowest values is represented by the Negro. . . . How else is one to explain, for example, that the unconscious representing the base and inferior traits is colored black?[16]

Commenting on this passage, Kovel notes that, "Whatever a white man experiences as bad in himself, as springing from what Fanon described as an 'inordinate black hollow' in 'the remotest depth of the European consciousness,' whatever is forbidden and horrifying in human nature, may be designated as black and projected onto a man whose dark skin and oppressed past fit him to receive the symbol."[17]

"Dominative" and "Aversive" Racism

The dynamics of these projections can take many forms, some obvious and some more subtle. Kovel suggests, however, that it is useful to distinguish two broad strands, which he refers to as "dominative" and "aversive" racism. Although these two types are closely related and overlapping in many respects, they nonetheless have somewhat different psychological roots and can have considerably different import. As he summarizes it, "In general, the dominative type has been marked by heat and the aversive type by coldness. . . . The dominative racist, when threatened by the black, resorts to direct violence; the aversive racist, in the same situation, turns away and walls himself off."[18]

In our present state, when dominative racism has become rather thoroughly disreputable in all but the most marginal sectors of our society, it is aversive racism that is the greatest source of pain. As Kovel frames it, "How can we understand the irony, so painful to black people who fled the South for the imagined justice and prosperity of the North and found, standing between them and those goals, coldness and disgust? This is indeed the central problem of our racism."[19]

In accounting for dominative racism, Kovel relies heavily on the Freudian theory of the Oedipus complex, emphasizing the conflicted envies and rages engendered by the images of sexual prowess and sexual appetite that are projected onto blacks.[20] But in attempting to explain aversive racism he suggests a different source. Every group that has been the object of prejudice, he suggests,

> has at some time been designated by the prejudiced group as dirty or smelly or both: thus have the Irish been regarded by the English, the Jews by the Poles, the Poles by Anglo-Saxon Americans . . . the reality of the situation does not directly affect the underlying belief. No matter how a prejudiced-against person scrubs himself, he will always smell dirty to the true bigot.[21]

Moreover, argues Kovel, although the irrational impulse behind such prejudices can find the fantasied dirtiness in any group of people, those with darker skin may be especially prone to be misperceived in this way by those with lighter skin.

Much of Kovel's account is rooted in highly speculative extra-
polations from classical Freudian theory. Although his analysis has
considerable merit in highlighting the ways in which racism can
reflect unconscious wishes, fears, and fantasies, and although his
account of the psychodynamics of the racist probably does offer useful insights into the psychology of at least some types of racist individuals, there are aspects of his approach that are potentially mischievous. In his emphasis on racism as an expression of such deep
and ubiquitous features of human nature that it seems more like a
simple fact of life than an aberration that can potentially be weeded
out, he gives short shrift to the enormous variations evident between
individuals and between cultures and historical eras.

Kovel does, to be sure, recognize the powerful role of culture and
history. Indeed, he argues that, "More can be derived about psychohistory from a study of the content of advertising . . . than from
the behavior of a neurotic on the analyst's couch."[22] He also addresses the possibility that social transformation and reform might, to at
least some extent, mitigate the severity of the conflicts he emphasizes and diminish their impact. Nonetheless, like many accounts of
social process that are heavily based on Freudian instinct theory, the
scent of inevitability hovers over his depiction of the body politic,
and toeholds for action or hope are few and far between.[23]

Other Views of Racism as "Needed" by the Racist

Kovel's account, while perhaps depicting racism as more "deeply"
rooted in our fundamental needs, is by no means the only important
formulation that can be viewed within the general rubric of "need-
based" accounts. Other writers, often in ways that are less bound to
theory and more to empirical observation, have also emphasized
ways in which people may *need* an "other" to disparage. We have
already noted Kenneth Clark's observation, shared by numerous
others, that lower-class whites and newly arrived immigrants could
always bolster their self-esteem by comparing their status to that of
blacks, and hence needed blacks to be "there, down below."[24] In this
regard, a number of classic studies have documented that prejudice
is far more likely among those whose status is low or declining than
among those with high or rising status, who presumably have less

need to find someone to place below them.[25] Moreover, there is evidence that lower self-esteem is associated with greater prejudice and that increases in self-esteem lead to more positive attitudes toward racial minorities[26] and, more generally, that those who feel threatened or diminished have a tendency to seek invidious "downward comparisons" with others perceived as even worse off.[27]

A somewhat related formulation stresses the notions of scapegoating and displacement, whereby frustrations engendered by the actions of those more powerful than oneself may be vented upon an innocent third party who is powerless and therefore a safer target for the aggression that is aroused. The cartoon version of this is embodied in the image of the man who has been unfairly treated by his boss and comes home and kicks the dog, but in fact varied and complex instances of this process may be observed in a wide range of settings. Often the source of the frustration and anger that is displaced is economic. Carl Hovland and Robert Sears, prominent members of an interdisciplinary group of psychologists and other social scientists at Yale who contributed significantly to the study of displacement, found that by examining historical data on cotton prices, they could predict the frequency with which blacks in the South were lynched. When cotton prices declined, lynchings increased. Blacks' victimization, it seems, increased with whites' economic frustrations.[28]

In addition to the specific economic and status threats that can motivate prejudiced attitudes, we are all confronted with even more fundamental threats by our mortality and vulnerability to illness and pain. Under the rubric of "terror management theory," some researchers have explored the ways in which our defenses against these powerful and basic perils can spur prejudice. Often, a key element in that defensive structure is our faith in the cultural values and vision of reality that give our lives meaning and implicitly promise a kind of symbolic immortality.[29] When confronted with the terrifying prospect of death, there is thus at times a tendency to heighten one's sense of solidarity with those who share a cultural vision and identity and, correspondingly, to disparage and reject those who are outside the identified group.[30] Consistent with this perspective is the finding that prejudices are often determined less by "stereotypical" beliefs that members of a particular group possess certain *traits* than by "symbolic" beliefs that they violate or threaten key *values* or *traditions* of the prejudiced person's cultural group.[31]

Prejudice as a Personality Trait

A prominent line of research has suggested that prejudice and ethnic and racial hatred may be associated with a particular personality type engendered by a particular form of child rearing. In a classic study motivated by an urge to understand the depravities of Nazi Germany, a group of prominent American and German émigré social scientists developed the concept of "the authoritarian personality" and initiated extensive investigations into the origins and correlates of this personality type.[32] Individuals high on the scale used to measure the authoritarian personality (the F scale) tend to be punitive in their attitudes and rigidly conformist to conventional and nationalistic ideas. They are highly obedient and deferent to authority, and expect similar obedience and deference from those below them. Associated with their rigidly hierarchical view of the world is usually an intolerance for anyone who is "different," and thus racial and ethnic prejudice is a common feature.

In this formulation, prejudice is again viewed as a phenomenon deeply rooted in the personality of the prejudiced individual, and thus far from easy to modify. Moreover, *The Authoritarian Personality* emphasized the childhood origins of this personality pattern, and the tendencies of the personality are seen as rather rigidly "set" early in life, with later experiences unlikely to bring about more than surface changes.

The concept of the authoritarian personality has been a highly influential one, indeed among the best known and most extensively investigated topics in all of social psychology. It has not, however, been without its severe critics. Some critics have emphasized that there are strong political biases and assumptions embedded in the research. Others have stressed that it is risky to assume that the traits identified were the result of a particular pattern of child rearing. Recollections of how one was brought up are notoriously unreliable and subject to retrospective filtering and rewriting. Moreover, even if the recollections are taken as valid, assuming causality from correlations is always risky. Some third factor, for example, might account for *both* the child rearing patterns *and* the personality patterns, which might then be evident in the same people but not necessarily because the one caused the other.

In recent years, research on the relation between prejudice and particular personality types has attempted to address some of the methodological limitations of the earlier research. Scales of "Right Wing Authoritarianism"[33] and "Social Dominance Orientation"[34] have yielded significant correlations with a variety of measures of racism, ethnocentrism, and other prejudices and authoritarian tendencies.

Underestimating the Pervasiveness of Prejudice

A number of lines of research suggest that prejudiced attitudes by whites toward blacks may be more widespread than is usually recognized or acknowledged, and that in certain respects even the most progressive and enlightened whites are unlikely to fully escape the legacy of our nation's racial history. Prejudiced attitudes are not necessarily conscious.[35] Thus, questionnaires asking straightforward questions may not accurately portray the degree of prejudice that people actually harbor. Moreover, there is ample evidence that individuals responding to such questions are subject to social desirability influences and alter their responses to appear the way they have learned is socially appropriate.[36]

One indication of the error potential of questionnaires that rely on people's explicit statements about their attitudes derives from a research paradigm that has been labeled the "bogus pipeline." In this kind of research, subjects are hooked up to an impressive looking set of purported physiological monitors and told that their real feelings will thereby be evident. When whites' attitudes toward blacks are assessed via questionnaires, their responses to the questionnaires are more negative when they think their real attitudes are being monitored in this way. The view of those who have conducted this research is that the prospect of being caught in a lie yields greater honesty in the subjects' responses, and that the more honest responses reveal a greater degree of prejudice and negative feeling than is ordinarily acknowledged.[37]

Indirect indicators of prejudice, tapping attitudes of which the individuals themselves may be unaware, are evident in several other lines of research as well. In one widely cited study the researchers chose a different approach to circumventing people's blandly giving the socially acceptable response. Rather than asking how they felt, these researchers assessed subjects' implicit attitudes via their behavior in a situation in which the element of racial comparison was not evident. Subjects in their research—white Princeton students—were ostensibly participating in a study of interviewing technique. What none of them knew was that the study was set up so that half of them were interviewing whites and half were interviewing blacks. Moreover, what was being assessed was not so much the more obvious indicators of whether they were being friendly or fair, but a variety of nonverbal behaviors of which the subjects were unlikely even to be aware. Thus, for example, the white interviewers sat further away from black interviewees than white interviewees, made more speech errors when talking to them, and ended the interviews sooner.[38]

These findings have particular relevance to the vicious circle perspective emphasized in this book, because such differences in treatment—subtle and unwitting, but powerful—can affect how interviewees actually perform in the interview. Consequently, white interviewers, whose own unconscious biases can create discomfort in black interviewees and impair their ability to present themselves effectively, have the direct experience that their biases are "confirmed," and are thus likely to behave similarly with the *next* African American they interview, and to perpetuate the pattern ad infinitum. Indeed, the researchers in this study found, in a subsequent experiment, that such impaired interview performance indeed occurred, even for white interviewees, when they encountered the nonverbal behavior patterns that blacks regularly encountered.[39]

In a particularly interesting—and disturbing—series of studies by Samuel Gaertner and John Dovidio, the focus was on what they called aversive racism, a concept derived to some degree from Kovel's similarly labeled notion, but possessing distinctive qualities as well. Gaertner and Dovidio's focus was on people whose consciously held views were liberal and nonprejudiced, but who "almost unavoidably [given our nation's history, economy, and culture], possess negative feelings and beliefs about blacks."[40] These negative attitudes, however, conflict uncomfortably with the rest of their value system, and hence are dissociated or excluded from awareness most of the time.

The negative feelings to which Gaertner and Dovidio are referring are not ones of hostility or hate. Rather, "this negativity involves discomfort, uneasiness, disgust, and sometimes fear, which tend to motivate avoidance rather than intentionally destructive behaviors."[41] Their studies indicated that where it could be readily apparent if they were acting in a rejecting way toward blacks, their subjects not only did not discriminate, but made a special effort to be helpful, responsive, or respectful. When the situation was more ambiguous, however, more negative responses to blacks became apparent.

In one study, for example, white subjects were asked to perform a complex cognitive task in a circumstance in which help from a partner could be available. When the subjects were directly asked by the partner if they wanted assistance, they accepted the help considerably more often if the help offerer was black than if he was white. However, in circumstances in which the subjects had to actively *solicit* the other's help, they requested help considerably *less* frequently from blacks than from whites. Thus, it seems, they went out of their way not to reject the black person's help offer, but when their own spontaneous preferences were the ruling determinant of what transpired and their choices were less conspicuous, a different attitude toward blacks seemed to be manifested. Gaertner and Dovidio suggest that because traditional role relationships between blacks and whites place blacks subordinate to and dependent upon whites, whites are likely to experience discomfort at the implicit reversal of this dependency relationship. Thus, they argue, whites in their study avoided the uncomfortable experience of relying on a black person for help when they could do so without appearing—even to themselves—as insensitive or prejudiced. Their lesser readiness really to regard blacks as equals became evident only when it could go unnoticed or be less conspicuous (again, even to themselves).[42]

In another interesting study that highlighted a very similar phenomenon,[43] white subjects were again paired with another person in the conduct of a task. For half the subjects, the other person was presented as the subject's supervisor in the task; for the other half, the

other person was presented as his subordinate. In fact, the other was
a confederate of the experimenter, and on each occasion "acciden-
tally" knocked to the floor a container of pencils. What happened
was very revealing. White subjects paired with the white confederate were more likely to help him pick up the pencils when he was in
the role of *supervisor*. In contrast, when they were paired with a
black confederate, they were more likely to help if he was in the role
of *subordinate*. Such a pattern suggests that the white subjects were
more uncomfortable with or resentful of a black in a supervisory
role than they might have been able to acknowledge.[44]

Conservative Values and "Symbolic Racism"

The work just described particularly emphasizes the conflicting attitudes that may be unacknowledged by whites who consciously hold
liberal egalitarian values. In contrast, other work exploring unrecognized or unacknowledged negative attitudes toward blacks has
focused especially on whites of a more conservative orientation.
Though not as thoroughly committed to egalitarianism as liberals,
most American conservatives share a general American creed that
emphasizes such values as fair play and equal opportunity. Consequently, conservatives too may experience some degree of conflict
between their ideals and both their own behavior and the reality of
contemporary American life. Studies exploring what the researchers
call "symbolic racism" or "modern racism" examine this conflict,
attempting to tap attitudes that may not be conscious but are
nonetheless manifested in a variety of ways.

The concept of "symbolic racism" was introduced by social psychologist David Sears and his colleagues at UCLA to account for
"disquieting evidence of continuing white resistance to full racial
equality."[45] In Sears's view, "old-fashioned" racism—the kind that
emphasized the grossest forms of racial stereotypes and tolerated,
or even advocated, legal restrictions on blacks' access to schools,
neighborhoods, jobs, and public facilities—had become unacceptable
to express publicly. Indeed, for many people it had become unacceptable to acknowledge even to themselves. Yet at the same time, a
powerful set of attitudes persisted that remained strongly antiblack.
What ensued, Sears suggested, was that the antiblack *feeling* was
cloaked in a cognitive content that stressed traditional American

moral values such as "individualism and self-reliance, the work ethic, obedience, and discipline."[46] When such attitudes serve to rationalize underlying negative feelings about blacks, they constitute what Sears and his colleagues call "symbolic racism."

This combination of antiblack affect and traditional values, Sears suggests, subtly shapes attitudes toward such matters as busing, welfare, and affirmative action. In Sears's studies, voting behavior and attitudes regarding these controversial issues correlated much better with measures based on his concept of symbolic racism than with measures of "old-fashioned" racist attitudes. He found as well that people's attitudes on these issues were better predicted by knowing their scores on his "symbolic racism" measures than by the direct impact of the policy on the individual's concrete self-interest (for example, whether the person had a child in the public schools who might be bussed or was in a vulnerable occupational situation with regard to affirmative action). Attitudes toward these issues, it seemed, derived from their *symbolic* value, their ability to stand in for larger affective and value questions, rather than from their concrete impact on the person's life. In Sears's view, the data indicate that in many instances attitudes about these issues are "an irrational response to long-standing predispositions rather than a reasonable response to the realities of life."[47]

John McConahay, one of Sears's original collaborators on the concept of symbolic racism, has suggested that the phenomenon that he, Sears, and others have studied might better be called "modern" racism than "symbolic" racism. This term is preferable, McConahay suggested, because the symbolic dimension is not unique to the more recent form of racism; "old-fashioned" racism too was rooted in symbolism, in "beliefs and stereotypes rooted in socialization and not in personal experience."[48] "Modern" racism, however, responds to those symbolic stimuli in different ways, reflecting changing public mores and the changing racial climate.

McConahay too contends that genuine antiblack feeling has not declined as much as suggested by standard opinion polls, which ask questions for which the socially acceptable response is easy to detect. By the mid-1960s, he argues, changes in manifest public attitudes had rendered many of the questions previously used to measure racism not very useful. A general antiracist consensus had developed such that few individuals would openly acknowledge attitudes that, not long before, were socially acceptable in broad segments of the population. Therefore, it was necessary to develop more subtle measures that did not so clearly scream out, "If I answer yes to this item, I'm admitting being a racist." Scales to measure "symbolic racism" or "modern racism" are designed to tap underlying attitudes in more subtle ways, so that respondents are less likely to alter their responses to present themselves in a socially acceptable manner.

It appears from the research of Sears, McConahay, and their colleagues that for many whites, considerable conflict is engendered by the coexistence of essentially prerational and largely unacknowledged negative attitudes toward blacks on the one hand, and a genuine belief in and commitment to values of justice and equality on the other. In fact, McConahay argues, "most white Americans are not univalently positive or negative in their attitudes toward black Americans. They are ambivalent."[49] It is this ambivalence, yielding behavior that is often interpreted differently by whites and blacks, that creates much of the confusion in contemporary American life and makes it so difficult for us to resolve our racial dilemmas or even fully to understand their nature.

Challenges to Theories of "Symbolic" or "Modern" Racism

The idea that covert antiblack attitudes have been obscured by being linked to a concern about traditional American values has not gone unchallenged. Paul Sniderman of Stanford and Philip Tetlock of Berkeley and their colleagues have performed a series of ingenious experiments designed to critically investigate these concepts, and have argued that their findings "pose fundamental challenges to symbolic and modern racism theories."[50]

In their studies, surveys were administered to a representative sample of whites, but unbeknownst to the respondents, different versions of the survey were presented to different subjects. For example, respondents were asked to indicate their attitude toward government assistance for a laid-off worker who was, depending on the version randomly assigned, portrayed as either black or white, married or single, with or without children, and someone with a history of being a dependable or not dependable worker. Sniderman et al. reasoned that this format afforded the possibility of eliciting biases against blacks without the subjects' awareness: if those expressing conservative values were using them to mask attitudes about blacks, they might be expected to be opposed to government assistance more when the individual described was black than when the (identically described) individual was white.[51] In fact, the reverse was found: where there were differences, the conservative respondents were more likely to support government assistance to the *black* worker than the white under similar circumstances.

Closer inspection, however, reveals a more complicated picture. The favoring of blacks was essentially limited to blacks portrayed in the survey as "dependable" workers. The conservative respondents, but not the liberals, were almost four times as likely to support government assistance to a dependable black as to a dependable white. If the worker was described as "undependable," there was little conservative support for assistance regardless of race. Sniderman et al. themselves explain this phenomenon in a way that, although they don't acknowledge it, undercuts their own criticism of the "modern racism" thesis. As they note from their own data,

> conservatives tend to see a hard-working black as an exception. So they tend to see a black who is dependable as an exception. "This one," they say to themselves, "is not like the others; he is really trying." And perceiving him to be an exception—perceiving him to be a person who exemplifies the values of individual effort and striving they admire—they make an exception for him. So, precisely because conservatives think less of blacks, paradoxically they can wind up wanting to do more for them.[52]

This is scarcely a ringing endorsement for the absence of racial bias among white conservatives! Indeed, it seems precisely what advocates of the modern racism concept have suggested. True, the conservative respondents wanted "to do more for them." But that is an artifact of the contrived circumstances of the study, in which the respondents were *told* the characteristics of the (black or white) worker, rather than forming their own judgments or employing their own preconceptions on this score. But since (as Sniderman et al. themselves highlight), blacks are perceived by conservatives as generally *not* dependable or hardworking, in real life this set of attitudes means that only a small percentage of blacks deserve assistance and, generally, that policies that maintain black inequality are perfectly acceptable because "it's their own fault."

Sniderman et al. argue that such considerations are trumped by the fact that conservatives in their study did not favor assistance to a dependable white over assistance to an undependable black. If the covert racism thesis were correct, they suggest, such a comparison would enable conservatives to favor whites while covering over racial bias with a veneer of concern for other matters, such as rewarding "dependability." This misses the point. As the authors themselves point out, conservatives are *generally* opposed to the government taking on responsibility for *anyone* to find a job. Whites are not favored by them *in this respect* simply because a dependable white does not seem unusual enough to them to merit overriding this general principle. It is only because blacks are generally viewed as *un*dependable that an exception can be made for what is perceived to be the rare black who is dependable. This general presumption that blacks are undependable, cited by Sniderman and Tetlock themselves, does not offer much reassurance about an absence of underlying negative attitudes or about the prospects of a fair shake for black job applicants.

Government assistance, after all, is not the only concern that confronts blacks in America today. Indeed, with the country's current conservative thrust, the role of government has been made less and less decisive; it is how one fares in the private sector that largely determines one's fate. What do Sniderman et al. think happens when an African American applies for a job in a company or division run by precisely the sort of individual they think they have exonerated in their studies—that is, when, under real life conditions, they are not "told" whether the black applicant is dependable or undependable but must make their own judgments?

This is not to suggest that there are not difficulties with the concepts of symbolic or modern racism. As discussed in Chapter Two, there are many problematic consequences when the term racism is used too loosely. Tetlock has objected, with some justification, to the "motive-mongering" that is entailed when attitudes on key public issues are ipso facto taken as indications of underlying racist motives.[53] And indeed, much of the substance of the ideas of symbolic or modern racism can be framed in a less provocative way that nonetheless attends to the essential moral and political concerns.[54]

Lawrence Bobo, for example, in discussing many of the same matters, has referred to "a gap between principles and implementation." Without invoking racism, he points out that, "Although there is continuing improvement in whites' beliefs about blacks and support for the general principles of racial equality and integration . . . , there is pronounced opposition to specific policies aimed at improving the social and economic position of blacks, as well as to participation in social settings where blacks are a substantial majority."[55] Similarly, Thomas Pettigrew has suggested that, "White Americans increasingly reject racial injustice in principle, but are reluctant to accept the measures necessary to eliminate the injustice."[56] Both statements can be understood in terms of the attitude of indifference discussed in Chapter Two.

Conclusion

Many of the particular formulations discussed in this chapter have been subjected to a variety of persuasive and effective critiques. As one examines the entire body of observation and evidence reviewed here, however, the general principle that we cannot judge the full range and depth of people's attitudes about the powerful issue of race by what they *say* those attitudes are remains sound and important. The findings and theories reviewed in this chapter suggest that we must be skeptical and sophisticated in interpreting what look like signs of diminished bias and prejudice.

But effective strategies must be rooted not only in skepticism but in people's experienced reality and experienced sense of self. Even if hypotheses about unconscious levels of racism have some validity, "cutting to the chase" and treating the more rational, hopeful, or generous-seeming manifestations as just so much cover or subterfuge is as poor a tactic in social change as it is in psychotherapy.[57] And there is much reason to think that in fact the changes in attitude, evident in so many ways, are as real as are the less salutary motives and feelings that are also revealed to the perceptive observer. What is most pervasively evident is complexity and conflict, a combination that, in almost every sphere, offers both danger and opportunity. Whites have manifested, in a confusing mixture, goodwill and tightly clasped wallets, compassion for blacks mistreated long ago or far away and averted eyes for those suffering closer to home, a sincere belief in the moral necessity of a level playing field and a blatant denial of the truly dramatic tilts that remain.

Those of us in the white community who believe we are people of goodwill and fairness must be willing to examine more closely the inconsistencies between our professed views and aims and our daily choices and behavior. In doing so, we must be careful not to succumb to an orgy of guilt and self-deprecation. Failure to appreciate what *has* been achieved will lead simply to discouragement. But we must not rest easy either. America is a racially more just society than it once was, but that is in good part because, in truth, our baseline left so much room for improvement.

I will be questioning, in the pages that follow, the idea that white society is fundamentally and irredeemably racist or that racism is inextricably linked to our most basic psychological needs. But there can be little doubt that racial prejudice is deeply embedded in our society and in the psyches of those who grow up in it. We cannot transcend those prejudices without owning up to them, and we cannot begin to break the vicious circles in which we are entangled without understanding how powerful a part of those circles are attitudes—conscious and unconscious—that differ less than we wish to suppose from those of an era we now regard with shame.

7

Prejudice without Intention?

"Cognitive" Foundations of White Racial Attitudes

The accounts of racism and prejudice discussed in the previous chapter emphasize the connections between racial prejudice and deeply rooted individual needs and conflicts. Through their lens, racism may appear to be an almost inevitable phenomenon, a set of attitudes so insistently woven into the fabric of the prejudiced individual's personality that efforts to overcome it merely mask inclinations that remain fundamentally unchanged. But the processes discussed thus far do not exhaust the explanations for prejudice and stereotyping. Many researchers have emphasized more *cognitive* sources, the ways in which the ordinary workings of human thought—the very same perceptual and cognitive operations that, most of the time, enable us to develop a reasonably accurate picture of the world and the way it works—can lead us into forming erroneous, overgeneralized, and harmful images of what people of other groups are like.

To be sure, "need-based" and "cognitive" explanations are not totally separate or antithetical. Our psychological functioning is always a complex mix. But the distinction is important because, whereas more "need-based" attitudes may seem to be relatively implacable, manifesting themselves almost regardless of the reality they encounter, prejudiced attitudes that are more "cognitively" based have a greater likelihood of being at least potentially open to change.

This does not mean that the latter change easily. As we shall see in more detail shortly, the cognitive operations that become hardened into stereotypes and prejudices can show quite considerable rigidity and a strong tendency to assimilate new situations into their procrustean pattern. Perhaps the best way to understand how this happens is to turn again to the concept of schema introduced in Chapter Four. Many definitions of the schema concept have been offered,[1] but the basic conception to which they all point is shared by almost all modern theories of human behavior: that we do not respond directly to environmental events but rather to events *as perceived*, and that perception is not a camera-like registration but an active and selective process. We *construct* the world we perceive, based not only on the input impinging on our senses at the moment but on expectations and readinesses rooted in past experiences.

Of the various conceptualizations of schemas and their operation, I find particularly useful that of Jean Piaget, the great Swiss student of children's psychological development. Piaget's is, to begin with, the most elaborated and comprehensive of all these efforts. One of the leading thinkers of the twentieth century, Piaget sought nothing less than an exhaustive account of the evolution of our knowledge of the world. Moreover, a central tenet of his work is that we come to know the world through acting upon it and interacting with it. Knowing does not just come about in the head but in our transactions with the world around us. Thus, although a theorist *par excellence* of the cognitive structures *within* each of us, Piaget was consistently attentive to the dynamic relation of those structures to the environment or context in which they evolve.

Equally significant for our present purposes, Piaget's emphasis on the dual processes of assimilation and accommodation, continuously in dialectical tension, offers an unusually complex and dynamic account of the way we apprehend the world as we simultaneously act upon it and are acted upon *by* it. Assimilation and accommodation, though in one sense opposing tendencies—the first pointing toward bringing to bear old categories and tactics in new situations, the second toward *changing* our approach and our assumptions as circumstances change—are nonetheless part and parcel of each other.[2]

To understand better why this is so, it is helpful to look at precisely how the processes of assimilation and accommodation actually function in the mundane acts of everyday life. The concept of assimilation, for example, points to the tendency to interpret new experiences in terms of the ideas, categories, and meanings available to us. Such a notion may seem rather straightforward, but it introduces what appears to be a paradox. On the one hand, we can only experience things in terms of the concepts we already possess. On the other, it is clear that over the course of the life span, the nature of those concepts differentiates and expands; the categories available to the adult are far richer and more complex than those with which the child tries to apprehend the world, and even throughout our adult lives we continue to form new concepts and ideas. This is not just a matter of what "intellectuals" do; how does anyone get to know that a machine she is seeing is a "computer" or a "microwave oven" or a "VCR" if, some time before, she had no such category in her head?

Piaget's answer to the question of how our schemas evolve and differentiate is to point out that assimilation of new experiences to existing structures implies *by its very nature* accommodation of those structures to the new experiences. When, for example, a child who has learned the concept of "dog" sees a kind of dog she has never seen before, say a dachshund or a Great Dane, it is an act of assimilation to incorporate this new dog into the already existing schema. But in the very act of doing so, the schema itself has changed. For it is now a mental picture of "dog" that has another element, another little wrinkle. To at least some degree, it has become a *different* schema than it was by the very act of being applied. And since virtually *every* experience we ever have is at least in some infinitesimal way different from every other that fits the same schema—are any two kisses ever totally alike, or even any two walks to the grocery store?—in the very act of applying the schemas that organize our mental life we are also changing them.

Assimilation and accommodation mediate our every act and experience, from the most basic physical movements like walking, standing, or reaching for something, to the most subtle nuances of personal relationships or the most abstruse products of a literate culture. But there are crucial differences between the ways our schemas are brought to bear in relation to the physical world and in our negotiations with the realm of the social and interpersonal. Accommodation, it turns out, proceeds more effectively and decisively in dealing with the physical world than in our interactions with other human beings. Indeed, therein lies one of the key roots of some of our most painful and intractible psychological problems, and of the racial impasse that is the topic of this book.[3]

In order to understand this difference and its implications, it is useful to remind ourselves of certain common experiences that are in one sense embarrassing and humbling, but in another, highlight for us the impressive complexity of even the homely, seemingly "mindless" acts we take for granted. Consider, for example, the simple act of sitting. All of us have had the experience of sitting on a chair or couch which we had somehow "read" wrongly—that is, of experiencing the act of sitting as one of falling, as the couch or chair turns out to have been just a bit lower than we had expected; or, alternately, of experiencing the hard landing, the surprising thud on our backside that occurs when the chair was just a bit *higher* than we had anticipated.

That the difference is usually just a matter of inches brings home even more sharply what an extraordinarily active and complicated process even the simple act of sitting is, for it highlights how closely calculated the act must actually be, how little leeway there really is. Most of the time the "calculations" we make and the virtually infinite series of cybernetic corrections are so accurate and so successful that we do not even notice we are "doing" anything other than "sitting." It is when we *mis*calculate that we can begin to give ourselves credit for how complex an achievement it really is to be able to sit in a chair in a way that does not *feel* like a complex achievement. (Much the same kind of experience is familiar to all of us when the curb from which we are stepping is just a bit higher or lower than we expected; here once again, the degree of physical jolt that can be experienced as a result of differences from expectation that cannot be more than a matter of centimeters should remind us of how remarkable it is that so much of the time we negotiate the task with a facility that approaches perfection.)

An important difference between our transactions with the physical world and those in the interpersonal realm is that in the former it is relatively easy to know when we are wrong. The jolt upon sitting or stepping off the curb is an excellent teacher, as is the experience of knocking over a glass one is reaching for because one has not paid sufficient attention. All these experiences not only testify to the skill entailed when we get it right, but they tell us loudly and clearly that this time we got it wrong. In the interpersonal world things are quite different. The ambiguity is usually much greater, and thus, although we probably make a good many *more* errors than we do in the physical realm, our ability to detect those errors is considerably less reliable.

If, for example, we enter an interaction with someone with the initial perception that that person does not like us, that perception is extremely difficult to disconfirm. For unlike the couch that virtually rises up and smacks us on the backside with the news that we have misperceived, or the glass whose shattered pieces on the floor leave us little opportunity to maintain that we had grasped it correctly, the messages from another person are very easy to reinterpret. Was his comment that he found what I said very interesting a sincere compliment, or was it in fact supercilious or condescending? Did his suggestion that we get together for lunch imply he wants to get to know me better, or that he intends to try to sell me something? When he laughed at my joke, was it genuinely appreciative, or was there mockery in the laughter?

What complicates these perceptions enormously is that each of the less flattering interpretations is truly possible, and, indeed, all but the most obtuse or defended of us have experienced the reality of these hidden attitudes more than once. Moreover, the ambiguity is of such a degree that even the other person himself may not really know what his attitude is. That is, he may indeed believe that he is being sincerely friendly and interested and yet unconsciously harbor the very attitudes the suspicious other thinks he is picking up.[4]

As a consequence of this complexity and ambiguity, it can be exceedingly difficult to disconfirm an erroneous perception regarding another person. Assimilation of the new experience to the assumptions we brought with us proceeds with much less correction from the process of accommodation, for there is much less recognition that we are indeed in a situation that requires some modification on our part. But since assimilation is not inexorable, and accommodation always proceeds apace at least to some degree, there is in principle always a prospect for correction of our erroneous impressions. If, say, the other person keeps manifesting signs of friendliness and interest, eventually our perception will accommodate to what is transpiring. But because of the extremely fluid and dynamic nature of interactions between people—because our perceptions have consequences for how we *act* toward others, and those actions in turn have consequences for how the other acts toward us—by the time we might be able to recognize that our perception was inaccurate, the other person may well have responded to our own behavior toward him in ways that seem to "confirm" our initial impression.[5]

Before too long, if we proceed with someone on the assumption that that person is hostile or uninterested or anxious, he or she *will* be hostile or uninterested or anxious. Moreover, when this happens, the strong likelihood is that we will simply conclude that we were right all along. Much of my work as a psychotherapist involves trying to intervene in sequences of precisely this sort, attempting to help people change both their perception and behavior before others are induced once more to provide a kind of pseudo-corroboration of what is in fact an erroneous view of what can be anticipated from interacting with other people.[6]

In matters of race and stereotyping, self-fulfilling prophecies of a very similar sort are essential constituents of the vicious circles that keep us divided and estranged. The behaviors and personal qualities to which stereotypic perceptions are directed are of a sort that makes it very difficult for stereotypes to be unambiguously disconfirmed. The equivalents in this realm of the chair or the curb telling us we have misperceived are few and far between.

Blacks encounter repeatedly the experience of not being seen or understood accurately, of being perceived through a cloud of prejudice, and they would have to be superhuman not to respond to the provocation in those experiences. Thus here too there is a "race" between erroneous perceptions and their specious "confirmation." Will the white person's attitude—admittedly entrenched but, from this perspective, not implacable—change with enough disconfirmations? Or will the black person, confronted with—one might even say, battered by—the provocative misperception over and over succumb to "confirming" an inherently false idea?[*]

---

[*] It is important to note that blacks' perceptions of whites often are similarly falsely "confirmed." I shall have more to say about this in the following chapters.

An example of this is offered in a generally perceptive and moving memoir by *New York Times* editorial writer Brent Staples.[7] Staples describes having been so angered by whites who fearfully shrunk from him when he walked down the street that he began to play with the misperception and intentionally act in ways that looked menacing. Although Staples's resentment is perfectly understandable—a graduate student in a Ph.D program, he was being perceived as a street criminal—the likely (and ironic) consequence of his behavior is that the whites who encountered his sardonic role-playing were strengthened in the very fear of blacks that Staples so resented.

In pointing out how Staples's own behavior contributed to perpetuating the stereotyping he so despised, am I simply blaming the victim? Some readers, I am sure, will perceive it as such. But my intent is certainly not to make Staples responsible for the prejudice of which he was indeed a victim, but rather to point out how insidiously and inexorably prejudices manage to elicit the behavior that seems to "confirm" them.

Of course it is not inevitable that the object of such prejudicial perceptions will respond precisely as Staples did. There are indeed a host of ways to respond. But over the long haul—as much of this book details—it is extremely difficult to find an exit from the ironic sequences that keep us mutually locked into our errors and confirmed in our misperceptions.

Stereotypes and Ordinary Cognition

Piaget's is not the only theory that lends itself to an understanding of the cognitive foundations of persistent stereotyping. Indeed, many other writers have devoted considerably more explicit attention to the role of cognitive processes in *social* behavior, and the study of what has come to be called social cognition is an influential thrust in contemporary psychology.[8] Many of the oddities and anomalies of our everyday social behavior can be understood by examining how ordinary and essential cognitive processes go awry in the complex sphere of social interaction.

Stereotypes are an extension—usually a problematic extension—of the general strategy we all find indispensible in sorting through the potentially overwhelming profusion of stimuli that assault our senses. Every feature of our thought and perception entails enormous filtering, latching onto features that roughly fit our expectations and screening out what would make our world, borrowing William James's memorable phrase, a "blooming, buzzing confusion." Stereotypes persist in part because they provide a schematic roadmap through the bewildering terrain of social complexity. They are usually not a very accurate map, and certainly not one that gets all the details right, but if they seem to get us through the day, they are likely to be valued and maintained.

Stereotypes are not limited to racial and ethnic categories; they are simply particularly mischievous in that arena. We have stereotypic expectations of what teachers will be like, of people dressed in three-piece suits, of construction workers, of men in leather jackets on motorcycles, and so forth. Conservatives have stereotypes of liberals; liberals have stereotypes of conservatives; men have stereotypes of women; women have stereotypes of men; and virtually everyone has stereotypes of psychologists. Any or all of these may be modified in a particularly striking encounter or relationship, but most often an accommodation is made in which one thinks, "He's not like other x's," and the exception virtually proves the rule to our stubborn consciousness.

Stereotypes are abetted by another necessity of effective cognitive functioning as well. An essential feature of the perceptual process is what Jerome Bruner has called "going beyond the information given."[9] Perception is almost always a kind of guessing game. If we waited until we had all the information necessary to confirm unambiguously what we think we are seeing, it would often be too late. Life requires us to make inferences, to fill in the missing pieces in what is almost always an imperfect picture.

So we simplify and screen out and leap to conclusions, and it is scarcely surprising that often we are in error. Indeed what is remarkable is how often our perceptions are accurate, or at least accurate enough to enable us to function effectively in the world. But not infrequently, we do indeed pay a price for the tricks in which perception engages, and the consequence is both that psychotherapists are kept in business and that stereotypes, the product of perception's short cuts, perpetuate injustice and social division.

Racial Stereotypes and "Illusory Correlation"

One of the most striking demonstrations of how the very nature of human cognition can generate stereotypes, quite apart from any hostile intent or rationalization of long-standing inequality, was offered in a study by David Hamilton and Robert Gifford of the University of California at Santa Barbara.[10] They asked people to read descriptions of actions by a series of individuals who were arbitrarily identified as belonging to one of two groups, simply called "Group A" and "Group B." The study was set up so that twice as many of the individuals described were labeled as "Group A" than as "Group B." For both groups, most of the behaviors described were socially desirable, and the proportion of desirable and undesirable behaviors was exactly the same for both groups. When the subjects in the study were later asked about the descriptions they had read, however, they remembered "Group B" members as having engaged in more of the undesirable behaviors than "Group A" members, despite the fact that the proportion of desirable and undesirable behaviors was exactly the same in the two groups.

What the researchers suggested—in a formulation that has subsequently been validated in a variety of studies—is that because undesirable behaviors were relatively unusual and there were also fewer "Group B" members than "Group A" members, the combination of undesirable behavior and "Group B" membership was especially unusual and therefore distinctive. As a consequence, instances of that combination stuck in the subjects' memories, and they were convinced that undesirable behavior was particularly associated with "Group B" even though it was not.

One of the important features of this study is that it was *not* a study of groups toward which the individuals already had some kind of bias. "Group A" and "Group B" were fictions, and there was nothing to suggest that they had any connection whatsoever to the particular racial or ethnic groups toward which the subjects might have had some bias. Moreover, the behaviors described were not behaviors particularly associated with race or ethnicity in our society, which could have falsely "clued" the subjects that "A" and "B" were, say, stand-ins for "white" and "black." The desirable behaviors described were acts such as visiting a friend in the hospital, and the undesirable actions were descriptions such as "John always talks about himself and his problems."

Hamilton and Gifford's findings thus suggest that stereotyping may arise from a characteristic of human information processing that almost "inadvertantly," as it were, leads to a false perception of minorities as engaged in more frequent undesirable behavior. Since, for example, only a minority of individuals, black *or* white, commit criminal acts, and only a minority of Americans are black, the sheer cognitive tendency for less frequently appearing combinations to be remembered as being more frequent than they actually are—a tendency that operates equally with "neutral" stimuli—will lead to a false perception that exaggerates the proportion of blacks who are criminals.[11]

The phenomenon just described is called "illusory correlation" in the literature of social psychology. The term points to the tendency to see a connection between two occurrences (such as particular behaviors and membership in a particular group) that does not actually exist, or, if there is in fact *some* connection between them, to experience it as considerably stronger than it actually is.

Illusory correlation is by now a well-established phenomenon, although there is some debate about the fine points of its exact mechanism.[12] Hamilton and Gifford's study highlights the *distinctiveness* of the relatively infrequent combination of unusual behavior and minority status as the source of the illusory correlation; such combinations stand out and consequently are more readily brought to mind when recalling what one has observed. Illusory correlation may derive as well from another source, the *expectations* with which we enter a situation. In contrast to the "distinctiveness-based" illusory correlations just discussed, "expectancy-based" illusory correlations have less to do with the *creation* of stereotypes than with their *perpetuation*. Once expectancies are established, what we remember about a complex set of events generally has as much to do with those expectancies as with what actually transpired.[13]

Indeed, expectancies can influence not only what we remember after the fact but what we pay attention to and the way we process and interpret experiences as they are unfolding.[14] For example, in a study by Birt Duncan at the University of California, white college students observed a videotaped interaction between two people in which an argument developed and one of the people shoved the other. When the shover was black, the behavior was coded as violent by the large majority of subjects. When subjects were shown a similar interaction, but with a white person doing the shoving, only a small fraction rated the behavior as violent.[15] Other studies too have shown that in situations in which there is some ambiguity about the meaning of a person's behavior, the same behavior is more likely to be interpreted as aggressive when it is performed by a black than when it is manifested by a white.[16]

Indeed, even flashing racially relevant words on a screen at a speed too fast for subjects to consciously register what they have seen can influence their judgments about how aggressive or hostile an individual's reactions were. In an influential study by Patricia Devine of the University of Wisconsin, subjects were given written descriptions, with no identification of race, of the actions of a fictional individual named "Donald," and told about behaviors such as refusing to pay his rent until his landlord painted his apartment or sending back a dirty glass at a restaurant. Those subjects for whom more of the subliminally presented words had stereotypical racial connotations judged Donald's actions to be more aggressive. Importantly, this influence of racial stereotypes on their judgments went on completely without awareness, and it was evident among subjects who scored very low on questionnaire measures of racism as well as among those who scored high.[17]

Indeed, *very often* the effects of stereotyping proceed without awareness on the part of the individual who is doing the stereotyping and without the conscious experience of being prejudiced. Individuals who manifest illusory correlations or expectancy effects believe that they are simply describing what they have seen with their own eyes. And while stereotypical expectations may *originate* in irrational fears and hatreds or venal defenses of privilege, once they are established in the culture, their "confirmation" via processes such as illusory correlation need not be motivated. It can be completely unintended, and yet powerfully shape how we see the world.

To those inclined to rationalize and justify stereotyping, these expectations might appear to simply reflect the contingencies and likelihoods that one finds in the world; different groups behave differently, and so our expectations about them differ.[18] What this exculpatory view omits is that these studies show that *the same* behavior is viewed differently. That is, at least a part of why blacks are "more aggressive" is that the very same behavior is *perceived* and *labeled* as more aggressive when it is manifested by a black.

Perhaps most important to the general thesis of this book is that such judgments themselves have consequences. If blacks find themselves being judged as aggressive or irresponsible or lazy for the same behavior that is labeled more benignly for whites, those judgments become a powerful psychological reality for the person being judged, and can influence how he or she reacts. Such perceptual biases also, by influencing how African Americans are viewed in job interviews, as prospective neighbors, and so forth, influence the concrete opportunities they will encounter over the course of their lives, and those reduced opportunities in turn also influence behavior. Thus, in one more vicious circle, the stereotypic perception alters the probability that the stereotypic behavior anticipated will eventually be forthcoming; and if it is, that will be experienced by the biased perceiver as "confirmation" of the stereotype. Especially is this the case because (a) it takes relatively little to come forth with behavior that is confirming, since even relatively harmless or neutral behavior will be *seen* as confirmatory, and (b) much of this goes on without awareness, so the biased perceiver is unaware of having an impact on the process at *any* point in the sequence.

Categories and the Perception of People as Members of Groups

From a slightly different angle, we may see that the sheer act of categorizing can play a significant role in perpetuating bias. We cannot avoid experiencing the world in terms of categories; and were it possible not to do so, we would be unable to learn from experience. If we responded to each new experience in all its uniqueness, we would have no way to apply what we have learned to the next situation we encountered. But the act of categorizing also can create mischief, especially in the social realm. Once established, the categories we employ shape what we are able to notice and how we experience what we do notice.[19]

Even setting aside the powerful social, historical, and emotional loadings associated with racial categorization in particular, the very process of sorting people into categories contributes to the creation and persistence of stereotypes. Even in studies in which people are assigned to categories that are completely abstract and arbitrary (for example, into groups randomly constituted and designated in terms such as "Group X" and "Group Y"), there is evidence that the categories shape our perceptions. Members of the "same" group are perceived as more like each other than they actually are, and people who are presented as members of "different" groups—even if this is a result of intentionally arbitrary groupings by the experimenter—are perceived as more different from each other than they really are. When judgments are made of the same array of people without their having been arranged into categories, the arbitrary "group differences" disappear.[20]

Moreover, not only are our perceptions and judgments of people influenced by the sheer act of categorizing, but so too is our memory. We *store* information in terms of categories, and at times our memories unwittingly treat people who belong to the same category almost as if they were interchangeable. In one very interesting study, for example, subjects were asked to observe a discussion group in which three of the participants were black and three were white. When they were later asked to identify which of the six group members made particular comments, there was a consistent tendency for the errors in recall to entail substituting one member of the same racial group for another. That is, if they didn't accurately remember precisely who said what, they were inclined to attribute the comments of one black person to another black or to recall what one white person said as having been said by another white. In effect, members of the category were "interchangeable." Put differently, what seemed to be most salient in what they remembered was not the particular individual but the fact that "a white person" said it or that "a black person" said it.[21]

"In-Group" and "Out-Group" Effects

The effects of categorization on our perceptions and recollections are exaggerated still further if we ourselves belong to one of the groups, and a number of additional phenomena are evident as well when this is the case. Not only do judgments tend to be more positive toward members of one's own group (the "in-group") than toward others (the "out-group"), but perceptions and evaluations of the in-group are more differentiated than are those of the out-group. The experience, it seems, is *"they* are all alike, whereas *we* are quite diverse."[22]

Although these phenomena should not be divorced from their social and historical context, it is important to be aware that to some degree they derive from basic features of human information processing, and thus can be elicited even by seemingly "neutral" distinctions. Simply categorizing people into groups, regardless of the content or nature of the categories, creates in-groups and out-groups, with favoritism toward one and invidious attitudes toward the other.[23]

Differences are evident as well in the causal attributions people make about the behavior of in-group and out-group members. For individuals who are members of one's own group, there is a tendency to understand their behavior in terms of the *situation* they are confronting. That is, their behavior is seen as a meaningful and particular response to what is going on around them. In contrast, the behavior of out-group members tends to be seen in terms of generalized and enduring *characterological* properties.

This difference has several important implications. In part, it reflects a phenomenon which has also been important in its own right in social psychologists' understanding of in-groups and out-groups: not only are individual differences between in-group members more readily noticed than between out-group members, but the differences *within* the behaviors of any individual are more recognized among in-group members. That is, in-group members are seen as acting differently in different situations; no single act can capture the diversity of who they are. But out-group members are seen as having characteristic ways of acting ("That's just what he's like").[24] This contributes to a generally more judgmental attitude toward the out-group; every act of theirs potentially reveals their "character" in a way that is much less true for in-group members, whose any particular act can be understood as an exception "due to circumstances." Moreover, the very act of seeing someone's behavior in context, as a meaningful response to the situation he or she is facing, fosters empathy. When behavior is not seen contextually, is not understood in relation to particular aims and perceptions, empathy necessarily diminishes.

Further compounding the bias governing perceptions of in-group and out-group members, the general tendency just noted—to see the behavior of in-group members as a response to specific circumstances and of out-group members as a reflection of character—is at times reversed, always to the detriment of the out-group. Specifically, there is *also* an inclination for the positive behaviors of in-group members to be attributed to internal causes and the negative behaviors to external causes. (In effect, in-group members do something good because of the kind of person they are, but do something bad because of the situation they found themselves in). The opposite attributions tend to be evident in explaining the behavior of out-group members. These additional perceptual inclinations add still further to in-group members being viewed more positively than out-group members.[25]

It is again noteworthy that these tendencies are evident not only with regard to membership in groups such as racial, national, ethnic, or gender categories, where membership is emotionally meaningful to many people and tied to long-standing allegiances and struggles. They are evident as well when the categorization is completely arbitrary. We may be assigned to "Group A" or "Group B" by an experimenter in a social psychology experiment, and almost instantly we seem to manifest much the same kind of differential perceptions as is evident in circumstances where there is a long-standing and emotionally rooted meaning to the categories.[26]

Apart from in-group and out-group effects, attributional influences operate in other ways as well to exacerbate bias and stereotyping. There is a *general* bias in American culture to attribute people's behavior and their success or failure to internal, dispositional characteristics of the person, rather than to situational or environmental influences. That is, in the individualistic worldview of our society, we tend to view people's fate as in their own hands, and to play down the ways in which the circumstances of some people make success more likely than for others (as well as the very considerable degree to which sheer luck is the determining factor).[27]

In the dominant American mythology, such considerations are just "excuses"; if the person really wants to succeed and is willing to work hard, he or she will. So pervasive is this tendency in our culture, and so one-sided is its understanding of the reasons for people's behavior, that it has been labeled by social psychologists "the fundamental attribution error."[28]*

This tendency, which significantly underplays the impact of history and social and economic circumstances on people's behavior, has further contributed to the stereotyping and prejudice African Americans encounter in our society. I have noted in the previous chapter how the need to believe in a "just world" can motivate people to assume that those who receive a smaller share of the pie must somehow deserve their disadvantaged status. Here we see a complementary influence that points in the same direction even without a specific motivation or need. The mere cognitive tendency to look for explanations in the characteristics of the individual, and to minimize the contribution of circumstance and environment, creates the same effect.

Stereotypes as Socially Shared

I have focused thus far on characteristics of human thought processes that can create error and prejudice even where there is no hostile intent or "need" being served, no *motive* to discriminate. Appreciation of these influences is essential in order for us not to make the error of assuming that *all* stereotyping and prejudice is motivated, that it always fills a personal or group need and therefore will "come out" in devious ways if it does not come out more directly. But it is also crucial to keep in mind that stereotypes do not derive just from characteristics of individual psyches, whether cognitive *or* motivational. They are usually socially learned and socially transmitted. Indeed, research indicates that prejudices toward particular racial and ethnic groups may develop before the individual has had any contact with members of those groups.[29]

Our behavior is powerfully influenced by reference groups, the set of people with whom we identify and whose views and standards we use to evaluate our own behavior and to calibrate our attitudes. Research has shown, for example, that a frequently crucial part of

---

* Interestingly, when it comes to *our own* behavior, we are much less prone to attribute everything to character. Perhaps because we are more intimately familiar with the ways our own behavior can vary from situation to situation, and because we know from inside "why" we behaved in one way rather than another, we are less inclined to manifest this fundamental attribution error with regard to ourselves.

the process of overcoming prejudices is a shift in reference group, entailing not only dissociation from a previous reference group whose attitudes were negative, but also an attachment to a *new* reference group with more positive attitudes.[30] Indeed, one study found that interracial behavior was better predicted by a subject's perception of the attitudes of friends, parents, roommates, and respected older people than by the subject's own attitudes.[31]

In this connection, Canadian psychologist R. C. Gardner has offered the interesting suggestion that stereotypes are particularly impervious to change because they do not require a negative attitude toward the group in order to be maintained. Even when people's *feelings* toward a group improve, they may still retain negative stereotypes because the information (or misinformation) is socially shared, and thus is perpetuated *simply by virtue of being so widely believed.* The stereotype, in essence, is experienced as a fact rather than as a belief or attitude.[32]

The Continuing Importance of Affect

Gardner's point should not be taken to imply that strongly held and affectively laden attitudes play no role in the process of perceiving another group. Even where certain perceptions of a group are widely shared as factual (which can be the case whether they are actually true or not), the *feelings* associated with these perceived group attributes may vary quite considerably. Writing from a Canadian vantage point, Gardner notes, for example, that

> an individual with a favorable attitude toward French Canadians might say what is so nice about them is that they are religious. An individual with a negative attitude might state that the problem with them is that they are too religious. Both individuals, however, might ascribe the attribute of religious to French Canadians.[33]

James M. Jones, one of the leading writers on the psychology of prejudice and racism, has put the limitations of purely cognitive approaches in strong and vivid language. "What about the passion, the fire, the drama of prejudice?" he asks.[34] Jones notes that the mere holding of a stereotype does not predict prejudiced behavior very well. Summarizing a number of recent studies that require greater complexity in our understanding of prejudice than purely cognitive

accounts provide, Jones concludes that our behavior toward a particular group is likely to depend not only on the content of our
stereotypes, but on the actual experiences we have with members of
the group and on how we *feel* about those experiences and about the
characteristics we attribute to the group.[35]

Here again, simple linear or unidimensional accounts of the
sources of our divisions and misunderstandings fail to capture the
circular and interactive complexity of human experience. Our feelings about other groups and about the experiences we have in interacting with them are shaped by the expectations and stereotypic
images with which we enter the situation. But those cognitive
schemas are neither inherent nor fixed; they not only shape but are
shaped by the feelings we hold about the people with whom we are
interacting and by what actually happens in that interaction. There
is no contradiction here. Thoughts, feelings, and behavior are part
and parcel of each other; indeed, they scarcely can be said to exist
apart from the context that includes all three.

In the interactions between people that maintain—or potentially can change—the prejudices each holds about the other's
group, each party experiences what is transpiring in light of past
experiences with that group, *ideas* about the group, *feelings* about the
group, and the concrete events that result between them as a consequence. And in the process of responding to and integrating these
multiple influences, each party shapes the *future* interactions
between them and sets the stage for the next round in this endless
process of behavior eating its own tail (or tale).

Cause for Hope?

Although the emphasis in this book is by no means exclusively on
"cognitive" explanations—indeed other points of view figure much
more prominently in the overall analysis the book offers—the reader
will certainly sense that I do share one important view in common
with those emphasizing cognitive factors in stereotyping and prejudice: a significant portion of the problematic stereotypes that afflict
race relations today results from distortions that are not necessarily
intended or "needed" by those who exhibit them. Put differently and
perhaps even more to the point, it is my intention to challenge, at

least in certain respects, the view that racism is so "deeply rooted" in American society that it is virtually inescapable.

Some of the findings reported in this chapter may seem to offer slim support for this more benign view. To the degree that I have been persuasive in arguing that cognitive factors play a greater role in producing and maintaining stereotypes than one might have previously thought, this success may also seem like a Pyrrhic victory for hope. If prejudice is less "needed" (in a motivational sense) by prejudiced individuals than we had thought, but is woven into the very fabric of our cognitive and perceptual apparatus, what is the cause for optimism? Indeed, may not such a "cognitive" view even imply that prejudice is still *more* inexorable than the motivational view does?

Certainly some of the findings reported in this chapter are chastening. In one sense, we must *add* to our understanding of the sources of prejudice—to the influence of historically rooted lies about various groups, current economic stakes in maintaining inequalities, and psychologically powerful needs to maintain self-esteem at the expense of others—still further powerful forces that generate and bolster prejudicial views. The factors considered in this chapter do not replace the factors discussed earlier, but rather complement and reinforce them.

But there is nonetheless a way in which this additional perspective offers hope rather than simply further cause for despair. For as powerful as the tendencies discussed in this chapter are, and as difficult as they make it to disconfirm the biases with which people approach perception of the social world, they are by no means inexorable. Understanding their operation enhances our ability to overcome their distorting and constraining effects.

Increased understanding of the "automatic" or "impersonal" factors that distort the thinking of all of us may also potentially give African Americans a new way of viewing some of the troubling behavior they encounter from whites. The aim of such understanding is not to absolve behavior that is offensive or insensitive; prejudiced behavior, and attitudes founded on ignorance and stereotype, must be *changed*, not excused. But I believe it can make some difference in the ways that African Americans experience the encounter with stereotypes if they recognize that the intent is not always hostile.

To be sure, the impact of bias and ignorant, stubborn misperception will continue to be painful. Moreover, the blows that accompany white stereotyping and prejudice are not only psychological; there are often concrete implications for African Americans' prospects for a job or promotion, for living where they choose, and so forth. But an understanding of the ways in which stereotyping derives in part from fault lines in the structure of perception that are our common human heritage may modify at least slightly both how the confrontation with stereotypes feels and how it is responded to. As a consequence, it can modify as well the repetitive back-and-forth between whites and blacks that creates such a powerfully self-perpetuating pattern. It thus might make it just a bit more possible for blacks to work *together* with whites to seek means of overcoming the misperceptions that flaw our entire society.

That asking such understanding of African Americans would seem unfair in the face of all they have had to endure is more than understandable. As an African American student in my class on race relations put it, in discussing the implications of the view I have been presenting, "What? Now *we* have to cure *them* too? It's all on us?"

An interesting insight developed, however, as this discussion proceeded. Upon questioning from some of the other students, it became clear to the woman who made the foregoing statement that although she had put it in terms of the responsibility being *all* on African Americans, in fact she was feeling that it was not right that *any* of the responsibility be placed upon them; they had been the wronged party, and it was up to whites to make it right.

One can understand the feelings that would lead to such a view, but it is not a workable or practical approach to overcoming the locked-in realities we face. As the early pages of this chapter particularly highlighted, the cognitions we hold regarding other people are not just "in our heads." They are maintained in part by the reactions we evoke in those toward whom we direct our expectations. I do believe that, for reasons both of history and of current economic and political power, whites hold the primary responsibility for initiating change. Calls for blacks to take responsibility for their own community have often been a covert way for whites to avoid *their* responsibility for changing inequitable circumstances, and at times little more than a ploy not to spend money to fix things. Nonetheless, the interconnections among us and the dynamic interplay of the ways we view each other are so substantial that unless African Americans actively consider the role they play in maintaining white attitudes—as, I hope it is crystal clear, whites must similarly do with regard to black views of them—we will be stuck in the same repetitive recriminations and misunderstandings for still another generation. Once again, to break the vicious circle, both sides must recognize its existence.

8

The Complexities of the Black Response to Oppression

Strengths and Vulnerabilities, Pride and Self-Doubt

The circumstances encountered by black people on these shores, from the extraordinary inhumanity of slavery to the poverty, violence, and virtual abandonment by mainstream society of today's inner cities, have presented a series of severe challenges to human resourcefulness. At times, as I shall discuss below, the adaptations that have arisen as a consequence have had painful and ironic consequences. But the response to these challenges has also included the development of noteworthy resources that have enabled African Americans not only to cope effectively and creatively with adversity but to transcend the adversity and construct lives of vitality and achievement. A primary concern of this and the following chapter will be to understand the diverse adaptations that have evolved in response to these circumstances—both those adaptations that, in one more vicious circle, end up perpetuating the very disadvantage that spurs them and those in which hardship becomes a forge in which the resources of individual and community are melded to yield uncommon strength and resiliency.

Whether one is discussing strengths or problems, one inevitably runs up against the issue of overgeneralizing. We are continually required to maneuver between overly broad and stereotypic generalizations on the one hand, and, on the other, failure to appreciate significant patterns, knowledge of which could guide us toward socially useful ends. Paulette Moore Hines and Nancy Boyd-Franklin, among the leading figures in the field of family therapy with black families, suggest that notwithstanding the very substantial diversity among black families, there is nonetheless "a set of core values and behavior, which in its gestalt remains distinctively characteristic of and understood by a majority of Black people."[1] Hines and Boyd-Franklin emphasize that although the stresses on black families are very considerable, and not infrequently lead to problematic adaptations, there are a number of noteworthy strengths that are found particularly often in the black community. These include "strong kinship bonds; flexibility of family roles; and high value placed on religion, education, and work."[2]

Offering an overview that places in perspective the images of poverty and the underclass that tend to dominate the media and our nation's discussion of racial issues, sociologist Andrew Billingsley points out that

> There are more than three times as many non-poor blacks as there are poor blacks. Every black community is peopled with them. The underclass is only half of that poor third [sic]. A majority of black working-class and middle-class individuals live in the inner cities of the nation and not in the white suburbs. There are more black adults who have graduated from high school and who know how to read and write than there are black high school dropouts. There are three times as many black youths who have managed to stay out of the criminal justice system than the celebrated 25 percent who have become engulfed in it. There are far more black persons who grow up in viable, stable, upward-striving black families than otherwise. And . . . they have millions of achieving, successful role models.[3]

Billingsley explores in detail a broad range of resources and communal values evident in the African American community, resources that are obscured when that community is viewed through a lens that takes the middle-class white family as standard and "normal." These include a much greater emphasis on extended family (so that many "single-parent" children have in fact several meaningful and available parental figures) and a very strong propensity in the African American community to take care of other people's children. This latter tendency is reflected not only in formal and informal adoption and a readiness to offer foster care but, more generally, in the widespread phenomenon of what Carol Stack has called "fictive kin."[4] Discussing this phenomenon, Billingsley notes that his own children "have so many 'aunts,' 'uncles,' and 'cousins' unrelated to them by blood that they can hardly keep track of them. Whenever they are in need, however, or reach a particular transition in their lives, they can count on assistance from these 'appropriated' family members."[5]

Creativity, Vitality, and the Cultural Contributions of African Americans

The strengths in the black community are evident not only in a range of familial and community adaptations largely unfamiliar in the white world, but in numerous manifestations of vitality and creativity that are evident on both an individual and a cultural level. Some of that creative energy is by now well known to whites; as discussed shortly, black contributions to the language and cultural life of our society have been noteworthy. But much of the creativity and vitality that have enabled blacks to cope effectively, and at times even to thrive, under circumstances that might be expected to yield simply resignation and despair has been expressed within the context of the harsh conditions of inner-city life. To many whites, this is an alien world, and appreciation of what constitutes creativity, inventiveness, and shrewd intellect within it is difficult.

The game of "the dozens," for example, a verbal sparring with few holds barred in which black youths turn insult into an art form, may be viewed simply as aggression and vulgar disrespect by white observers who fail to appreciate how creatively and playfully this competition serves to *contain* and *transform* aggression. Even more signficantly, the white observer who is distracted by the often scatological content of what is going on may miss the virtuoso use of language, the wit and inventiveness, that put to the lie the stereotype that blacks are "not verbal." As a youth growing up in a lower-middle-class white neighborhood in the Bronx, a neighborhood not quite as removed from interaction with blacks as were the suburbs where wealthier whites lived, I recall vividly our efforts to "sound" each other, and how inadequate those efforts seemed to all of us—a group of putatively highly verbal youths almost all on the way to college—when we let ourselves compare our efforts to be clever to the "real thing" occasionally overheard in the halls of our junior high school.

The contributions of blacks to the broader cultural life of our nation have been more difficult for whites to disparage or ignore. So pervasive have these contributions been that it is difficult to picture what contemporary American culture would be like without them. (I will return to this point in the next chapter when I consider the concern of some blacks that "assimilation" means losing one's identity by merging into "white" culture.)

Throughout the world, oppressed people have learned to express their abilities in those areas where opportunity is least denied them. And because their prospects are much more limited in other realms, because they are in essence "channeled" in certain directions whereas others in society can express their talents in a wide variety of settings, the oppressed or excluded tend to excel in the areas permitted them. Thus, although there is nothing inherent in Jewishness that entails any particular skill with money, Jews became associated with finance very early in the emergence of a money economy in Europe largely because they were excluded from owning land and from other kinds of participation in society.

In circular fashion, stereotypes then developed based on observation of this relative success without appreciation of the oppression that underlay its particular emphasis. As Jews in the United States have encountered broader opportunities, their successes have been evident in a much wider array of occupations, but the stereotype of Jews being associated with money and finance has persisted.

In similar fashion, sports and the arts have been fields in which blacks have had more opportunity than in many other occupations (though one need only mention the name Jackie Robinson to recall for how long even these channels were closed). As a consequence, some of the greatest contributions of African Americans to American society have been in these realms. Black athletes dominate professional sports such as basketball and football[*]—in 1998, twenty-three out of the twenty-four players chosen for the NBA All-Star

---

[*] Blacks continue, however, to be significantly underrepresented as coaches, managers, and general managers in comparison with their level of participation as athletes. Here the barriers remain substantial.

game were black—and their contributions virtually define many of the key developments in American music. Blues and jazz, perhaps the two most distinctly American art forms, were essentially invented by blacks, and a variety of other musical forms (soul, gospel, rock and roll, and rap, for example) derive from black culture as well. The number of renowned African American contributors in these areas is so enormous that listing them would seem both superfluous and tedious. I could name a hundred and almost every reader could readily say with justification, "But what about so-and-so? Is he/she not an outstanding talent?"

But sports and music are not the only cultural arenas in which African Americans have made especially important contributions. They have been a vivid presence in our literature from the days of Frederick Douglass through the accelerating contributions in this century of writers such as Langston Hughes, Zora Neale Hurston, Richard Wright, Ralph Ellison, and James Baldwin, and at present, they are perhaps the single cultural group that is most creatively and prodigiously contributing to American literature. It is aptly symbolic of the prominence that African American writers have achieved that the most recent American to win the Nobel Prize for literature is Toni Morrison, but she is by no means the only jewel in the crown. One simply cannot be abreast of contemporary American literature without some knowledge of the contributions of the African American novelists, essayists, and poets who are reshaping our language and our sensibility.

In the realm of cultural criticism and social and philosophical analysis, it is much the same. Articles have appeared with increasing regularity in our leading serious journals and magazines attesting to the influence of black intellectuals, and a number of commentators have suggested that contemporary African American critics have virtually reinvented the role of the "public intellectual."[6] Writers such as Cornel West, Henry Louis Gates, Jr., and Stephen Carter, to name just a few, are well known for important works on issues related to race, but their interests and their influence upon fellow intellectuals goes well beyond the bounds of race alone.

In other cultural and artistic domains as well, African Americans have made increasingly important contributions. In film, a number of young black filmmakers, perhaps inspired by the success of Spike Lee, have recently appeared on the scene with fresh explorations of African American life, often achieved on budgets but a small fraction of the typical Hollywood product. In television, the prodigious success of Bill Cosby is of course best known, but it is equally worthy of note that portrayals of African American families have more generally become a regular part of network fare, and have provided outlets for the talents of African Americans in all phases of the creation of such shows. In dance, blacks have become an absolutely central presence in the art form. It is virtually impossible to think of contemporary dance without thinking of the contributions of Alvin Ailey, the Dance Theatre of Harlem, Bill T. Jones, and numerous other black individuals and groups.

Finally, there is the still broader cultural influence of black language. Although, as I shall discuss in the next chapter, white prejudice toward the accent and linguistic forms of the inner city has been a significant factor in impeding the progress of blacks attempting to enter middle-class occupations, at the same time those very forms and rhythms have been the single most vibrant source of linguistic innovation and revitalization in the culture at large. The number of phrases that white Americans have adopted from the fertile phrase factory of the inner city is legion. Equally evident are the efforts of countless whites to appropriate the styles and cadences of black speech, to affect the cool, wry, mellifluous manner that characterizes the communication style of many African Americans. These white appropriations are sometimes labored, sometimes quite successful. They are usually not, however, as the cliche would have it, the sincerest form of flattery. For the originators of these vivid and captivating modes of expression are less often honored than disparaged, and the whites who profit from these infusions of linguistic vitality tend to leave them home like Cinderella when more "formal" or "serious" occasions arise.

The Psychological Toll of Oppression and Discrimination

The resources and creativity, then, that African Americans have brought to bear in their struggles with the inequities and injustices they have faced have been noteworthy, as have the achievements. Nonetheless, the harsh circumstances have surely taken their toll. Everything we know about the effects of disparagement and privation suggests that, although such circumstances can at times bring out unexpected reserves of courage and resourcefulness, eventually they wear most people down and block the realization of their full potential.

A key underpinning of the movement toward primary prevention of psychological disorder is an understanding of the debilitating effects of poverty, belittlement, and absence of opportunity. Those of us who wish to fight these inhuman tendencies and circumstances cannot do so effectively if we try simultaneously to maintain that they are a formula for bringing out the best in human beings. Despite many notable exceptions, the sad reality is that terrible conditions take a terrible psychological toll.[7]

Addressing the psychological harm that oppression has induced, however, is a complex and difficult task. For the *recognition* of these difficulties may become itself a new source of stress and pain, a new challenge to people who have already had more than their share. It can be more comfortable, at least in the short run, for the victims of injustice to deny that it has affected how they think about themselves and their ability to compete effectively with those who have not had to endure what they did.

How best to address the consequences of our nation's legacy of racism is a question fraught with ambiguities and painful choices at every turn. Is discussion of the harm resulting from years of oppression and systematic disparagement—and from stereotypes and inequities that persist to this day—a helpful and progressive effort to get at the truth and lay bare the full costs of injustice? Or, far from reflecting a sympathetic and realistic assessment of the pain whites have caused blacks (and the debt we owe), is it just *one more* instance of slander and putdown, one more way to say that blacks are not equal to whites? The complexities and contradictions are such that the dominant extant ideologies do not point clearly to an answer, and positions may be shared by strange bedfellows. Thus, the highly conservative position of Clarence Thomas—viewed by many blacks as insensitive to the realities most of them face and as shutting the door after *he* got in—has ironic affinities with that of many militant black nationalists, who, like Thomas, argue that it is insulting to talk of persisting psychological handicaps.[8]

Further complicating matters is that the same behaviors and adaptations that are seen as signs of strength by some observers may also be understood as contributing to the *difficulties* blacks have had in improving their economic circumstances and successfully moving out of the harsh world of the inner city. Joseph White, for example, in a chapter that has been called "the watershed paper on modern black psychology,"[9] argues that

> Many . . . so-called culturally deprived youngsters have developed the kind of mental toughness and survival skills, in terms of coping with life, which make them in many ways superior to their white age-mates who are growing up in the material affluence of Little League suburbias. These black youngsters know how to deal effectively with bill collectors, building superintendents, corner grocery stores, hypes, pimps, whores, sickness, and death. They know how to jive school counselors, principals, teachers, welfare workers, juvenile authorities, and, in doing so, display a lot of psychological cleverness and originality.[10]

Such a portrayal once again confronts us with the vicious circles that are at the heart of this book's analysis. For the very attitudes and behaviors that enable these youngsters to survive in the harsh environment to which our society consigns them—and thus are indeed strengths in coping with the circumstances of their lives—are also likely to play a role in *preventing them from leaving* that environment.

It is sometimes argued that pointing to these characteristics as the reason why blacks are unable to move out of the inner city or achieve success in the mainstream job market is a misleading distraction, and that the real cause is racism and discrimination. I do not disagree that racism and discrimination continue to play a substantial role. But as will be apparent, I also believe that a single-minded fixation on such factors—as important (and frequently denied) as they are—averts our eyes from other *also* important dimensions of our impasse and, ultimately, undermines our ability to overcome the discriminatory attitudes themselves.

The Clarks' Studies of Racial Preference and Identification and the Issue of "Black Self-Hatred"

The conflicting and ambivalent attitudes about how to address the psychological consequences of oppression are especially well illustrated in the shifting views of the work of Kenneth Clark, probably our nation's most renowned black psychologist. Of all the indicators suggesting that slavery, segregation, and continuing disparagement and discrimination had damaged the self-esteem of black Americans, the most influential and widely cited were the studies of Kenneth and Mamie Clark exploring the racial identifications of young black children. It was their studies in particular that constituted the core of the social science data considered by the Supreme Court in the landmark school desegration case, *Brown v Board of Education*

Using line drawings, dolls, and a coloring task, in which some of the stimulus figures were white and some were black, the Clarks asked such questions as (for the drawings) "Show me all those that you want to be in your class at school"; "Show me all those that you want to come to your party"; "Show me all those that you like"; and for the dolls, "Give me the doll that is a nice doll"; "Give me the doll that is a nice color"; "Give me the doll that looks bad"; and "Give me the doll that looks like you."

As I will discuss in more detail shortly, the results of these and like studies were in fact complex and ambiguous, and lent themselves to widely diverging interpretations. The interpretation that became dominant and most widely known, however, was that racism had induced in blacks damaging feelings of shame, self-hatred, and self-rejection. Interviewed years later, Kenneth Clark noted that he and his wife

> were really disturbed by our findings. . . . What was surprising
> was the degree to which the children suffered from self-rejection,
> with its truncating effect on their personalities, and the earliness
> of the corrosive awareness of color. I don't think we had quite
> realized the *extent* of the cruelty of racism and how hard it hit. . . .
> Some of these children, particularly in the North, were reduced to
> crying when presented with the dolls and asked to identify with
> them.[11]

One implication of the Clarks' work that was especially significant in its historical context was that separate was *not* equal, that the very fact of segregation had a psychological impact. In essence, what the Clarks' research seemed to demonstrate was that no one had been fooled into believing that blacks and whites were being kept separate simply because they were "different," with no value judgment implied; implications of superiority and inferiority were inherent in the system of segregation, and they were not lost on participants from either side of the divide. The very fact of segregating a portion of the population in separate facilities, the Clarks' work suggested, induced feelings of shame and self-disparagement in the group that was historically in the less advantaged position.

The Idea of Self-Hatred and the Shift in Identity from "Negro" to "Black"

The decade following the Brown decision was one marked by a great intensification of the struggle for black civil rights. Buoyed by the landmark implications of the Court's decision, and supported at the time even by a significant segment of the white population, civil rights activists overturned the system of legalized segregation in the South and succeeded in passing historic legislation making it illegal throughout the country to discriminate on the basis of race in employment, housing, schooling, and other areas.

The results of these efforts could be—and still are—viewed in rather contradictory ways. On the one hand, they were an enormous success. Sweeping changes were achieved in the legal foundations of our society and in the thinking of most Americans about what was acceptable and just. The black middle class began to gain rapidly in size, and those who were inclined toward optimism could see as not too far away the day when inequality would be a thing of the past.

On the other hand, poverty stubbornly persisted in many black communities, and the growth of the black middle class seemed to have the unexpected consequence of leaving many other blacks even more isolated than before.[12] At least as significantly—and affecting even those blacks who were "making it" under the new rules—the judicial and legislative efforts left largely untouched some of the deeper hurts and some of the most insidious indignities that racism can inflict. Although political and economic aims remain central to the black struggle—we are still very far from having achieved anything approaching parity between blacks and whites in average income, rate of unemployment, access to housing, or a host of other indicators of fairness—increasingly the emphasis has shifted to what might be described as matters of perception and psychology: to how blacks view themselves and are viewed by others, and especially to pride, affirmation, and self-determination. The oppression blacks experienced for so many years was not only political and economic. Daily humiliations—from grown men being called "boy," to being followed suspiciously in stores or passed up by taxi drivers—have been a regular feature of the black experience.

Not surprisingly, therefore, once significant progress was made on the legal front, increasingly greater emphasis was placed on a different kind of change: black pride and an emphasis on blacks taking responsibility for their own movement and their own communities began to take center stage. The aim was not only to change the laws but to live with dignity.

In the early stages of this new direction in the movement, its underlying foundations remained quite consistent with the ideas of self-hatred and self-rejection put forth by Kenneth Clark and others. Indeed, central to the very effort to forge a new identity rooted in black pride and affirmation was an emphasis on the damage to black psyches attendant upon the older (pre-movement) identification. One product of the militancy of the late 1960s was a change in the way Americans of African descent referred to themselves. The change, from "Negro" to "Black," was more than merely linguistic; it was a powerful, emotionally loaded shift in the basic sense of identity, and it carried with it a highly critical view of the older identity of "Negro." In the view of many leading black thinkers, the "Negro" *was* a self-hating, self-rejecting black person, and the pervasiveness of that mind-set was one of the key problems the black community had to overcome.

In attempting to explicate the shift in identity from "Negro" to "Black" and all its implications, a variety of writers formulated accounts of what came to be called *nigrescence*—a French word meaning "the process of becoming black." As depicted by William E. Cross, Jr., a leading theorist of the nigresence process (and, as we shall see shortly, later a severe critic of the Clark self-hatred formulation), nigrescence theory originally depicted "a process of Black identity change that transformed self-hating Negroes into committed and self-accepting Blacks."[13] Commenting on his own thinking at the time, Cross notes that

> Like other observers of nigrescence in the early 1970s, I assumed that Negro self-hatred was an established fact; consequently, my model, and every nigrescence model of the time, implied that the

> average Negro American was "self-hating and deracinated," and thus very much in need of identity change . . . my depiction of the identity to be changed was a recapitulation of Kenneth Clark's self-hating Negro—thus the title of my model, *The Negro-to-Black Conversion Experience.*[14]

In light of later developments to be discussed shortly, it is significant to note that at the stage in the historical development of black consciousness to which Cross is referring, the idea that self-hatred and low self-esteem had been a significant feature of the psychology of African Americans, far from being anathema to proponents of black pride or black nationalism, was in fact *particularly prominent among the most militant.* What was felt urgently to be necessary was to purge the black community of the "Uncle Tom" mentality, to expose the self-hatred and weakness that inhered in cooperation with whites and acceptance of white standards and values, and to *contrast* the old way with the new, strong, proud, defiant identity of being "Black."[15]

Rejection of the Self-Hatred Hypothesis

In recent years, there has been a shift in the way many blacks, and especially many black intellectuals and militants, have thought about black identity. The same underlying attitudes that, some years before, had led to the disparagement of the self-hating "Negro" mentality are now at the root of what might seem to be a quite opposite view—that it is erroneous and demeaning to suggest that prior to the Black Power movement and the advent of black nationalism, self-hatred had been endemic to the black community. Beneath these differing surface expressions lies the same emphasis on the assertion of black pride. Now, however, the vanguard view entails a reexamination of the very idea of the "self-hating Negro," which has come to be seen by many leading thinkers in the black community as just one more instance of blacks being put down and pathologized.

A key casualty of this shift in viewpoint among many black intellectuals has been the reputation of Kenneth Clark and his work. For many years, Clarks's writings and his research with his wife, Mamie, were a central pillar of the psychological understanding of racism and oppression, a powerful demonstration of the psychological harm that an unjust system can inflict. Now he is regarded by some as a thinker who, as William Cross puts it, promoted "a pejorative interpretation of Negro identity"[16] and "was predisposed to see Negro life from a pathogenic perspective."[17] This judgment seems rather harsh, especially since Cross himself recognizes that a significant influence upon Clark's interpretation of his data was the wish to assist in the historic task of challenging the foundations of legally sanctioned segregation. The needs of a movement change over time, and what the black liberation struggle needed for the legal challenge to segregation was, as Thurgood Marshall noted, strong evidence of the *damage* that segregation had wrought. Clark's data seemed to Marshall a good way of showing that damage.[18]

There is indeed some basis for questioning the formulations that evolved out of the Clark studies and related work, and for working harder to develop a more differentiated account of black identity and of the impact of deprivation and discrimination. To begin with, in much of the literature bearing on these studies, matters of identification or similarity are confused with matters of preference. Thus, although some studies do include questions such as "Give me the doll that is a nice doll" or "Give me the doll that is a nice color," in interpretations of the literature such questions are sometimes merged with questions such as "Give me the doll that looks like you," which is not at all equivalent.

The methodology of these studies tended to give the children just two choices to identify with; the drawings or dolls were either light or dark colored (or sometimes, white or brown colored). The children's actual skin colors, however, varied from very light to very dark, so that some of the children's skin color was in fact closer to the "white" or "light" stimulus object than to the "dark" or "brown." Thus, it is fallacious to assume that when such children choose as looking most like them the "white" doll or drawing, they are exhibiting self-hatred or self-rejection. In fact, they are being accurate.[19]

Interestingly, apropos Cross's captious depiction of Clark, it was the Clarks themselves who initially pointed out some of the limitations and bases for alternative interpretations of their findings. It was they, for example, who first noted that, given the dichotomous nature of the stimulus materials typically used in such studies, the identification of some of the lighter-skinned black children with the "white" drawing or doll was physically more accurate than would be

a "racially" correct choice. Moreover, consistent with later critics'
questioning the appropriateness of basing notions of racial attitudes
almost exclusively on the responses of very young children, it was
the Clarks themselves who pointed out that the *older* black children
in their study were more likely to identify with the *black* stimulus
figure, and who persuasively explained and integrated these two
tendencies in their data: "It is obvious that these [younger] children
are not identifying on the basis of 'race' because 'race' is a social concept which they learn at a higher stage in their development. They
are, however, definitely identifying on the basis of their own skin
color, which is to them a concrete reality."[20]

Finally, it is important to note that in studies such as the Clarks',
which were interpreted as revealing black self-rejection, the black
subjects did *not* as a rule show a preference for white.[21] Rather, they
simply did not show a strong preference for black. In effect, blacks
were viewed as having lower self-esteem than whites because they
did not show the preponderant preference for their own group that
whites did.[22]

Taking into account the whole range of critiques of the Clark
studies and the self-hatred hypothesis, William Cross, writing in
1991, suggests that the positive identity shift that was initiated in
much of the black community in the 1960s has been misunderstood.
In stressing the positive features of the new identity, he argues, he
and others had been too negative about what came before. A valuable and important shift had indeed occurred, but it was not a shift
that entailed overcoming self-hatred, for the self-hatred was never
there.[23]

"Black Self-Hatred" and the Zeitgeist: Where are We Now?

Part of the way the Clark studies were interpreted, Cross suggests,
derived from a zeitgeist in which ideas of pathology and self-hatred
among blacks were current, even among progressive and sympathetic observers. Given the oppression that blacks had endured, it
seemed only logical that they would be damaged, and so damage was
what was seen. What didn't fit was treated as "noise in the data," and
"researchers who tried to depict *any* portion of Negro life as a reflection of strength and a unique culture were simply labeled 'roman-

tics.'"[24] The result was "an image of the Negro dominated by feelings of inferiority."[25]

Cross is certainly correct that fashions and underlying social attitudes shape considerably how investigators collect and interpret their data, and that interpretations of the black experience have at times been plagued by an often well-meaning but nonetheless unwarranted tendency to see that experience through a pathocentrically tinted lens. But while it is necessary to be alert to the ways in which unexamined assumptions about psychological harm and a readiness to see pathology can bias our understanding of the black experience, it is essential as well to be alert to the dangers of an equal and opposite bias that can similarly distort our understanding: As a result of the very oppressions that contributed to shaping the "self-hatred thesis," *and* as a result as well of the impact of the self-hatred thesis itself, many blacks have felt an understandable need to assert the health, strength, and vitality of the black community and of blacks as individuals. This raises the danger that the *new* zeitgeist can similarly bias interpretations and skew observations, and that ways in which African Americans *have* been harmed by injustice can be swept under the rug. Such a strategy may bolster self-esteem in the short run, while in the long run eroding the foundations for more enduring change in the fundamental inequalities that continue to afflict us.

Just as the zeitgeist at the time of the Clark studies was one in which it seemed very natural to assume self-hatred, the zeitgeist today is increasingly unfriendly to *any* examination of conflict and self-doubts among African Americans. Where once the dominant currents in the movement emphasized the sickness of the "Negro" identity, a sickness that only militant "Blackness" could overcome, today the dominant currents among black intellectuals emphasize a long, unacknowledged tradition of strength in the black community (sometimes traced all the way back to Africa) and a keen alertness to anything that can be viewed as "pathologizing."

Concern about how years of oppression and disparagement may have induced conflicts and doubts that can impede the acquisition of fundamental skills, and thereby obscure the true potential of many African Americans, is today more likely to be viewed as hostile and insulting than as helpful. Accounts of psychological harm or dam-

age are seen as necessary to repudiate, and at times the very exploration of such matters is seen as the biased and inappropriate application of "white" or "Eurocentric" psychology. Joseph L. White, for
example, in the lead article to a major book on black psychology,
states that

> It is very difficult, if not impossible, to understand the life styles of
> black people using traditional theories developed by white psy-
> chologists to explain white people. Moreover, when these tradi-
> tional theories are applied to the lives of black folks many incor-
> rect, weakness-dominated and inferiority-oriented conclusions
> come about."[26]

The emphasis on seeing strengths and opposition to pathologizing is, in fact, an attitude with which I am very much in accord.
One of the key features of my own writings on psychotherapy, for
example, has been an emphasis on highlighting the debilitating and
counterproductive consequences of a pathology-centered view of
people.[27] But it is essential not to let a guideline become a constricting ideology. If *all* discussion of self-doubts among blacks is written
off as pathologizing, much of the understanding that is required to
finally and effectively achieve racial equality in our society will be
foregone. Indeed, as should be apparent from the discussion in Chapter Five, without being able to explore the impact of years of racism
and disparagement upon the self-confidence of African Americans
as they go through school, take examinations, and enter the work-
force, we are hampered in countering the defamatory claims and
self-serving misrepresentations in works such as *The Bell Curve*.

The Complexities of Self-Esteem

Part of the confusion in interpreting findings like the Clarks', and
in understanding the import of the shifting sense of identity among
African Americans over the past several decades, derives from the
multidimensional nature of self-esteem itself. Simple conceptions of
"high" or "low" self-esteem fail to capture much of the complexity
of the sense of self as it is experienced in daily living.[28]

William Cross, arguing against the interpretation that the Clark
studies revealed a significant degree of self-hatred among black chil-

dren, attempts to address this complexity by distinguishing between feelings about oneself as an individual and feelings about oneself as a member of a group.[29] One can feel perfectly competent to deal with the challenges of one's daily life and still feel defensive about one's group or eager to show one is "not like them." And one can be flushed with racial or ethnic pride but still be apprehensive about one's ability to perform well on tests or to deal with customers or the boss. Moreover, one may choose to orient oneself toward the greater opportunities offered by the larger society or think of oneself primarily as a member of the nation as a whole without necessarily feeling negatively or disparagingly toward one's specific racial or ethnic group. Such distinctions are experienced by members of *all* ethnic groups in a multiethnic society, and there is little reason to think that they are any less characteristic of blacks than of Jews, Latinos, Italians, Poles, or any other group.

But notwithstanding the usefulness of the distinction between the personal sense of self and one's feelings about the group to which one belongs, it needs to be supplemented by still further differentiation and analysis if we are to avoid misleadingly global conclusions. The distinction does raise useful cautions about inferring personal self-hatred or low self-esteem from measures like the choice of a brown-skinned or white-skinned doll. But although useful, the distinction is far from absolute; feelings about one's group and feelings about oneself are often far from irrelevant to each other. Some studies have indicated very low correlations between the two,[30] but this reflects in part the limitations of present social psychological methodology, which often attempts to measure self-esteem through simple questionnaires. Given these limitations, it is wise to supplement the findings of formal academic studies with attention to the experience of everyday life. As any sports fan knows, for example, when the home team scores a basket or hits a home run, one feels *personally* bigger and stronger for the moment. Sports fans chant *"We're* number one," not *"They* (the team) are number one," and the very blurring of self-boundaries that this implies is one of the key reasons many people *are* sports fans.

The identifications that arise from racial and ethnic solidarity, of course, are more profound and significant than those deriving from rooting for a sports team. But the two have in common not only a

bolstering sense of "we-ness," but a we-ness that has at least two dis-
tinguishable elements with rather different implications. One important part of the experience might be described as "non-competitive,"
the strength and security that comes simply from *belonging*, from
the sense of solidarity with others to whom one feels linked. But a
second part has a distinctly competitive or comparative element, and
depends upon the fluctuating fortunes of the group with which one
identifies. The intensity of the celebrations that follow an NCAA basketball championship or World Series or World Cup victory derives
from the way even this peripheral and transient element of group
identification can, at least for a brief time, powerfully infuse individuals with a sense of greater self-worth and efficacy.

Ethnic and racial identifications too have components both of
belonging and competitive group standing—the first more endur-
ingly sustaining, the second more vulnerable to the fortunes of the
group in comparison with others. But since racial and ethnic identifications are deeper and less voluntary, injuries to the group's standing can more profoundly affect how people feel about themselves,
and can at times at least partially undermine the comfort that
derives from the simple sense of belonging.[31]

Moreover, even where "personal" identity or self-esteem and
group identification and esteem are usefully distinguished, it is necessary to be clear that neither is a unitary trait. How one feels about
oneself and how one feels about or orients oneself toward one's
group can vary considerably depending on the domain or context
(with friends, in school, in bed, at work, etc.) as well as simply on
one's mood. Certain individuals, at the extremes of either high or
low self-esteem, seem to feel the same about themselves almost all
the time, but most of us can vary quite considerably from day to day
or situation to situation. Although there is certainly meaning in
referring to some people as having greater self-esteem than others,
those characterizations essentially refer to a kind of averaging of
experience; there will be times or situations (and they are not necessarily rare) when the person with "lower" self-esteem will feel
more confident or better about him- or herself than the person who
generally can be characterized as having "greater" self-esteem.

As Adelbert Jenkins, another perceptive writer on the psychology of the African American experience, puts it in attempting to

make sense of the conflicting claims about the self-esteem of African Americans,

> tests of self-concept that measure a person's general level of self-esteem are not necessarily good at describing a more specific aspect of self-esteem. For example, if you use global measures of self-esteem you are less likely to be able to predict academic achievement than if you use specific measures of *academic* self-esteem. . . .
>
> Related to that measurement issue is the fact that self-esteem is affected by the situation a person is confronting. . . . For example, students may justifiably be able to think of themselves as academically competent in one context, say in a small high school in the rural South. But upon entering a different setting, let's say a large prestigious Black college, they may find this aspect of self-esteem being challenged considerably by the more rigorous classroom demands and the better student body. . . . Both the lack of specificity of a test and the situational quality of self-esteem may be reflected in the contradictory literature on self-esteem in black children.[32]

This phenomenon may be exacerbated still further for blacks at predominantly white colleges or in other settings where they are competing with whites. It is here where the psychological impact of centuries of invidious racist messages are most likely to have left residual insecurities. Elaborating further on the points made by Jenkins, one may consider that some of the contradictory findings with regard to self-esteem among blacks may depend on whether they are comparing themselves to whites or to other blacks. Jennifer Crocker and Brenda Major of the State University of New York at Buffalo, for example, have reviewed considerable research on the ways that individuals from stigmatized groups maintain their self-esteem in the face of the indignities and disparagement they encounter, and one of the key implicit strategies entails comparing oneself to members of one's own group rather than to members of the dominant group.[33]

Some of the indications of high self-esteem in spite of all of the demeaning characterizations that blacks have had to endure in American society may thus derive from the many situations in which the reference group with which they compare themselves is other blacks. They may feel good about themselves in *that* comparison (which, given the racial divisions that still characterize our society, is the one relevant to a good part of their daily experience), and yet feel much less good about themselves if the comparison is with whites. There is where the long history of assaultively disparaging characterizations may most readily evoke unfairly self-derogatory images, whether consciously acknowledged or not.[34] It is also where differentials in test scores, previous educational advantage, and familiarity with the cultural styles and cultural referents of the faculty can all create challenges to maintaining self-esteem.

Indeed, notwithstanding his objections to accounts that point to the impact of racial disparagement on the self-esteem of African Americans, Cross too notes that global self-esteem measures can miss the specific impact of racial stereotyping on black children's sense of "self-as-student" or "self-as-learner." Discussing the findings of a national panel on Head Start, he notes that minority status does not necessarily induce an overall sense of inferiority— young minority children enter school with "a strong and positive global self-concept"—but that "the stigma of racism, ethnocentrism, and poverty" can have specific effects on the children's confidence and sense of self in the academic realm. This suggests, he says, "that global self-esteem and context-specific academic self-esteem may not be related."[35]

It suggests as well, as I shall discuss further in later chapters, that attempts to address the specific anxieties that African American children and adults may have in confronting school and job challenges are not the foolish or demeaning "social work"* or "reforming the poor" that some radical critics have disparagingly depicted them as. Rather, attention to these issues of self-esteem and their behavioral consequences is crucial to any successful attempt to deal with the persisting residues of past and continuing discrimination. Without such efforts, programs conceived in strictly political and economic terms will yield disappointing results, and the vicious circles that maintain our inequities will grind on.[36]

---

* My point, it should be clear, is not that there is anything foolish about social work. I am depicting the way the term "social work" is used disparagingly by those whose view I am criticizing.

Concluding Comments

It should be apparent that the question of whether living in a racist society has made African Americans particularly vulnerable to self-doubts or diminished self-esteem is one that elicits sharply contending views, and that those views cut across ideological lines. On the one hand, an emphasis on precisely such a phenomenon is consistent with an effort to highlight the psychic toll of racism and oppression. Such was the aim of the Clarks, for example, and of Thurgood Marshall in citing their work. It is consistent as well with efforts to combat the demeaning interpretations of black-white differences on IQ and performance tests by writers such as Herrnstein and Murray and their ilk. Test anxiety and lack of self-confidence have been clearly demonstrated to impair performance on such tests,[37] and the self-doubts that Clark and others have pointed to have been one basis for effective rebuttals to those who claim that test score differences reflect differences in basic intelligence. Finally, the idea of self-hatred was for a time embraced by the most militant vanguard of the black liberation movement as precisely the pervasive mind-set that needed to be overcome and that the black power and black pride movements were designed to change.

On the other hand, the black struggle has increasingly been concerned with countering what is seen as a pathocentric view of black individuals, families, and communities. We saw this in earlier chapters with regard to the Moynihan Report and the concept of the culture of poverty, and much of this chapter has depicted the shifting ground around the idea of self-hatred and low self-esteem. What was once an idea mostly associated with a progressive perspective has increasingly been viewed by blacks as demeaning and undermining.

These matters are highly value laden and virtually impossible to resolve on a purely empirical basis. The challenge we face, in my view, is to address the consequences of years of disparagement without, in the very act of addressing them, disparaging still further. In part, the path toward doing so is to keep clearly in mind that whatever damage we find is the responsibility primarily of American society at large, a society that, for all its very real virtues, has a history with regard to racial matters that is nothing short of disgraceful. But if we are finally to right the wrongs that derive from that history, we will have to look at them with fully open eyes. There are enormous strengths in the African American community, and for many whites it is those strengths that remain most invisible and must be seen clearly if we are to progress. But there are also more destructive stigmata of suffering—doubts, conflicts, and debilitating gaps in the development of many African Americans' God-given potential—that, understandably but problematically, have been pushed out of sight from the *black* side of our tortured and divided national community. Our problems are too severe and our challenges too great to afford us the luxury of trying to attack them without full awareness of what they are and where they come from. Unless blacks can find a way to face the pain of seeing fully what has been done to them, and whites can face the guilt most of us would prefer to rationalize or deny, we are in for many more years of grief and danger.

9

Integration, Assimilation, and Separatism

The Ambiguities of Identity

Blacks and whites in America inhabit the same country but at times seem to live in different worlds. Although they see each other more and more at work, they tend to live in separate neighborhoods, attend separate schools, and have separate friends.[1] They also, it is sometimes contended, belong to different cultures.

It is not very surprising that whites would reveal an absence of ardor for changing this situation. Although the consequences of inequality and separation ultimately take a toll on the nation as a whole, in the short run it is clearly whites who live in greater comfort in our still divided society. The embrace of separation by many blacks, in contrast, more clearly presents a challenge to our understanding.

To be sure, blacks' contacts with whites often tend to be far from heartwarming. The experiences of blacks who have tried to move into white neighborhoods have generally been painful, and in work settings, whether it is consciously intended by whites or not, African Americans frequently feel disrespected. The wish for a private zone, free from the stresses so often experienced in interracial contacts, should thus not be difficult to appreciate. Yet the concept of "separate but equal" has had such terrible connotations in our history and such injurious concrete consequences for African Americans that the powerful pull of separatism in one form or another in the black community presents us with a phenomenon which it behooves both whites and blacks to understand better. My aim in this chapter is to explore the assumptions, experiences, and psychological orientations out of which both the assimilationist and separatist perspectives arise, and to consider their implications for our ability to resolve the tenacious conflicts and inequalities that continue to plague our society.

Du Bois's Dilemma

At least since Emancipation, African Americans have struggled with the question of whether to think of themselves as Americans, as a group apart, or as some combination of the two. In a passage that has been called "probably the most famous in all African American literature,"[2] W. E. B. Du Bois depicted the psychological condition of the African American in words both poignant and powerful:

> It is a peculiar sensation, this double-consciousness, this sense of always looking at one's self through the eyes of others. . . . One ever feels his twoness—an American, a Negro; two warring ideals in one dark body, whose dogged strength alone keeps it from being torn asunder.
>
> The history of the American Negro is the history of this strife—this longing to attain self-conscious manhood, to merge his double self into a better and truer self. In this merging, he wishes neither of the older selves to be lost. He would not African-ize America, for America has too much to teach the world and Africa. He would not bleach his Negro soul in a flood of white Americanism, for he knows that Negro blood has a message for the world. He simply wishes to make it possible for a man to be both a Negro and an American, without being cursed and spit upon by his fellows, without having the doors of opportunity closed roughly in his face.[3]

Many different approaches have been offered over the years to come to terms with these dual images of identity—what might be called Du Bois's Dilemma—from rather thoroughly assimilationist visions at one pole, to black nationalist or Afrocentric visions at the other. At present, for a variety of reasons, the influence of the assimilationist or integrationist pole seems to be in decline.[4] The hopeful mood that accompanied the dismantling of legally sanctioned segregation has given way, for many in both the black and white communities, to discouragement over whether meaningful integration can ever be achieved and to a questioning of even the value of such a goal. This is a development about which I have considerable reservations and concerns. It is, however, one which it is essential we understand.

To be sure, this propensity toward separatism is by no means unique to the present moment. It has been manifested in the white community in the decades-long trend of leaving the city and moving to suburbs that, far from coincidentally, are almost exclusively white. It was manifested even more explicitly when whites responded to court-ordered busing by either sending their children to private schools or moving to districts outside the purview of such court orders. It is perhaps most dramatically evident in the increasing tendency toward walled or gated communities.

Among African Americans as well, separatist attitudes are by no means a new phenomenon. As reflected in the quote from Du Bois, the tensions between assimilation and separatism in the black community are long-standing. In both groups, however, there are forces today intensifying and accelerating the separatist inclination. Consistent with the central theme of this book, we shall see that these separate influences intertwine powerfully. Ironically parodying the very structure of the genetic material that unites us all, they form a kind of double helix, a pair of strands that wrap around each other and reproduce themselves again and again.

The Ambiguities of Assimilation

For many African Americans, assimilation is both the tempting siren and the mark of the traitor. But just what it means to assimilate is far from clear. The term "assimilation" has taken on powerful political and emotional connotations, and its surplus meanings, often unstated, impede rational or dispassionate discourse.

For those to whom assimilation is a questionable goal, the concept implies a self-defeating or even cowardly effort to shave off the rough edges of who one is in order to "fit in." It calls forth images of self-deception, of pathetic "wannabees," at times even of collaboration with the enemy. And, very significantly, it evokes images of "deracination." This term, frequently misunderstood as implying removing one's race or, in effect, bleaching one's soul, actually derives not from "race" but from the French word for "root." But its precise definition is itself both apt and chilling: "to pluck or tear up by the roots; to uproot, eradicate, exterminate."[5] Assimilation, it is frequently feared, will obliterate all traces of African Americans' unique culture, and hence a fundamental aspect of their identity.

These negative views of assimilation seem to me to be based on several false premises, which have contributed to the persistence of a pattern of separation that is ultimately of benefit to practically no one in our society, least of all African Americans. The first of these misconceptions is that the culture into which blacks would assimilate is "white." Such a view denies the enormous impact blacks have in fact had on American culture. As discussed in Chapter Eight, our language, music, dance, literature, art, and humor have all been deeply influenced by African Americans. Even the ethical principles to which our society subscribes, at least "officially," owe much to the black liberation struggle: the veneration of the idea of a "color blind" society—though now often invoked *against* the interests of African Americans—is scarcely the product of "white" America's original traditions.

Assimilation, it must be understood, is not a static or one-way process. It does not entail becoming a carbon copy of those who already are participants in the mainstream culture. In the very process of assimilating to mainstream American culture, those who are assimilating *change* that culture.

We may see this process in its purest form with the successive waves of immigrant groups that have become a part of American society. Immigrants come closest to having to fit into a culture of which they have not been a part. They must "become" Americans, must change themselves (or must encourage—or at least permit—change in their children) in order for the process of assimilation to be achieved. Yet at the same time, the very process of their assimilating produces profound changes in the society itself. Over time, it becomes a *joint* product of what it was, who they were, and how the two interact with and change each other.

This is, of course, not a precise fifty-fifty proposition. No single immigrant group has so altered the institutions of our society that those institutions are now as much a reflection of the new group's influence as of what they were before. But over time, America has become a strikingly different country as a consequence of its successive waves of immigration. The society whose "ropes" the immigrants first had to learn now has many of their threads woven through it.

Even more is this the case for blacks. To say that the culture into which blacks are being asked to assimilate is "white" culture is a distortion that one would hope blacks most of all would not countenance. That America is a "white" country is a myth of the white supremicist movement, not the reality of our nation's history, and especially of its history in recent years.

It is true that in many places in our society, blacks are still made to feel unwelcome, not only by the persistence in some quarters of outright racism and hostility, but even by the unwitting actions and insensitivities of people who do not think of themselves as prejudiced. Settings that whites regard as integrated, or as not particularly about color at all, often do not feel that way to blacks. As one African American friend put it, even when blacks are welcomed, they are welcomed as "that lovely black family" that moved in down the block rather than as "that lovely family." I would have to be blind not to acknowledge that it is easier to be a white person in this country, easier to be comfortable in far more contexts. But it is not a "white" society, and it concedes far too much to racist ideas when blacks too, even if with different meaning and intent, affirm this false idea.

What Must Be Given Up?: Confronting Concerns about Loss, "Betrayal," and Abandonment

Perhaps the most difficult question regarding assimilation has to do with what has to be given up. The habits, customs, styles, and rhythms with which we have grown up are a central source of our sense of security and comfort in the world, and their loss exacts a high price. For all of us, our identities are made up of innumerable elements which are part of the texture of our daily lives, and without which we would feel not quite ourselves. Most Americans don't have to think about this very much, because these cultural identity elements are relatively unconflicted and unlikely to change. They are like the proverbial water to the fish, a background without which the self we know could not survive, but so reliable and constant we scarcely register them. But when that crucial background is felt to be threatened, its elements rise to the forefront of consciousness, and become consciously valued—and fiercely defended—badges of identity. Something like this was experienced, I believe, by the white Christian right in the face of the profound cultural changes of the 1960s, and the reaction it triggered has had a profound impact on American politics. Something similar is experienced, for different but obvious reasons, by many blacks, for whom the idea of assimilation can feel like pulling out the bricks that hold up the endangered edifice of their identity.

For blacks, so long *kept* out of the social and economic mainstream of our society, the issue of what has to be "given up" in order to now enter can be difficult and loaded. The students in my classes on race and ethnicity have described fearing getting caught in a no-man's-land in which they are no longer accepted in the black community yet not really accepted in the white world either. They worry, moreover, whether mainstream success means abandoning those in their community who have not shared their good fortune. That sense of having turned their backs on their people can be felt not only with regard to their economic plight, but with respect to their culture as well. I have been told by some black undergraduates, for example, that they feel guilty about liking classical music, because it feels as though they are being implicitly critical of the people they grew up with.

Some African Americans deal with the tensions between the styles and mores of the community in which they were reared and those of the middle-class white world, within which their greatest professional and economic opportunities are likely to lie, by engaging in what is called "code switching." They speak, act, and dress one way on the job or in interactions with whites, and another when they are "home." In part, this is a sensible and workable solution, enabling many blacks to pursue success in the larger arena of society as a whole, while maintaining their ties to the community in which they were raised. Speaking and acting "black" when with other blacks can be both an affirmation of personal identity and an act of loyalty, a sign that one has not tried to "become white" or come to view white styles and mores as better.

But although some African Americans find this a relatively satisfactory solution, many—including quite a few who can do it well—find it uncomfortable and troubling. They may feel "false" or "phony" in their behavior in the "white" world, or worry that they are being complicitous in its implicit assumption that white ways are superior. Whites certainly also can experience conflicts between career advancement and issues of personal integrity or comfort—how much to go along with the boss or the corporate culture, whether to take credit for work done by subordinates, how much to "sell" oneself, and so forth. There is certainly a kind of code switching that distinguishes behavior in the boardroom from behavior in the bedroom. But there is not the same degree of conflict at the core of most whites' participation in the wider world of society, the sense that the very way they speak or dress or relate at work may reflect not only personal compromises but a kind of betrayal of their people or abandonment of their identity.[6]

In *Thirteen Ways of Looking at a Black Man*, Henry Louis Gates, Jr., states that, "to be a black man in twentieth-century America is to be heir to a set of anxieties: beginning with what it means to *be* a black man."[7] Giving voice to the complexities that confront every black in America, Gates further notes that,

> You can rebel against the content of an identity you didn't get to choose—and yet badly stitched vestments are not easily cast off. It's a version of the predicament faced by the wolf who would have to gnaw off a limb to escape from a trap. Hence the appeal of that comforting old lie: I'm not a black *x* (poet, president, whatever), I'm an *x* who happens to be black. Alas, circumstances won't have it so. Nobody happens to be black: this is a definitional truth. For a world in which blackness is elective or incidental—a world where you can "happen to be" black—is a world without blackness, a world, that is, where the concept has been dismantled or transfigured beyond recognition.[8]

There is no one way to look at—or to be—a black man. Gates, like the men he sensitively describes, "rages against the dread requirement *to represent*; against the demands of 'authenticity.'"[9] But he adds, "railing against something doesn't mean you've escaped from it . . . it follows you everywhere like your own shadow. It isn't a thing of your own making, and it won't succumb to your powers of unmaking—not yet, anyway."[10] Other Americans too must contend with the tensions between their uniqueness and their membership in a group, whether chosen or assigned. But for African Americans, it can never be a small matter that they "happen to be" a member of the group for whom our society has reserved its severest tests. When pressures do not come from outside the group, they are likely to come from within.

The Complexities of Solidarity

Hardships and doubts that are difficult to bear individually become more manageable when they are undergone as a shared experience. Strengthened not only by privation but by positive traditions of mutual aid and support that some have suggested can be traced all the way back to Africa,[11] the psychic ties of African Americans to their group, the sense of racial and cultural affinity and of shared fate, are often extremely powerful.

I do not mean to romanticize the solidarity among African Americans. Mistrust among African American men, and between African American men and African American women, has been extensively reported and widely represented in essays, novels, and films. The reports of students in my classes on race relations affirm and parallel these accounts. Black friends, colleagues, and students who attended the Million Man March have described a special thrill in their warm and emotional encounters with other African American men, and explicitly noted the contrast with their usual experience. Some referred specifically to the "look of threat" that they often have encountered in other circumstances, and to how much it meant to them to be able to look another African American man (a stranger) in the eye and feel safe.

Well-documented divisions can be found as well based on skin color and hair texture. Both African American and black Latino students in my classes have described painful experiences of conflict with their families over the skin color of a boyfriend or girlfriend and the sense of favoritism in the family that went with light skin and "good hair."

Nonetheless, there are many indicators suggesting that solidarity, identification, and a sense of shared fate are pivotally important features of the African American experience. In the same race relations classes that revealed certain tensions and divisions in the black community, it has also been striking how frequently the black students have referred to what "we" have experienced. Their emphasis on the sense of "we" was not nearly as characteristic of the students from other groups. The phrase "when we were slaves" was a frequent part of the dialogue. When students from other groups pointed out that none of the students in the class, nor their parents or grandparents, had ever been slaves, a number of the black students described the strong sense of identification with their slave forebears, and some described family rituals in which visits to relatives in the South included storytelling passed on from generation to generation to keep alive the knowledge—and the shared experience—of slavery.

The bonds of "fictive kin" discussed in the last chapter are another reflection of the strong sense of solidarity and identification that characterizes many African American communities. Ties of this sort are an enormous strength to any group, but are especially important for a people struggling to overcome the effects of oppression and discrimination. At the same time, however, they may lead to drawing a tight boundary around the group, and thereby to a potentially restrictive separation of the group from the rest of society.

Here again, it is important to understand the dynamics of this separation in a way that includes the powerful role of the larger society. The boundary is a *joint* product of whites and blacks. It is hardly irrelevant, for example, that whites frequently work so hard to keep blacks out of their neighborhoods, or move when that effort is unsuccessful. If many blacks live within a tightly bounded world, many whites like that just fine.

Nonetheless, these boundaries are strongly affirmed by many African Americans, and, in the circular fashion that this book highlights, they can contribute to perpetuating the circumstances to which they are a response. Although the emphasis on solidarity is understandable and in many respects salutary, it is potentially in tension both with the urge to individuate and with efforts to negotiate one's way in the larger society.

The first of the two tensions—between solidarity on the one hand and the urge to individuate on the other—is common to a variety of ethnic groups attempting to retain their unique traditions and group identity in the midst of a multicultural society in which they are a minority. Many of the novels of Philip Roth and other Jewish American writers of his generation depict a similar conflict between maintaining group traditions and solidarity and the wish to become "modern" or "American," which can include a sense of self that is differentiated from family or ethnic group affiliation. More recently, such conflicts have been increasingly depicted by artists from Asian immigrant groups, for example, in the Chinese-Canadian film *Double Happiness* or in novels such as Chang-Rae Lee's *Native Speaker* or Wayson Choy's *The Jade Peony.*[12]

The second of the two tensions, however—between separateness and "making it" in the larger society—seems especially acute among African Americans. There is nothing that is *in principle* contradictory between solidarity and success. One can strive to make it in the larger world and still be committed to affirming one's group identity and helping others of the group who have not yet been as fortunate. Indeed, one can strive to make it *in order* to do so (both to be a role model or inspiration and to obtain the resources to be able effectively to make a difference). But in daily life, many blacks do experience the tension, do feel that their success is a sign that they have betrayed, or at the very least have left, the group. As the participants in my interracial dialogue groups and the students in my classes on race and ethnicity have described it, there is concern that they will appear (and perhaps feel) "too good for the folks they grew up with," that they will "forget where they came from," that they will begin to be *embarrassed* by their family and community, will begin to talk differently, dress differently, listen to different music, and start to "turn white." As one African American student put it in his course paper, "If you extricate yourself, you get labeled as 'taking on airs' or thinking yourself better than others. There is jealousy, anger and envy from those left behind and tremendous guilt and self-doubt on the part of the one leaving. The power of these connections can be immobilizing."

In my classes—and especially in supervising cases involving blacks and Hispanics in the psychological clinic at City College—I have repeatedly observed indications of guilt over making it while one's childhood peers, siblings, and other family members fall by the wayside, ending up in prison, succumbing to the influence of drugs, struggling to survive on welfare, or remaining mired in neighborhoods in which crime and despair are pervasive. This guilt, which resembles other forms of "survivor guilt," can create painful conflict that makes whatever success is achieved fragile and vulnerable.

To be sure, the individualistic striving for success that is characteristic of middle-class American culture is by no means a necessary token of mental health. Many successful cultures, from Norway to Japan, have a philosophy of "the nail that sticks out gets hammered down," and encourage solidarity rather than differentiation. I vividly recall giving a workshop in Norway and worrying that the participants were not very stimulated because they were not commenting and raising questions the way an American group would if they were engaged. My host reassured me that in fact they were responding very positively, but that it was not the tradition in Norway to raise questions in the public session, especially in the beginning; that would appear too much like showing off or trying to appear smarter than the others.

But that attitude is addressed to showing off, presenting oneself as better than others or separate from the group. It does *not* imply that studying hard or working hard is questionable or will alienate one from the group. In Japan, for example, where the philosophy of not sticking out is very strong, students study extraordinarily hard in a race for grades whose competitive fierceness is well beyond what is characteristic in the United States.

Many African Americans, in contrast, experience pressure from peers that does inhibit their individual efforts to strive for excellence (at least in certain spheres) and to achieve their full potential. As A. J. Franklin, professor of psychology at City College and former director of its doctoral program in clinical psychology, puts it,

> African-American boys must also battle the attitude that if they succeed in school, they are "copping out" or "being white." The gifted kids are then pressured to bury or underplay their talent to be accepted by their peers.[13]

In a similar vein, James Comer and Alvin Poussaint, two distinguished black psychiatrists and authors of *Raising Black Children*, note the impact of stereotypes that lead blacks who achieve to be perceived as "white," "not black," or "not black enough." Comer and Poussaint describe the

> absolute terror and psychosocial paralysis we see in some black students from low-income families whose status as students means passage out of this black stereotype. It is a source of great

conflict for black teens who would like to maintain friendships
with blacks and whites, who enjoy Beethoven as much as Stevie
Wonder, who prefer algebra to football, and so on. This confusion
reaches its extreme when black students accuse other black students of 'acting white' because they work hard and achieve academic success.[14]

To be sure, one must place Comer and Poussaint's account in its
context. They note that the pressures they describe derive from
stereotypes, and it ill behooves us to create still another stereotype out
of the ways blacks have responded to those they already have to contend with. When they describe how black teenagers may be made to
feel unacceptable if they are "too smart" or take their studies seriously, or how fear that they will be "called 'dork' or 'white' or worse
. . . may cause a black teenager to fear success and try to fit in with
his group,"[15] we must not forget that anti-intellectual attitudes are
common among white teenagers as well. They may not accuse their
studious peers of being "white," but certainly would not find words
like "dork" or "nerd" exotic.

But it is a distortion as well to read Comer and Poussaint's volume as simply a standard child-rearing manual in sepia, or to minimize the pain and pressure depicted in Franklin's description as
merely about how all kids face peer pressure that puts them in conflict about devoting themselves to their studies. Certainly neither
Franklin nor Comer and Poussaint wish to contribute to further
stereotyping of their own people. But they believe it is important to
call attention to the special and distinctive pressures that black children and teenagers—especially black boys—must contend with.
Whites do the black community no service when we minimize the
impact of the pressures Franklin, Comer, Poussaint, and many others have described.

The Question of Language

The conflicts over solidarity and maintaining one's "black" identity
versus working to make one's place in the mainstream of American
society are especially poignant and difficult with regard to language.
Unlike the problematic adaptations to oppression that restrict the
development of abilities needed to succeed in the larger world of

American society, black language forms are simply alternative ways of creating and structuring an English grammar, with a complexity and subtlety that are equivalent to that which we call "standard English."[16]

Contentions that "Black English" (or, more recently, "Ebonics"*) is a separate language seem to me misguided. Speakers of the two versions understand each other too readily for that notion to make sense.[17] But the grammar and style of speech of many African Americans most certainly do differ from that of most white Americans, and there can be little question that those differences impact negatively on their educational and job prospects.

Interestingly, the very fact that African Americans are native speakers, not immigrants who have to learn a new language, has in certain respects actually made it more difficult for them to assimilate. Both immigrants with foreign accents and blacks with the accent of the inner city have been discriminated against in our society. Prejudices in both instances have led potential employers to hear their words through a filter, as it were, paying more attention to the accent and sentence structure than to the substance. But differences arise in the persistence of this source of prejudice from generation to generation.

People who are learning a second language do not tend to regard their own way of speaking the new language as just as good as a native speaker's. They see it as an appropriate aim to speak the language as much like the native speaker as they possibly can, and they hope and expect that their children will speak it in a way that does not detectably differ from the speech of people whose families have been here for generations. But such an aim for blacks, who *already* speak English, would require them to view the way whites speak English as somehow better. It takes very little psychological sophistication to understand why such a view of one's own way of speaking and of one's parents' would be less than welcome to anyone, much less to people for whom disparagement has been so central a theme of their interactions with the white world.

Consequently, blacks' speech patterns are much less likely to

---

* The widely publicized controversy over the Oakland School Board's proposed policy on Ebonics erupted after this section was essentially completed. The relevance of the discussion here to the Ebonics controversy will surely be evident to the reader.

change drastically from one generation to the next than are the speech patterns of immigrants and their children. And although there is terrible injustice and prejudice in judging people by their accents and speech patterns rather than by what they are saying, the reality is that such judgments are made constantly, and they add to the difficulties blacks encounter in advancing in mainstream society in a way that other groups in our society have not had to face.[18]

Thus, for many African Americans, the affirmation of identity and the perfectly justifiable feeling that one's own way of speaking the language is equally meritorious can have the consequence of impeding their chances to rise in society. Blacks who speak with an accent and a grammar closer to "standard English" are perceived more positively by most whites than blacks who speak in the accent and linguistic structure of the inner city. If truth be told, they are probably even perceived as more intelligent. A number of whites I know have acknowledged, with some shame, that on trips to England they were startled to hear black newscasters speak with what sounded like Oxford accents, the very accents they had found so intimidating when uttered by white Englishmen. They would recognize, with distress and chagrin, that they perceived these Oxford-sounding blacks as more intelligent than American blacks. They would recognize as well that such a perception was completely unfair. And it is. But it is part of what many African Americans are up against. As one African American student in my class on racial and ethnic stereotyping put it, "Whatever we do, we're in a no-win situation. I hate the idea of having to speak 'like a white man,' as if the way my own people speak is not good enough. But I also know that if I don't, I'm likely to get screwed. Some days it feels like I don't even know where to put my tongue in my mouth, I get so messed up and angry."

Changing the way they speak English can improve African Americans' prospects for advancement in American society; but doing so may stir painful conflict. Whether they refuse—either as an explicit and conscious choice or in a way that is more automatic and perhaps scarcely noticed—or whether they decide to speak the accent of upward mobility, they face a burden that, ironically, immigrant whites did not confront precisely *because* their parents did not speak very good English.

The Deeper Roots of Separatism: Some Speculations on the Painful Consequences of Ambiguity

For many African Americans, being a part of American society has meant being hurt. For years, the chief sources of that hurt were overt and unambiguous. But therein lay as well some basis for protecting against it (or at least moderating its impact).

To be sure, the overtness of oppression does not provide absolute protection against internalizing the unjust disparagement or the experience of pain. Even in the face of the most blatant oppression, there is a tendency, common among all peoples, to take in the values and attitudes of the powerful, whether the power be that of a parent over a child or of an oppressor group over one's own. Anna Freud called this tendency "identification with the aggressor."

It is very likely, however, that African Americans were afforded at least some protection from self-blame by the utterly unmistakable evidence that their deprived position in our society derived from sources outside themselves. The actions by the white majority that prevented them from exercising their potentials were crystal clear. When confronted with laws that say you must drink from a separate fountain or ride in the back of the bus, or with the unfettered and unhidden discrimination that existed until the civil rights laws of the 1960s were enacted, it is much less likely that one will tell oneself that being poor or failing to advance in the social hierarchy is due to limitations within oneself.

In general, differences in wealth or poverty, in job or position, tend to be seen in our society as a reflection of individual merit, not external circumstance.[19] And whereas laws and legal doctrines that explicitly relegated blacks to the margins of society were sufficiently overt that they offered a clear alternative explanation for the subordinate status of African Americans, today we are officially an "equal opportunity" society. What, then, are we to make of those who "don't take proper advantage" of that opportunity? If people are in a lesser position and there are *not* laws explicitly relegating them to that position, then it must be their own fault.

This view is nonsense, as I shall elaborate in Part Three. It utterly ignores history, social position, the accidents of birth, and a host of other powerful determinants of where one ends up in the social hierarchy. But it is a myth that sufficiently pervades American society that it is capable of being embraced not only by those for whom it is a comforting justification of their privilege, but by those who find themselves at the bottom of the hierarchy as well. It thus can create in the latter a need to *defend* themselves against the doubts and self-accusations that being part of America induces, a need that makes hesitancy to further assimilate into American society and to accept its values more readily understandable. Although it is no doubt true that African Americans tend to be more skeptical than whites about the extent to which racism and discrimination have been overcome in our society, there are many indications that the troubling doubts Spike Lee had his black "chorus" express in *Do the Right Thing*—for example, their hilarious but deeply painful dialogue about why the Koreans had been able to open businesses in their neighborhood but their own people had not—are a common product of our present confusing state.

Defending Self-Esteem: Effective Strategies and Painful Ironies

African Americans are by no means helpless in the face of these doubts and anxieties. Jennifer Crocker and Brenda Major, psychologists who have done extensive research on the ways in which members of stigmatized groups protect their self-esteem, note that "stigmatized individuals are not merely passive victims but are frequently able actively to protect and buffer their self-esteem from prejudice and discrimination."[20] They cite three strategies in particular as commonly employed in this regard: viewing failure or negative feedback as a consequence of prejudice and discrimination (and hence protecting *the self* from responsibility); selectively comparing one's performance and status with that of other members of one's own group rather than with that of individuals from more privileged groups, who may have better outcomes; selectively devaluing those dimensions on which one's group performs poorly and emphasizing those on which it excels.

These efforts can be of substantial subjective value, but they can also be a source of painful ironies, contributing to restrictive definitions of identity that make embracing the opportunities of the larger society appear a danger or a sell-out. At times, these psychological operations serve to protect self-esteem against the consequences of injustice and disadvantage and thus can aid in finding the strength to persist in the face of substantial obstacles. But maintaining self-esteem by attributing failure to prejudice and discrimination can also create a *stake* in seeing continuing prejudice and discrimination, and thus can lead to overestimations of how much discrimination still endures. For some people, far from encouraging them to persist, this may *undermine* their motivation, leaving them convinced that what-ever they do they will still be excluded.

The work of Berkeley ethnographer John Ogbu, discussed in Chapter Five, points in much the same direction. Ogbu notes that discriminatory treatment tends to disillusion blacks about whether hard work in school will really bring rewards and prevents them from developing what he calls "effort optimism," the conviction that enables people to persevere. Because they have experienced so many obstacles, Ogbu argues, "they have reduced their academic efforts, even though they still believe in the overall value of education. This apparent reduction in academic effort is not necessarily conscious, but rather may be an adaptive response to a history of unequal and inadequate rewards for their educational efforts."[21]

These reactions are responses to real injustices, but they also tragically end up feeding the sources of those injustices and con-tributing to the maintenance of the stereotypes that keep us locked into a divided and inequitable state. This process is further exacer-bated by the employment of the other two key strategies for pro-tecting self-esteem described by Crocker and Major. When self-esteem is based on comparing one's successes only to those of one's own group, it increases the motivation to define oneself as belonging to a group apart and to view assimilation into the larger social matrix as an impossible and even undesirable goal. But in a society where educational and occupational opportunities are much greater in the largely white mainstream, a stake in keeping separate to pro-tect self-esteem can have as a consequence negative educational and occupational outcomes. These can, in turn, require still further sep-aration in order to protect self-esteem against the impact of those outcomes.

The third strategy described by Crocker and Major for protect-ing self-esteem—disparaging those activities in which one's group has been less successful—can create still other self-fulfilling prophe-cies. Educational psychologist Jason Osborne, in research based on large national samples of youths from all ethnic backgrounds, found that in comparison to youths from other groups, the degree to which the self-esteem of African American boys depended on achievement in school declined substantially between eighth and twelfth grade, eventually reaching close to a zero correlation.[22] Osborne sees this as a demonstration of the "disidentification" with the academic realm described by Claude Steele.[23] In a similar vein, education researcher Laurence Steinberg, in a study of 20,000 teenagers, reports that

> Black and Latino students . . . are far more likely than other students to find themselves in peer groups that actually devalue academic achievement. Indeed, peer presure among Black and Latino students *not* to excel in school is so strong in many communities—even among middle-class adolescents—that many positive steps that Black and Latino parents have taken to facilitate their children's school success are undermined.[24]

Such pressures and such skewing of values and priorities are in large measure a response to the perception that academics is an area in which African Americans do poorly; but the result is likely to be still another self-fulfilling prophecy. As Claude Steele has pointed out,[25] academic success requires putting oneself on the line, *caring* about doing well. If the response to poor performance by previous cohorts is to devalue academic achievement, then the stage is set for failure to repeat itself. And although there is nothing intrinsic about that failure, which is rooted in a long history of injustice and inequity, its continuing repetition can make it *look like* it is inevitable—and hence spur once again the defensive devaluation of academic achievement that over time becomes as much cause as effect.

This is by no means to suggest that these defensive efforts are the only reason for poor school performance. The generally lower grades and SAT scores of African American students result from a host of factors, from poorly funded schools and crowded classrooms, to neighborhoods that create enormous stresses and pressures, to disparaging stereotypes that confront almost all African Americans whether poor or solidly middle-class. But the psychological operations I have been describing—a response to these conditions but also, over time, a factor in their own right—add to the forces keeping us unequal and apart.

The Link between Separatism and the Defense of Self-Esteem

In *Dark Ghetto*, Kenneth Clark's classic study of inner-city life, Clark observed that, "the invisible walls of a segregated society are not only damaging but protective in a debilitating way. There is considerable psychological safety in the ghetto; there one lives among one's own and does not risk rejection among strangers."[26] At the present time, several decades since Clark began his studies of the psychological consequences of racial injustice, the opportunities available to African Americans have increased substantially. But in various ways, the sequelae of oppression remain for many blacks, and attitudes generated by the need to protect self-esteem have become self-fulfilling prophecies that obscure those new opportunities or seem to prove them false. Frankly confronting these attitudes, Douglas Massey and Nancy Denton, authors of *American Apartheid*, a powerful study of the impact of America's persisting residential segregation, state starkly that

> As a psychological defense mechanism, . . . ghetto dwellers evolve a cultural identity defined in opposition to the larger ideals of white society. . . . Black identity is thus constructed as a series of oppositions to conventional middle-class "white" attitudes and behavior. If whites speak Standard American English, succeed in school, work hard at routine jobs, marry, and support their children, then to be "black" requires one to speak Black English, do poorly in school, denigrate conventional employment, shun marriage, and raise children outside of marriage. To do otherwise would be to "act white."[27]

Among the many sad ironies resulting from such a way of coping with massive inequities, one of the most powerfully consequential and most poorly understood is the way this adaptation aids whites in warding off recognition of those very inequities. Rather than seeing or acknowledging the enormous tilt in a playing field in which one side grows up in tree-lined suburbs with good schools and stable communities and the other in neighborhoods that are deprived, abandoned, and dangerous, whites are enabled to focus on behavior and attitudes that seem like *they* are the explanation for our inequalities. Thus decent people can feel comfortable ignoring indecent conditions. "They bring it on themselves" is a gravely simplistic social falsehood. But it is given a patina of seeming truth by the very way that the victims of this falsehood have defended their self-esteem against continual assault and by the implicit ideology that has built up upon this defensive stance.

Discrimination as Contested Territory in the Imaginations of Blacks and Whites

A key dilemma confronting us is that, to a significant degree, the path toward resolving our historic injustices leads through pain. It is tempting to deal with differences in test scores by alluding to different cultures with their own separate mode of cognition[28] or by "race norming" (evaluating scores relative to the applicant's group norm rather than overall norms). And it is more comfortable to focus on direct discrimination, to note the instances when *qualified* blacks are turned away, than to address the unjust circumstances that prevent many blacks from developing the skills to *be* qualified.

But in emphasizing continuing discrimination, as real as it still is in many particular situations, the psychological defenses of African Americans can intersect in problematic ways with the defenses of whites. For many whites, focusing on discrimination as the issue of contention can be a means of diverting attention from inequities that, at present, may be more responsible for the continuing disparities in the positions of blacks and whites in our society. For these whites, our nation's history of massive and undeniable discrimination can be a kind of ironic friend, a lightning rod that identifies the "bad old days" and highlights for them the *difference* between their world and the world of their parents and grandparents. The very egregiousness and overtness of past discrimination provide a baseline from which it is easy to detect change in the present circumstances and to be comforted by the substantial progress we have made.

The potentially defensive aspect of this focus does not necessarily imply insincerity in the belief that discrimination is wrong or in the pride many whites feel in our progress in overcoming it. In most instances, I believe, these sentiments are quite genuine. Rather, I include these perceptions as instances of defensiveness because the strong emphasis on ending discrimination—notwithstanding its sincerity—often serves another function for whites as well. *It directs attention to the task that has been largely accomplished (outlawing dis-crimination) and away from the task that still remains largely to be achieved (creating a genuinely level playing field).* In effect, the already largely accomplished task takes center stage in whites' attention, comfortingly conveying that any continuing differences in circumstances are primarily the responsibility of blacks.

Getting whites to confront these ongoing inequities is essential to the task of achieving genuine equality. But shifting our societal attention, from discrimination in the usual sense of that word to the roots of our inequalities in a wider and more complex set of life circumstances, can confront African Americans with the *consequences* of those unfairly differential circumstances in a way that may be dis-comforting. The emphasis on discrimination enables readily observable differences in income, educational attainment, and occupational status to be addressed in a more familiar and reassuring way. But it can have the unfortunate side effect of distracting attention from inequities that create real differences in skills and in readiness to advance in the educational and occupational world. These inequities—differences in economic starting point, schools, neighborhoods, etc., along with the cultural and attitudinal responses to those differences I have discussed through much of this book—play an enormous role in maintaining our social inequalities. Directing our attention to the issue of discrimination can contribute to an already strong tendency among whites to overlook them.

It is ultimately true that all that African Americans need is a fair chance. But the nature of that fair chance is more complicated than simply ending discrimination in the usual sense of the word. It includes offering them a fair chance to develop their talents, so that by the time they apply for a job or for admission to a college, they do not come with grades or test scores that set them apart.

Discrimination has by no means disappeared from American life. It remains an obstacle to black progress, but it is an obstacle that may be tempting to exaggerate because it is the *kind* of obstacle that is easier to acknowledge: not only does the fault lie completely outside oneself and even one's community, but it implies one's skills and attitudes have been unaffected despite the assaults of disparagement and injustice. What is most painful to acknowledge is that the more pervasive, sometimes subtle, and usually lifelong obstacles that are addressed throughout this book can exact a powerful psychological toll, at times limiting the ability to benefit from opportunities that are now available. It is far more comfortable to see oneself as a victim of *simple* injustice—*I am fully qualified and am simply being discriminated against*—than as the victim of the more complex, and in some ways more debilitating, injustice I am describing. And make no mistake: I am indeed describing injustice. It is society at large that permits these conditions to persist, that allows babies—innocent in the eyes of any but the most extreme racists—to be born into, and then to have to lead their lives within, circumstances so likely to limit their prospects and even their very capacities.

Anxiety, Assimilation, and the Black Middle Class

The conflicts and doubts I have been discussing are particularly evident among the black poor in our inner cities, but there is reason to think that middle-class blacks experience equivalent stresses and develop coping strategies that similarly separate them psychologically from the American mainstream.[29] The slights and assaults on dignity depicted in vivid detail by writers such as Ellis Cose, A. J. Franklin, Joe Feagin, and Melvin Sikes all play a role in shaping (and at times constraining) the ways in which many middle-class African Americans express and develop their potential. As A. J. Franklin has put it, elaborating on what he calls the "invisibility syndrome," "We are not literally invisible—that might sometimes be preferable. But on the streets, in stores, in elevators, and in restaurants, we are seen as potential criminals or as servants, not as ourselves. Within a single hour we may be viewed as a potential rapist—hugely frightening—and as a doorman—absolutely insignificant."[30]

Moreover, many middle-class blacks are confronted with burdens their white colleagues are much less likely to encounter. Even if doing quite well, they may privately worry, for example, that they are only in the position they are in because of affirmative action and did not achieve their position strictly on their merits—or that they are *perceived* this way, a source of stress in its own right. This eventuality is increased by the persisting difference in grades and standardized test scores between blacks and whites, even when researchers control for income.[31]

Thus, middle-class blacks often work or attend school side by side with whites whose grades and scores are significantly higher.

At the University of Texas Law School, for example, the court found in *Hopwood v. Texas* that "the presumptive denial score for nonminorities was higher than the presumptive admissions score for minorities."[32] In a study of the ten top American law schools, the mean first-year grades for black students were only at the eighth percentile for the total student body.[33] And in a study of students entering the nation's most elite colleges in 1991 and 1992, "the average African American student had an SAT at the tenth percentile of white students."[34]

To be sure, it is important not to confuse these differences in scores with differences in innate ability. I have already discussed in Chapter Five the many social forces that suppress the performance of African Americans on such tests. But the awareness of a low score can nonetheless be a source of doubt and distress, even for individuals who have gained jobs or university admissions despite those scores.

The long-lasting psychological impact of standardized test scores is evident among whites as well as blacks. I know quite a few impressively high-achieving whites who still feel some residual sense of shame and self-doubt because years before, when they were applying to college or graduate school, their test scores were relatively low. To view such tests as an unfailing gauge of someone's true intellect, especially in the face of achievements that clearly demonstrate the individual's real ability, is a serious error; but in a number-obsessed society such as ours, such scores can leave long-lasting scars and doubts.

Perhaps least often appreciated is an onus experienced by many middle-class blacks that is generally far less significant for successful members of other groups in our society. The very pressures for group identification that are at the heart of this chapter foster a particularly strong identification among middle-class blacks with the circumstances of the black poor. As a consequence, middle-class blacks are likely to be in much greater touch with the misery of others who share their racial or ethnic identity than are middle-class members of other ethnic groups. Put differently, they may be more inclined to identify with their racial compeers than with the whites who share their incomes or professions but not some of their most profound daily experiences. The result can be an identity in which being a member of an oppressed group lies at the very center, fostering an experienced sense of deprivation and exclusion that does not necessarily comport with their actual economic circumstances. The pain of those in the ghetto thus becomes the pain of the black middle class as well.

This identification with those in quite different economic circumstances is fostered as well by the numerous ways in which middle-class blacks *do* share the fate of their less successful ethnic peers. Experiences such as getting passed up by taxis, being trailed in department stores, being subtly but definitely steered away from certain homes or apartments by real estate agents, or simply feeling out of place in various social or business settings contribute to the view of many middle-class blacks that there is considerable truth in Malcolm X's bitter rhetorical riddle: *What do you call a black person with a Ph.D.? Answer: A nigger.*

To be sure, compassion, solidarity, and refusal to distance oneself from those less fortunate are virtues all too lacking in our highly individualistic society, and the presence of such attitudes among many middle-class blacks is to be admired, not faulted or pitied. Yet it must also be appreciated that forms of separatism and solidarity that evolved to provide solace in the face of stresses created in dealing with whites may exacerbate the very distress and alienation they are designed to alleviate. Thus, when black college students hang out mostly with other blacks, a kind of comfort is clearly derived. But there is also a kind of magnifying of the experience of marginalization—both because relations with whites never do get worked out, since there is not the contact and process necessary to do that, and because if one's identification remains so centrally as a "black student" rather than as a "Harvard student" or a "Michigan student" or what have you, that in itself heightens the sense that one is part of an oppressed group rather than a privileged group. How one *thinks* about who one is contributes significantly to how one *feels* about who one is.

Concluding Comments

For most of us, it is easier to talk about the political or economic dimensions of our racial difficulties than to look within at how we attempt to ward off guilt, shame, or self-doubts. Thus, working-class whites who feel their status threatened can more comfortably explain their racial attitudes by contending that blacks are getting jobs they would otherwise have gotten; it is much more difficult to acknowledge the need, when feeling unmanned because of being unemployed, to have someone to look down on. Similarly, African Americans who must cope with the internalized residues of disparaging messages can usually more easily address the manifest inequities that clearly still exist than the doubts those inequities have engendered. Issues regarding assimilation, separatism, Afrocentrism, multiculturalism, and a host of related trends and ideas deserve to be discussed on their substantive merits, apart from the motives that influence attitudes about them. But ultimately, if we do not pay attention to the anxieties, doubts, and conflicts our history and our continuing inequities have generated, we are depriving ourselves of valuable weapons in the struggle to understand and overcome those inequities. Both in my arguments for a more positive reconsideration of assimilation and in my more speculative venture into examining attitudes in this realm in terms of defenses, anxiety, and self-esteem, I have been guided by the view of Harry Stack Sullivan that "we are all much more simply human than otherwise."

PART THREE

The Seamless Web of Problems and Solutions

Crime and the Multiple Causes and Effects of Inequality

When problems are interconnected, so too must be solutions. The vicious circles that characterize our persisting divisions do not respect the boundaries that politicians and social scientists often like to draw. There is no isolated "crime problem" that can be solved by criminal justice measures alone, leaving for other efforts the solution to housing segregation, poorly functioning schools, joblessness, or the cultural values and adaptations that derive from all of these. Our problems form a seamless web, and so too must the solutions we fashion. That is one of the key lessons of the vicious circle perspective that guides this book.

No matter where our starting point, pursuing the causes and consequences of any one of our pressing social problems leads us to the others. In this chapter, I will focus on the issue of crime, but it is of the very essence of what I am saying that these chapters cannot be read in isolation; they are all very much about each other.

The problem of crime—like most of our social problems—tends to be approached with an adversarial mindset. The views that presently dominate public attitudes and public debate are steeped in either-or thinking that obscures the way multiple influences feed back and reinforce each other, with each both cause and effect at once. This narrow and problematic way of thinking is succinctly captured by Fox Butterfield in a *New York Times* article about the causes of increases or decreases in the crime rate:

> For liberals, crime must be traced to its roots in poverty, jobless-
> ness and racism, deep-seated social and economic ills. Nonsense,
> conservatives counter, the origins are cultural, stemming from the
> decline of the family along with the rise of welfare dependency,
> single-motherhood and a permissive social ethos.[1]

In such debates, each side, in telling its half of the story, leaves out, or pushes to the margins, the observations and insights that lie at the core of the other side's understanding. But rather than one or another of the favored explanations being the fundamental cause of our difficulties, what we are actually faced with is a complex of influences by now so thoroughly intertwined that each strand of the ropes that bind us tightens all the others.

Thus, liberals are correct that family decay, welfare dependency, and a decline in the venerable middle-class virtues are in large measure a product of poverty, joblessness, racism, and social inequity. But family and community disorganization in turn contribute powerfully *to* joblessness, poverty, and even, to some extent, racism. The circle is seamless and repetitive. Any effort to portray only one half of the circle as the "real" cause—whichever half it might be—condemns us to repeat it once again.[2]

Crime, like most of our social ills, must be understood not only as the product of multiple and complexly interacting influences, but as itself a link in the causal chain. That is, the social problems that from one perspective constitute the *roots* of crime can be seen from another as among its *consequences.* Appreciating this has profound implications for how we attempt to approach *both* crime *and* the social ills to which it is linked. If crime is viewed merely as a "symptom," an indication that something else is wrong, something "deeper" and more significant, then attention to crime in its own right may be seen as misguided or regressive, as attempting to shut down the expression of a deeper well of misery. Focusing on crime is thus seen as *antithetical* to the needs or interests of poor and minority communities.

But if crime has a causal impact as well, if crime exacerbates the very evils advocates for minorities and the poor wish to remedy, then the interests of poor and minority communities virtually *require* aggressive efforts to address crime itself. Far from being illiberal, getting tough on crime may be essential to achieving liberal ends.

Liberals are very largely right about the root causes of crime. Where they err is in failing to notice how powerfully crime in turn strengthens and maintains those very root causes. Even apart from the more specific influences I shall elaborate shortly, the sheer impact of crime on the residents of inner-city neighborhoods, the toll in human misery crime exacts, should be enough to persuade us to take crime more seriously. It is by now widely known that murder is the single greatest cause of death among young black men, and blacks are victims of murder at a rate that is four times higher than for whites.[3] Moreover, the pervasive atmosphere of violence creates a fatalism in a still larger number of black youths. As has been frequently reported, in some neighborhoods it is not uncommon to hear youngsters say that they do not expect to survive past their twenties. This is not only a horrifying psychological state for a young person to be burdened with; it also has an impact on the inclination to delay gratification and plan for the future, and thus on acquiring the training and skills that are necessary for successful employment later in life.[4]

The Reciprocal Relationship between Crime and Its Roots

In addition to its direct and painful impact on its victims, crime has repercussions on employment prospects, educational opportunity, housing segregation, racial prejudice, and ultimately the very perpetuation of crime itself. Because crime contributes to businesses moving out of, or being reluctant to locate in, inner-city neighborhoods, it contributes to the high unemployment rate in those neighborhoods (which in turn further contributes to the high crime rate). Crime also affects the quality of education kids receive in school. The violence and weapons that have become a part of life in many inner-city schools are bound to be a distraction to both teachers and students. It is not surprising that children who hear gunfire while they are trying to do their homework do not score as high on standardized tests as those for whom that sound implies simply that the television set must be on.[5]

One of the most important ways in which crime feeds back to maintain its own root causes is in its relation to racially segregated

housing. Housing segregation is one of the most persistent residues
of our nation's racist past, and as I shall discuss below, it is almost
certainly a significant factor in the elevation of the black crime rate.
Notwithstanding the passage of fair housing laws, housing in America remains nearly as segregated today as it was before the advent
of the civil rights movement. And as Douglas Massey and Nancy
Denton have argued persuasively in their important and compelling
book *American Apartheid*, residential segregation lies close to the
center of the causal nexus that maintains our society's racial difficulties and divisions.

There are many causes to this persistence of residential segregation. Much of whites' resistance to living side by side with blacks
is clearly the result of prejudices that are long-standing and virtually unrelated to actual experience. But that resistance is also maintained by fear of crime. The fear may be magnified by selective perception and stereotypes, but those perceptions and stereotypes are
fed by actual events. It is a fact that blacks commit violent crimes at
a far higher rate than whites, and it is a fact with significant social
consequences. Blacks constitute slightly under 13% of the population, but they represent 44.8% of those arrested for murder, rape,
aggravated assault, and robbery.[6] As put by Randall Kennedy, a
prominent African American professor at the Harvard Law School,
"That relative to their percentage of the population, blacks commit
more street crime than whites is a fact and not a figment of a Negro-
phobe's imagination. . . . This proposition has ceased to be controversial among most careful students of crime in America."[7]

Consequently, when whites start to see significant numbers of
blacks in their neighborhoods, they get nervous. Even if they know
that the majority of blacks do *not* commit crimes, they may feel, as
one interviewee put it, that "you read that one out of four young
black males is involved with the criminal justice system—either in
prison, on parole, or on probation. That means three out of four have
done nothing wrong. I know abstractly that it's not fair to that three
out of four to penalize them for what the others have done, but can I
live with the idea that there's one chance in four that the guy walking down my block will mug me? I don't think so."

Now to be sure, this narrowly self-interested attitude is not very
ennobling. Moreover, although seemingly rooted in a "hardheaded"
analysis of unfortunate but objective realities, it in fact includes sig-

nificant distortions. Even putting aside how unfair this position is to the large majority of blacks, who even by this interviewee's own calculations are no less innocent than he is, it must be recognized that not all of the "one in four" are muggers. Many have committed offenses that needn't make one fear if they walk down one's block (though it could be countered that selling drugs, for example, even if not in itself a violent offense, is part of a culture of violence that one might rationally wish to keep out of one's neighborhood).[8]

Perhaps the most important limitation of attitudes like those of the interviewee just described is that they fail to probe very deeply into *why* it is that blacks commit a disproportionate number of violent crimes. The honest pursuit of this question would point to a wide variety of persisting inequities and deprivations. A still deeper probe would suggest that the very way of thinking manifested by the interviewee—his readiness to lump people together on the basis of skin color alone and to treat the safety and opportunities of acknowledgedly innocent blacks as an "unfortunate but necessary" sacrifice to the interests of whites—itself limits the options available to many African Americans and contributes to the very rage and crime that the interviewee fears.

Thus, the point of the above discussion is clearly not that white resistance to blacks living in their neighborhoods is "justified."[9] Rather, my pointing out that the de facto exclusion of most blacks from white neighborhoods is at least in part a *result* of black crime rates as well as a cause stems from a search for more comprehensive and effective solutions to the repetitive circular patterns in which we are caught. As it is the aim of this chapter (and this book) to demonstrate, the tangled complexity of our difficulties is so considerable, and the prospects for problems perpetuating themselves through their own consequences so substantial, that we must detect and apply our leverage at every point where forces are aligned against progress.

This is by no means to suggest that black crime is "the" explanation for white resistance to more integrated communities. Ellis Cose is surely correct when he argues, in a different context, that, "Notwithstanding currently fashionable arguments that blame white racism on black crime, it's unlikely that discrimination against certifiably 'safe' blacks stems primarily from fear of black violence. Black executives, for instance, are not barred from private country clubs because white members fear their African-American peers will rob them."[10] But high black crime rates assuredly do *exacerbate* existing prejudices, giving them an anchor that increases the difficulty in rooting them out. It is in the very nature of prejudice that it entails poorly examined overgeneralizations. The distinction between street criminals from impoverished ghettoes and African American college graduates wearing suits and ties is easy to make in principle. But the psychological dynamics of prejudiced cognition are such that fears associated with the former impact on the perception of the latter, making crime a matter that affects all African Americans.[11]

It is important to note as well that the dynamics of prejudice change over time. Cose points out that "even the most superficial and charitable reading of American history reveals that the stereotypes, and the justifications for them, were in place long before anyone imagined a so-called underclass of the type that exists today. These stereotypes have never needed much confirmation in reality in order to endure."[12] Cose's point seems to me indisputable, but is nonetheless limited by his implicit assumption that prejudices are static, monolithic entities. In fact, although prejudices are by their very nature rather rigid psychological entities, like all of our thoughts and attitudes they are maintained by the constant interplay between preexisting inclinations and the continuous environmental input that must be processed and interpreted.[13] Although change in rigid psychological structures is much slower and more limited than in more flexible and adaptive structures, they too are always potentially in flux (see again Chapter Seven). There is much evidence that white attitudes toward blacks have continued to evolve and that an important impact of the civil rights movement has been to shake up long-entrenched assumptions and perceptions. This certainly does not mean that prejudice or racism have disappeared, but the dynamics of white prejudice are different now. Crime likely plays a considerably larger role in *maintaining* prejudice now than it did in generating it originally.

Crime and the Decline of Liberalism

Crime also contributes to the perpetuation of inequality in another way, which is more indirect but no less substantial. One significant source of the ill favor into which liberalism has fallen has been the perception by large segments of the public that liberals' search for "root causes" of crime reflects a "softness" toward crime that is dangerous and perverse. In my view this evolving public attitude has been very unfortunate. We do need to get at the "root causes" of crime, and they indeed do lie in many of the very inequalities and impediments to equal opportunity that liberals have pointed to for years. But if we regard crime as only a *result* of these circumstances, and fail to see how crime contributes to perpetuating them and erodes support for the very programs and initiatives needed to address them, our prospects for effectively addressing those root causes are seriously diminished. It is not that liberals are wrong that those conditions breed crime. It is that they leave out that *crime also breeds those conditions.*

Thus, slogans like "build schools, not prisons" are dangerously simplistic. To be sure, resources are limited and, in one sense, money spent on one may seem to diminish what is available for the other. Building prisons can be seen as an *alternative* to building schools, and as a way of treating the symptoms while allowing the disease to continue to rage. Moreover, in the present political climate, that is indeed often the reality.

But such a view is entirely too static. It implies that the size of the pool of public funds available to address our social ills is fixed. The question we really need to ask is: How have we arrived at the views we now hold regarding what resources are appropriate to devote to the public sector and what should be reserved for private consumption? Even after correcting for inflation, our gross national product is larger today by hundreds of billions of dollars than it was in the 1960s. Yet then there was a strong national consensus supporting a war on poverty, and today we feel we "cannot afford" social programs.

There are many reasons for this changed perception. Some of them derive from widely shared misconceptions about the sources of satisfaction and security in our lives.[14] Some derive from a view, which I intend to challenge, that social programs do not work, that they have been tried and have failed. But a good deal of the responsibility for this state of affairs must be placed on the way liberals have painted themselves into a corner, undermining their valid insights and potential influence by taking positions on crime and social decay that feel to the majority of Americans like they are just not paying attention. Crime is certainly not the only factor that has reduced the support for liberal views in recent years, but it is a serious error for liberals to overlook the emotional and symbolic freight that crime carries.

In the overly dichotomous way that political attitudes tend to get categorized, being tough on crime is almost automatically assumed to be a "conservative" position. But there is nothing intrinsic about this connection, no logic that links commitment to a governmental role in promoting equality to a view that criminal sentences are too severe or that necessitates that concern about the victims of crime must be associated with a *lack* of concern about the victims of economic or racial injustice.

The sources of dominant liberal attitudes about crime are not difficult to understand. The fact that such a huge number of black men are in jail or otherwise entangled in the criminal justice system—a recent study in Baltimore, for example, reported that on any given day more than fifty percent of black males between the ages of eighteen and thirty-five were in prison or under criminal justice supervision[15]—is a symptom of a serious failure to address the obstacles that keep African Americans from entering the social and economic mainstream. But the ready assumption by many liberals that African Americans accused or even convicted of crimes are more victims than victimizers does not contribute to the resolution of our inequalities. All too often it contributes to their perpetuation.

The Destructive Solidarity between Black Victims and Their Victimizers

One implication of the argument I have been developing is that the interests of the minority of African Americans who commit serious crimes and the interests of the larger African American community diverge quite sharply. It would be an advance in our efforts to achieve racial justice, I believe, if the ties of sympathy and solidarity that lead so many blacks to see black prisoners as victims, and to rejoice when a black defendant is acquitted, were to diminish. Though it is viewed almost as heresy in the circles that in other ways share my deepest values, it seems to me that black criminals are as significant an obstacle to black progress and black interests as the complacent white middle class. Not only are the majority of

their victims law-abiding blacks who are forced to live in close proximity to them because of either poverty or housing discrimination,
but as I shall elaborate below, they help perpetuate the stereotypes
that impact so powerfully on those blacks whose behavior and way of
life are in fact quite different.

A good example of the problematic solidarity which I am
addressing here is evident in the views of Bruce Wright, a prominent and controversial African American judge on the New York
State Supreme Court. Judge Wright paints a Kafkaesque portrait of
the criminal justice system, in which "practically anonymous prisoners or defendants come before an unknown judge" and never get
to know the name of the prosecutor who, in Wright's words, "zeal-
ously seeks to abort such freedom as they have."[16]

Wright's account struck an especially personal note for me
when he added that, "even more sadly, the poor defendants who rely
upon appointed counsel often never know the names of the lawyers
who are the trustees of their destiny or doom. They have come to
believe that everything is predetermined and that nothing a defendant can do will make a difference."[17] This depiction evoked a vivid
recollection of a chagrined friend, a dedicated advocate for the poor,
who experienced a crisis of conscience in his work as a Legal Aid
lawyer when a black teenager whom he had successfully defended in
Juvenile Court proceedings just the week before in a case involving
a purse snatching, came into the office after being arrested again,
asking, "Where's Fishman? I gotta see my man Fishman." Far from
feeling helpless in the face of anonymous forces, this youth felt he
knew exactly to whom to go to get off for the knifing he had just
committed![18]

To be sure, Wright's views are not necessarily representative of
the black community, whose members, after all, are the primary victims of violent crime. But to a disturbing degree, what *is* widely
shared is a profound skepticism and mistrust toward the criminal
justice system, resulting in an increasingly reported hesitation by
black jurors to send blacks who have committed crimes to jail. For
many whites, it was the O. J. Simpson trial that particularly brought
to their attention these powerful misgivings. But whatever role such
attitudes may have played in the Simpson jury's decision, their
declared reason for acquittal was that questions raised by the defense
introduced "reasonable doubt" as to Simpson's guilt. In other less

high-profile trials, the reluctance of black jurors to convict a black defendant has been more explicit. Jerome Miller, president of the National Center on Institutions and Alternatives and by no means a "law and order" advocate, reports the following example as reflecting an increasingly common attitude among African Americans:

> On March 6, 1990, an 18-year-old African-American man was acquitted of a felony by a black jury in the District of Columbia. "One young juror was crying when the verdict came. The prosecutor gaped as it was read. The crashing sound in the courtroom was the defendant, whose elation propelled him backward over his chair." Three weeks later, a letter arrived at D.C. Superior Court from one of the jurors, who wrote that though most of the jury believed the defendant to be guilty, they had bowed to those who "didn't want to send anymore Young Black Men to Jail."[19]

Jeffrey Rosen, writing in the *New Yorker*, describes a number of similar cases, some where the jurors used almost the exact same words to describe their reluctance to convict a black defendant despite overwhelming evidence—and despite the *victims,* in many of the cases, being black.[20] Both Miller and Rosen note that similar occurrences have been repeated in jurisdictions throughout the country.

Along similar lines, black prosecutors report that they are frequently perceived by other blacks as traitors, notwithstanding that their efforts contribute significantly to the safety of the most vulnerable black communities. In a book aptly titled *The Darden Dilemma*[21] (because of the way in which Christopher Darden became a figure of considerable controversy in the black community for his role in prosecuting O. J. Simpson), several black prosecutors describe this phenomenon. Jeffrey Craig, for example, a black deputy attorney general in Pennsylvania, notes that, "Sometimes I'm very apprehensive even telling black people what I do." In the eyes of many blacks, he reports, "I'm a turncoat, . . . I'm not helping my brothers and sisters."[22] In fact, the kinds of cases Craig prosecutes involve mostly white-collar crimes committed by whites, but the very fact that this would seem relevant in his defense, as it were, implies that prosecuting *black* criminals—who in fact prey particularly on the black community—is somehow shameful.

Another black prosecutor, Robert Grace, describes being viewed negatively even by other black prosecutors because he was the prosecutor in the high-profile murder trial of Calvin Broadus, better known as the rapper Snoop Doggy Dogg. Notwithstanding that Broadus was being tried for the murder of another black man, the reaction to Grace was that he was "another brother trying to take another brother down."[23]

How Fair is the Criminal Justice System?

My emphasis on the destructive and counterproductive consequences of minimizing the impact of black crime or viewing blacks who commit violent crimes under the umbrella of victimhood should not be taken to dismiss the very legitimate misgivings many blacks have about the criminal justice system and especially about the police. Concerns over fairness have been raised about every stage of the process from arrest to sentencing. With regard to police behavior in relation to blacks, there can be no doubt that abuses—indeed, frequent abuses—occur. The implications of these abuses, and the ways they are instantiations of the kinds of vicious circles I have been discussing throughout this book, are, in fact, of sufficient importance that I will discuss them in a separate section below. With regard to questions such as whether blacks are arrested out of proportion to the percentage of crimes they commit, whether they are more likely to be convicted in the face of similar evidence, or whether they receive harsher sentences for the same crimes, the evidence is mixed, but certain tentative conclusions can be drawn. On the one hand, certain indications of unfairness are striking and strong. These include the very strong evidence that defendants who kill whites are more than four times as likely to be sentenced to death as defendants who kill blacks,[24] and that black men convicted of raping white women have been up to *eighteen* times more likely to receive a death sentence than white rapists or rapists whose victims were black.[25]

On the other hand, the overall argument for unfairness in the criminal justice system is often marred by tendentious arguments. Jerome Miller, for example, tells us that "Most people probably think that violent crimes as reported by the FBI involve a murder, a mugging, or a bloody assault. This is seldom true. In most cases, the violent crime consists of a threat or a perceived threat."[26] Miller would have us believe that there is a sharp difference between crimes that result in serious injury and hospitalization and those that "merely" involve a threat. Perhaps I am just too squeamish, but I regard being held up at gunpoint or having a knife held to one's throat as more than just a mildly unpleasant inconvenience, *regardless* of whether the victim ends up in the hospital or not. Miller's distinction reflects a minimizing mindset that is obtuse to the experience of being terrorized—and to its impact not only on the victim but on the way in which black men in general are viewed.[27] For Miller, fears of black crime are all exaggeration and distortion, and our concern about high black crime rates is glibly dismissed as "crime kitsch" offered by "coifed TV hosts and news readers."[28]

In contrast, the evidence seems to me overwhelming that the primary reason that so much higher a proportion of blacks are imprisoned for committing violent crimes than whites is that blacks really do commit such crimes at a much higher rate.[29] In 1990, for example, blacks (12 to 13% of the overall population) accounted for 61.2% of all arrests for robbery, 54.7% of arrests for murder and manslaughter, and 43.2% of arrests for rape.[30] Do these figures merely reflect police bias, a greater tendency to arrest blacks that has little to do with their actual rate of criminal activity? There are data that make this interpretation unlikely. The Census Bureau conducts an annual survey to determine what percentage of households has been victimized by crime, and that survey includes questions about the race of the victim and the assailant. In that survey, 65.1% of the people who had been robbed reported that the robber had been black. Obviously, in cases of murder or manslaughter the victim him- or herself could not be questioned, but in cases where others could clearly identify the race of the assailant, 53.9% were black. These figures compare quite closely to the figures of 61.2% and 54.7% for arrests, and suggest that the high arrest rate of blacks for those crimes corresponds to a real high rate of black criminal activity.

With regard to rape, the comparison between arrest rates and reports on the Census survey do suggest that, for this specific crime, black offenders are in fact more likely to be arrested than whites. Whereas 43.2% of those arrested for rape were black, only 33.2% of the women interviewed indicated that their attacker was black. It is possible that this disparity reflects a greater zeal by police in arresting blacks accused of rape than whites. But it may also reflect a variety of factors that lead to rapes by whites being *reported* less often by the victim, and in light of the fact that no such disparity exists with regard to murder, manslaughter, or robbery, the latter seems a more likely explanation. In any event, another disturbing reality remains, quite apart from arrest rates: blacks, constituting 12 to 13% of the population, commit 33.2% of reported rapes.

No amount of racial bias in enforcing the law is acceptable, and I am convinced we still have much work to do before we can rest easy that racial prejudice is not an element in the administration of justice. But it also seems clear that the critical issue with regard to the arrest and incarceration of African Americans is not that we are arresting and convicting black defendants out of proportion to the crimes they commit, but that the high rates of arrest and incarceration essentially reflect genuinely high black crime rates. *This* is the heart of the tragedy: that our society continues to expose so many African Americans to conditions that generate crime, and that that very crime, in turn, contributes to perpetuating those same conditions.

The Black Community and the Police

The realm in which the indications are strongest that blacks do encounter unfair differential treatment from the criminal justice system is in their interactions with the police. Instances of police brutality or insensivity, of abuses or humiliations, are so widespread and so widely reported that detailed documentation seems unnecessary. Racial slurs by police and orders laced with curses and contempt are daily occurrences in our nation's inner cities. Moreover, countless descriptions by successful middle-class blacks attest that they too experience the same humiliations. Not only do they get stopped by police when they are walking in a neighborhood in which they are not expected to be seen or driving a car that the police do not associate with African Americans (or, in their stereotypes, associate with African American drug dealers only), but they are frequently treated on those occasions in a manner that would be almost unthinkable in the interactions of police with middle-class whites.

Indeed, the likelihood of a black man being arrested is so high— the National Center on Institutions and Alternatives estimated that seventy-five percent of black males in the city of Washington, D.C., could expect to be arrested and jailed at least once between the ages of eighteen and thirty-five[31]—that one mostly black high school outside of the city offers a course in how to behave when stopped by police. The course, sponsored by the police themselves, along with educators, the local chapter of the NAACP, and the Black Lawyers' Association, covers such topics as how to assume the position with legs spread apart and hands on the floor, how to respond to being patted down, and how the police maintain control while handcuffing by holding the suspect's thumbs.[32]

Of course, not all interactions blacks have with the police are unfair, insensitive, or overly aggressive. Indeed—and this is the irony I wish to address here—it is the police that stand as the clearest barrier between the healthy elements of the inner-city community and chaos. In a recent long article in the *New York Times* on the relation between the police and minority communities (aptly titled, "When the Saviors Are Seen as Sinners"), one community leader stated, "It's a really tough situation. We're living in a war zone with both sides coming at us with arms. We need the police so badly, but we also need them to be professional."[33] The article documents both the occurence of inexcusable police abuses and the yearning of the neighborhood's residents for freedom from drug dealers and violent crime.

Whatever the percentage of police officers who act abusively and in a biased fashion toward blacks and other minorities, we can agree that it is unacceptably high. We should also be able to agree that this does not mean that all, or even most, police officers are racists. The problem is much more complicated than that. To some extent, the problem reflects a police culture that is partly a product of who is drawn to police work, partly of the tasks society assigns to the police, and partly of the kinds of encounters cops are likely to confront. There is much evidence that black cops also engage in the kinds of behavior toward minorities that, if seen in a white cop, would be prone to be described simply as racist. As put by Ron Hampton, the executive director of the National Black Police Association, "The way you police in an affluent white community is not the way you police in a poor black community." Hampton goes on to describe an interaction with a black police officer in training that highlights the problem in poignant terms: "I asked him a few questions about his assignment. He said he was assigned to Georgetown, which is about ninety percent white, but he'd been training in a ninety-nine percent black community. He said, 'I'm disappointed. I don't want to go to Georgetown.' He said he wanted to work where the police tell the people what to do, not where the people tell the police. That kid wouldn't have said that before he went into the police academy. Now he's calling the people he grew up with trash; he's calling them scum."[34]

But the problematic behavior cannot be singularly or unidimensionally attributed to police culture alone. Here, once again, we are confronted with a vicious circle, into which it behooves us to intervene at every point possible. However the pattern I have been discussing began, by now new recruits are constantly inducted on both sides, confirming their worst fears of how the other side will act by confirming the other side's worst fears of how *they* will act. Police regard the black community warily and often with some hostility because they experience the hostility toward them *from* the black community. And the black community regards the police with the same set of emotions and expectations because they too have experienced behavior that daily serves to corroborate their attitude.

The mutual mistrust is fed, it might be said, by both the truth and the falsity of each side's perception. What is true in each case is the daily sense impressions that seem to justify the hostility; what is false is the failure to perceive one's own role in creating similar sense impressions in the other.

The Consequences of Long Sentences for Nonviolent Crimes: More Vicious Circles

Exacerbating still further the alienation of the black community from the criminal justice system has been a failure of that system to distinguish sufficiently between violent crime and other illegal activities. As I have already suggested and will further elaborate below, it is by no means socially regressive or counter to the interests of minorities and the poor to sentence violent offenders to long terms in prison. But in many states, low-level drug dealers receive longer sentences than offenders who commit crimes that are a much greater threat to public safety, and a large proportion of those in prison as a consequence are African American. Here again we encounter an ironic vicious circle: Harsh sentences for drug dealers are a response to fear of inner-city crime and disorder. But some of the consequences of those long sentences have ended up contributing to the very social conditions that *generate* crime and disorder.

By far the largest segment of the more than half million black men presently incarcerated are in prison for street-level drug sales or other nonviolent offenses,[35] and as criminologists Michael Tonry and Jerome Miller have each forcefully pointed out, the consequences of dealing with these offenses by long prison sentences have been devastating.[36] On any given day, almost one out of every twelve black men between the ages of eighteen and fifty-four are in prison or jail,[37] and the reverberations of this significant absence of young men affect the entire community. William Julius Wilson,[38] for example, has shown how powerfully the relative scarcity of marriageable men in many inner-city neighborhoods has contributed to those neighborhoods' problematic state. Wilson has focused particularly on the restricted *economic* opportunities that lead many black men to absent themselves from the marriage market, but the *literal* absence of so many men from the community, who are locked up in prison or otherwise embroiled in the criminal justice system, is another powerful factor in this tragically self-perpetuating pattern.

The impact of imprisonment on these men's prospects for making a healthy contribution to their communities, moreover, does not end when they leave prison. Having been in prison has a powerful effect on their chances of landing a decent job afterwards. In essence, for many it is *one* strike and you're out. Those we have imprisoned, even if they do not learn habits in prison that point them to engage in criminal activities again, are more likely to become permanent members of the unemployed or marginally employed. Even if they do not commit further crimes, a life of hanging out on the street corner with nothing to do indirectly contributes to the discouragement of the *next* generation, and in still another ironic circle, to the prospect that they too will see selling drugs as their only option.

It is important to be clear that, notwithstanding their less than promising beginnings, not all of the young men who end up incarcerated and then marginalized were on an inevitable collision course with disaster at the time they were arrested. Many youths, of all races and ethnic groups, drift aimlessly and even somewhat destructively or self-destructively for a time before taking hold as productive citizens. Youths from more advantaged backgrounds have many more supports in place to help them finally to gain traction and move on with their lives, but many disadvantaged youths too eventually find a way to move beyond false starts and difficult beginnings. When prison intervenes, however, the likelihood that they will pick themselves up and move on diminishes substantially, and a stage that might have been temporary can easily become relatively permanent.

Harsh sentences for nonviolent offenses yield further ironies as well that undermine the very aims that underlie such penalties. Current sentencing policies, and the attendant reality that so many African American youths are behind bars, powerfully affect attitudes toward crime and the criminal justice system in the black community, strengthening the perception that blacks are treated unfairly and heightening alienation. And, apropos one of the central themes of this chapter, by contributing to the sense that black prisoners have been the victims of injustice, such policies foster identifications that are inimical to the black community's deepest interests and impede solidarity in condemning and isolating those who commit offenses that do the community so much harm. Relatedly, criminologist Alfred Blumstein of Carnegie Mellon University has argued that "we have locked up so many people that we have lost the stigmatizing effect," thereby weakening the entire criminal justice system.[39]

How Should We Deal with the Nonviolent Offender?

Precisely how to deal with nonviolent offenses, especially street-level drug sales, remains a question about which continuing discussion and debate is essential. Advocates of decriminalizing drug use or sales point to the destructive side effects of applying criminal sanctions to behavior that is often more *self*-destructive than a direct assault on others and to the lessons learned from the failure and enormous social costs of Prohibition earlier in this century. They point as well to the irrationality of policies that single out certain drugs while permitting the use of alcohol and tobacco, substances which cause far more bodily harm and premature deaths (including, in the case of drunk driving and alcohol-related partner or child abuse, widespread death and injury to innocent parties). Opponents of legalization, on the other hand, point to the likelihood that use of individually and socially destructive drugs would increase significantly and to the prospect that the very community to whose concerns we are trying to respond will feel abandoned and betrayed by policies that sanction the ready availability of drugs on their streets.

What seems clearest is that it has been an error to deal with drug dealing and other crimes that do not involve acts of violence in the same way we have dealt with violent offenders. But recognizing this error does not necessarily imply we should simply ignore such activities. If we do not legalize the sale and use of presently illegal drugs, and put in place the structures and safeguards that legalization would require, then we must find an alternative to present policies that does not simply ignore the issue. Failure to enforce the law, winking at illegal activity, can be demoralizing to the health of the community, conveying a sense of "anything goes" that is profoundly disturbing to the sustenance of stable institutions or individual motivations. As criminologist and police consultant George Kelling has documented, there is much evidence that permitting disorder, much less felonious, even if nonviolent, behavior, breeds further disorder, as well as more serious crime.[40]

In the highly dichotomous way that positions are staked out in our current adversarial approach to social questions, Kelling's analysis is generally seen simply as a conservative or (in the buzzword sense) "law and order" view. But in fact, Kelling's emphasis on how a critical mass of seemingly minor offenses can lead to rapidly accelerating demoralization and fear in a neighborhood, and hence can yield frightening escalations of crime, decay, and social disorder, is consonant with a growing literature undertaken to a considerable degree from a progressive point of view. This literature applies the concepts and methodology of epidemiology to the study of social phenomena, examining how crime or other social problems can spread and escalate like an epidemic, and how unexpected escalations and deescalations can occur when previously unnoticed trends go beyond a crucial "tipping point."[41] Indeed, as I shall discuss further in later chapters, the very same concept can be used to make the case for investing more money in social programs than we have thus far and for understanding why it is premature to conclude that liberal social programs have failed or are unworkable.

It is important to notice, moreover, that central to Kelling's approach is *not* so much arresting people as disrupting their activities, and that even for those arrested, Kelling, like many to his left, advocates a variety of alternatives to imprisonment for those involved in nonviolent offenses. These include drug treatment programs, counseling, and carefully targeted and immediately performed community service in the neighborhood in which the offense was committed.[42] Where incarceration is part of the response to an offense, Kelling advocates placing low-level offenders in local county jails rather than in state prisons and keeping them separate from violent offenders, "so that they can receive appropriate punishment, treatment, and counseling, remain close to the community, and be reintegrated into it upon release. The goal is to restore and maintain the health of the community by changing the behavior of offenders so that they become contributing members—a much harder task than simply locking them away, and one that, if successfully achieved, will prevent recidivism."[43]

The inclination of many on the left to view an active police presence in minority communities as equivalent to a hostile occupation force has seriously hampered the very effort to revitalize the communities the left wishes most to aid. Some of the roots of this attitude lie in very real abuses I have discussed earlier in this chapter, but some of its source lies in an adversarial mindset that it is one of the aims of this book to critique.

When Long Prison Sentences *Are* Appropriate

None of what I have said about the counterproductive results of long sentences for nonviolent offenders offers any reason not to arrest, or imprison for a long time, those who commit violent crimes. Far from the victims of injustice they are sometimes portrayed as being, the vast majority of those in prison for crimes such as armed robbery, aggravated assault, or weapons possession, not to mention murder or rape, are brutal enemies of their own people, who create untold human misery, in the neighborhoods of the poor and helpless most of all. The glamorizing of the "gangsta" image in the black community and the readiness of many white liberals and progressives to identify with black prisoners are, in part, one more unfortunate side effect of the misguided drug policies discussed above: there *are* people in prison who probably shouldn't be there, and concern that *they* are receiving overly harsh sentences, for reasons not unrelated to race, can spill over to embrace those who do not deserve much of our sympathy. But it is essential that we move past the erroneous perception that sees an underdog in those who in fact do such terrible harm, on so many levels, to all of us but especially to their own community.

Confusions abound in this realm, as do sentiments masquerading as considered analyses. Sound ideas slide almost imperceptibly into incoherence or moral obtuseness. Thus, Michael Tonry, whose useful views regarding the destructive impact of our current drug enforcement policies I cited above, tells us appropriately, in considering the vastly higher rate at which young black males from poor urban neighborhoods are arrested than youths from affluent suburbs, that "Unless invidious assumptions are make [sic] about constitutional differences between the two groups of men, it must be the case that the environments of the young urban men provide more temptations and fewer disincentives."[44] But this important and valid point shades into another that sounds similar, but has potentially troubling implications: "crime by young disadvantaged black men does not result primarily from their individual moral failures but from their misfortune of being born in places and times and under circumstances that make crime, drug use, and gang membership look like reasonable choices from a narrow range of not very attractive options."[45]

But standing in a dark corner waiting to hold a knife to someone's throat in order to take their money is not just another boring day at the office. "I wish I had a better job, but this is the best I could get" may indeed capture an aspect of the implicit mindset of the low-level drug dealer, but it does not capture very well the true brutality that is entailed when someone shoots or stabs or stomps on or simply (!) terrorizes another human being. If that is not a moral failure, then the very idea of moral failure is trivialized. Or, since Tonry clearly *does* hold morally responsible the whites who formulated the crime and imprisonment policies he condemns,[46] something even more disturbing seems to be implied—that moral responsibility is somehow reserved only for whites.

To be fair, Tonry is most disturbed—and appropriately, for the reasons discussed above—with the harsh sentences meted out to nonviolent offenders. But to be fair to truth as well—and to understand the mindset that I believe is killing liberalism (for Tonry's sentiments are not isolated ones)—we must note that he also recommends that *all* sentences be scaled down "at least by half," and argues that every prisoner who has served ten years or more be considered for parole or release. Moreover,

> The only valid general criterion for denying release would be that, on actuarial grounds, the offender presents an unacceptable risk of future violent criminality. Denying release *might* also be justified for especially notorious offenders like political assassins and serial murderers." (emphasis added)[47]

Apparently, killing just one person, especially if the victim did not hold high office, is not sufficiently notorious for Tonry. And people who rape and brutalize, who rob people at gunpoint or knifepoint, who engage in drive-by shootings (but just once or twice), are simply *ordinarily* notorious, and it is *we* who are morally deficient and inhumane if we keep them in prison too long.

To be sure, prison in general and long sentences in particular do bring risks. The harshness and brutality often encountered in prison can have the result of producing more "hardened" individuals. Moreover, long sentences can impede the prospects for rehabilitation. It is hard enough to come back into society with a record; to do so after years of being out of circulation in society is even harder. Indeed, there is some evidence that, for offenders who committed the same crime, those who received longer sentences were more likely to be recidivists and/or to be rearrested sooner after their release.[48]

When it comes to violent crimes, however, the balance is quite different. Concern about the brutalizing impact of prison on people who were not violent when they went in is not very relevant when we are talking about people who behaved brutally *before* they went to prison, who went to prison *because of* violent behavior. Moreover, if the aim of long sentences is to keep dangerous people off the streets for a very long time, concerns about how they will adapt when they get out are less pressing; the whole point of long sentences is that they will *not* be out in just a few years.

Whether long sentences act as a deterrent is a topic of considerable controversy, and there is a substantial body of research that challenges that idea. But there can be little doubt about the effectiveness of what is referred to as incapacitation. Even if no *other* potential criminal is deterred by the long sentence any particular violent offender receives, we can be certain that the offender himself will not threaten our homes or our streets while he is incarcerated.

There have been challenges to what seems like the airtight logic of the foregoing argument, largely on the empirical ground that periods when sentences have been increased have not uniformly been associated with reduced crime rates.[49] The number of variables influencing crime rates, however, is so large that it is difficult to control for them across periods, and many extraneous factors could account for the lack of a clear association. Moreover, much of the research that has been done has focused on sentences in general or on what might be called quasi-economic crimes rather than on violent street crimes in particular. It is important to recognize that drug dealing, for example, is a free-market crime, a crime of salesmanship, not violence. It is not really very surprising that when competitors are incapacitated through arrest, and the demand for the product remains high, there will be replacements, new sellers looking to fill the newly available niche in the market. There is not a similar "demand" for being mugged or murdered, and much less reason to think that replacements will automatically appear out of the woodwork if we remove the most heinous perpetrators from society.

What does need to be clear, however, is that if we do not complement arrests and imprisonments with efforts to improve the conditions of our poorest neighborhoods, we are indeed keeping open the factories that produce muggers as their product. It should be obvious that a central tenet of the overall point of view presented here is that relying on prisons without social programs that promote genuine opportunity and equality is as certain to be ineffective as is relying on social programs without addressing the destructive effects of violent crime.

What Should Prisons Be Like?

Calls for longer sentences are often linked to proposals for "making hard time harder" or "restoring fear to prisons."[50] These latter sentiments can lead us in very problematic directions. If our moral need for retribution regresses to the most primitive forms of vengeance, if we, even vicariously, engage in the same kind of brutality as the people we wish to punish, then in an important sense the bad guys will have won. They will have imposed their standards and values on us rather than vice versa.

Prisons should be a place where we *control* violence, not a place where violence is rampant. Such an outlook requires that we exercise considerably greater disciplinary control over guards—it is scarcely a state secret that violence toward prisoners by prison guards is widespread—and that we exercise greater control over prisoners. Long sentences are one thing. Sentencing people—even the violent offenders I view with repugnance—to a real possibility of gang rape, savage beatings, stabbings, or simply humiliating intimidation is quite another. Prisons must be run according to *our* standards, to *civilized* standards, not according to the laws of the street. There are plenty of ways of limiting and controlling prisoners' physical contact with each other that do not constitute solitary confinement.

Views such as that of former Massachusetts governor William Weld that "prison should be like a tour through the circles of hell"[51] are misguided in another respect as well. The last thing we need in our inner cities is to add to the mythic status of prisoners. Macho images of prisoners as heroic survivors of everything The Man can dish out, of prison as a rite of manliness, are already part of the plague that endangers youngsters in our inner cities, adding to the destructive pull of the oppositional culture described by Elijah Anderson[52] or of the "cool pose" described by Richard Majors and Janet Billson.[53] Prisons should be Spartan, but should offer very few macho points. The terrible cachet that prison now holds in the inner city, reflected in rap music or in pants worn falling almost to the knees in homage to the most recalcitrant prisoners whose belts have been taken away, is but one more cost that the perpetrators of violence have exacted upon their communities. It ill behooves us to aid them.

I do, however, understand the sentiments that lie behind these misguided calls to "make hard time harder." Although there is no denying that prisons are frightening and degrading places, there is also a sense that they have too many amenities. Where is the point of intersection between our wish to make prison unpleasant and our need to uphold *our own* standards in the way prisoners are treated? Clearly, for almost all of us, heat in the winter, running water, sanitary facilities, proper nutrition, and adequate health care are all requirements. But where do weight rooms fit? Why do prisoners have access to facilities that many hardworking people on the outside have difficulty affording—especially when they are facilities that enable prisoners to hone their macho image and indeed, might give them the extra strength to be more successful in a violent endeavor once they are released?

Access to television or the music of their choice is less of a luxury good in one sense; virtually all prisoners could afford these things before being confined, and they are indeed now fairly standard aspects of American life. But I am not convinced that television is a human right. Did all prisoners prior to the 1950s, when television became widely available, experience cruel and unusual punishment? Television is a useful soporific for prison authorities, keeping the inmates occupied and thus less of a management problem. But does it contribute to their rehabilitation, or, for that matter, their reflection on whether they want to risk enduring this experience again when they get out? Should we permit *color* televisions to enhance the experience? Perhaps small black and white sets, with restricted channel access that provided only the options of news or intelligent talk shows would better serve society's purposes.

Eliminating most of the television options presently available might lead some inmates to read instead as a way of passing the time. This, in my view, is a social good. Many, of course, have come from neighborhoods and schools where genuine literacy is not high, and literacy efforts are one cost of the kinds of prisons I am advocating that I would gladly pay. Similarly, drug rehab programs and programs that would help inmates gain employment when released represent money wisely spent. Computers should be widely available, along with high-quality training in their use. (But—in marked contrast to what is appropriate for the rest of the population—access to the internet should be strictly monitored, and sites that are titillating or that could be potentially implicated in criminal activities should be restricted. And games should not be a part of the computer fare.)

Is what I am suggesting an instance of imposing middle-class values? While I would not agree that such values are shared only by the middle class, the answer to whether we are imposing the mainstream values of our society (to put the question slightly differently) is an unambiguous yes. Such a restriction of options or imposition of values would and should be utterly unacceptable in other realms of our society. But prison is *not* a realm of freedom. Prisoners, by their actions, have forfeited some of the rights the rest of us have. As I have indicated, those forfeitures should not include humane living conditions or freedom from violence. But they do include many of the choices the rest of us both cherish and take for granted.

Is Toughness Enough?

To the reader who wishes to deny the extent of the injustices that persist in our society, and the extraordinary obstacles many African Americans face in being able to pursue the American Dream, it may be tempting to conclude from this chapter that crime is the linchpin for solving our racial difficulties, that if we only get tough about crime everything else will follow. Nothing could be further from the spirit of my views. The whole point of the vicious circle analysis is that there *is no* single point to which all our efforts should be applied, no place to position Archimedes' lever so that it can lift the world.

I do view crime as having ramifications far beyond what is usually acknowledged by the left in viewing crime almost exclusively as a symptom. But one can demonstrate equally the powerful consequences of poverty, of racial prejudices and stereotypes, of restricted employment opportunities, of poorly funded and demoralized schools, or of the segregated housing that persists to an extraordinary extent in our supposedly color blind society. Each of those factors must be understood as having powerful consequences in its own right and, at the same time, as the product of all the others. It is only in seeing how reciprocally reinforcing are these separate yet complexly interlaced forces that we can formulate an approach to our difficulties that has a chance for success.

11

Separate Neighborhoods, Separate Destinies

The stubborn persistence of segregated housing lies close to the core of our society's racial impasse. Notwithstanding a variety of laws and court decisions designed to put an end to housing discrimination, America remains a land in which the phrases "white neighborhood" and "black neighborhood" are saturated with meaning, and in which the term "mixed neighborhood," far from signifying the norm, is often a euphemism for a neighborhood in decline. This state of affairs is perhaps the most undeniable sign that we have not yet transcended the tragedy of slavery and its more than century-long aftermath.

The restrictions African Americans face in seeking housing are clearly a circumstance imposed, not chosen. Nonetheless, even in this realm the pervasive influence of vicious circles is very much in evidence. Just as violent crime can contribute to maintaining the very circumstances that breed it, there are similarly reciprocal relations between housing segregation and such other factors as poor schools, limited job opportunities, and the oppositional culture that sometimes derives from them. It is the aim of this chapter to spell out those interconnections.

Explanations and Pseudo-Explanations

There are many reasons people live where they do, and certainly both economic circumstances and simple preference play a considerable role. But these two explanations are not sufficient to account for the extreme degree of separation or for the particular patterns we find. Starkly summarizing the extent of the separation, Reynolds Farley noted in 1977 that "whites who have more than a college education are more residentially segregated from similarly well-educated blacks than they are from whites who have never completed a year of school."[1] A decade later, Farley, together with Walter Allen, found some small declines in the level of segregation, but the overall levels remained very high.[2] Moreover, when they again looked at the relation between residential segregation and economic status, they found that "blacks of every economic level are highly segregated from whites of the same economic level." Indeed, "the segregation score for families in the $50,000 and over range . . . is close to that for . . . families with incomes under $5000."[3]

Analyzing data from the 1990 census, Roderick Harrison and Claudette Bennett observed that although there were some declines in segregation levels compared to the previous decade, they were so small that "the modest declines in the residential segregation of blacks, more than two decades after the passage of equal housing opportunity laws and despite considerable suburbanization, suggest that present patterns of residential segregation may remain with us for decades to come." Indeed, they noted that the rate of change was so slow it "would leave blacks as segregated 50 years from now as Hispanics were in 1990."[4] In a related vein, the distinguished sociologist and social psychologist Thomas Pettigrew pointed out that, "Urban blacks are residentially segregated from their fellow Americans far more intensively than any other urban ethnic or racial group. Puerto Ricans, for example, in one generation dispersed more in Chicago than blacks managed throughout the century."[5]

Some of the explanation for residential segregration, to be sure, is economic; whites tend to be wealthier than blacks, and so can afford to live in neighborhoods that many blacks cannot afford.[*] As findings such as Farley's show, however, the patterns of segregation

---

[*] This second explanation, of course, does not exactly stand as a ringing endorsement of America as a land of equal opportunity.

are not simply a matter of economic level—of economic like living with economic like. Rather, they suggest strongly the impact of simple racial prejudice. Summarizing the results of numerous studies, Douglas Massey and Nancy Denton noted that

> Whereas segregation declines steadily for most minority groups as socioeconomic status rises, levels of black-white segregation do not vary significantly by social class. Because segregation reflects the effects of white prejudice rather than objective market forces, blacks are segregated no matter how much money they earn.[6]

Equally insufficient is the contention that the sorting out by race is simply voluntary. Although it is indeed true that some African Americans, both poor and well-to-do, feel more comfortable living with others of their own race and choose to do so, it is difficult to escape the conclusion that much of the separation is imposed. The obstacles blacks face in the free pursuit of housing outside of minority neighborhoods range from being told that a house or apartment they wish to look at in a predominantly white area is already rented or sold, when in fact it is not, to outright threats to blacks who move into certain neighborhoods.

What *is* probably true is that discrimination *in turn* produces "voluntary" segregation. That is, in response to the hostility and rejection they encounter, some blacks may conclude that they would rather live among their own. But choosing to live in an all black neighborhood as a "preference" over living with people who don't want to live with you is not equivalent to simply preferring to be separated.

Where preference and voluntary segregation most clearly play a role is not in the behavior of blacks but of whites. As Massey and Denton put it (and I suspect few white readers will really disagree),

> although whites now accept open housing in principle, they remain prejudiced against black neighbors in practice. Despite whites' endorsement of the ideal that people should be able to live wherever they can afford to regardless of race, a majority still feel uncomfortable in any neighborhood that contains more than a few black residents; and as the percentage of blacks rises, the number of whites who say they would refuse to enter or would try to move out increases sharply.[7]

Clearly what Massey and Denton are pointing to is a disjunction between ideals and behavior; what whites say they believe in in
principle is not necessarily what they live by. But it is not simply
hypocrisy or racism. The disjunction reflects in substantial measure
the concerns about crime, values, and divergent styles of behavior
discussed in the previous chapter and below.*

It is therefore essential, if we are to overcome the foot-dragging
and subterfuges that have maintained massive segregation in a nom-
inally equal access society, to link the battle against housing discrimination to other initiatives that can help to sever the perceived
link between integrated housing and diminished safety. *Both* the
black and white communities will benefit if segregation is overcome
not simply by forcing whites and blacks to live together, but by
working to ensure that an end to segregated housing will not
require the substantial sacrifice of safety many whites believe it
implies. Most blacks, after all, *also* want to live in neighborhoods that
are free of crime, and similarly have a stake in keeping their neighborhoods in such a state.

The Role of White Violence in Generating and Maintaining Segregation

As I discussed in Chapter One, appreciating the role of the vicious
circles in which we all are caught does not mean that moral responsibility is therefore equally apportioned or that no beginning points
can be discerned. In this regard, it is useful to remind ourselves that,
whatever role fear of black crime or disorder may currently contribute to perpetuating our pattern of segregation, it was *white* violence that very largely brought it about. Segregation did not occur
"naturally," as an innocent sorting into economic or cultural kin.
Rather, it was a product of the violent response of the white community when industrialization and the new opportunities it brought
drew large numbers of blacks to Northern cities for the first time.

Prior to about 1900, the relatively small numbers of blacks in
Northern cities in fact lived reasonably interspersed with whites. A
large proportion of them, to be sure, were poor, and lived in the

---

* This is by no means to imply that hypocrisy or racism are absent. Both, along with stereotyping that exaggerates real tendencies so that they appear more frightening and fixed than
they really are, clearly play a significant role.

worst parts of the city. But they shared their neighborhoods with whites of similar economic circumstance, and those blacks who did achieve economic success could be found in many of the best neighborhoods. All in all, their degree of segregation did not differ substantially from that of European immigrant groups.[8]

The situation changed radically, however, as the flow of blacks to the cities increased. As Massey and Denton describe it,

> In city after northern city, a series of communal riots broke out between 1900 and 1920 in the wake of massive black migration. . . . In each case, individual blacks were attacked because of the color of their skin. Those living away from recognized "black" neighborhoods had their houses ransacked or burned. Those unlucky or unwise enough to be caught trespassing in "white" neighborhoods were beaten, shot, or lynched. Blacks on their way to work were pulled from trolleys and pummelled. Rampaging bands of whites roamed the streets for days, attacking blacks at will.[9]

As a consequence of this violence, blacks found it necessary to retreat for safety to black enclaves, where there could be safety in numbers. Even well-to-do blacks, who had been living in the best neighborhoods throughout the city, had to retreat to the newly formed ghettoes in order to escape this lawlessness. The color of their skin, rather than any specifics of behavior or character, was the cue that triggered the attacks.

Today, the forces maintaining black segregation are usually more subtle: blacks are steered to certain areas by real estate agents; they are told a house has been sold or an apartment has been rented when it actually has not; and they find that when more than a few of them do manage to move into a neighborhood, whites begin to move out,[10] leaving them again living in an area that is almost exclusively black.[*] But the threat of violence is not completely absent even today. There are many neighborhoods in which blacks moving in receive threats; even bombings of the homes of blacks who move into neighborhoods where they are "not wanted" are not completely a thing of the past.[11]

---

*At times, it may instead be mixed black and Hispanic, as Hispanics often encounter similar receptions from whites.

All of this is essential to bear in mind as we consider the complexity of the dynamics that maintain residential segregation today. Both historically and in the present, segregation is primarily a product of white choices, and its poisonous consequences—further detailed below—lie very largely on the white side of the moral ledger. But we will be stymied in the very aim of overcoming the unjust isolation and constraints blacks encounter if we limit our understanding of the dynamics maintaining this state of affairs to white racism alone.

Deeply rooted prejudices and fantasies, to be sure, play a very considerable role in the hesitancy of whites to live side by side with blacks, but so too do responses to actual behavior and attitudes that whites perceive in the black community. Here we must confront another of the painful ironies that so thoroughly pervade our racial difficulties: behavior patterns induced very largely by the isolation of segregated neighborhoods contribute significantly to maintaining that very isolation.

"The Culture of Segregation"

Among the deleterious effects of residential segregation, perhaps none is more pervasively debilitating than what Massey and Denton have called the culture of segregation—*"an oppositional culture that devalues work, schooling, and marriage and that stresses attitudes and behaviors that are antithetical and often hostile to success in the larger economy."*[12] Massey and Denton are by no means the only writers to call attention to these attitudes and behaviors,[13] but they have been particularly illuminating in demonstrating the powerful role of residential segregation in shaping and maintaining them.

Compounding the tragedy that Massey and Denton describe is that these patterns do not just *result* from residential segregation; they also contribute to *perpetuating* the isolation and disadvantaged status of those who live within the segregated district. Once a certain dynamic develops in a neighborhood, it takes on a life of its own, and it becomes necessary for the young men who live there to maintain a stance—for purposes of survival in that very cultural system—that is experienced as highly problematic by people *outside of* that system. The residents of such a neighborhood are often caught in what Elijah Anderson, a leading student of inner-city life, calls a "cultural catch-22" that entraps many black youths:

> [T]o appear harmless to others might make him seem weak or square to those he feels a need to impress. If he does not dress the part of a young black man on the streets, it is difficult for him to "act right." If he is unable to "act right," then he may be victimized by strangers in his general peer group. The uniform—radio, sneakers, gold chain, athletic suit—and the selective use of the "grit," the quasi-military swagger to the beat of "rap" songs, in public places, are all part of the young man's pose. *Law-abiding and crime-prone youths alike adopt such poses, in effect camouflaging themselves and making it difficult for more conventional people to know how to behave around them, since those for whom they may not be performing directly may see them as threatening.* By connecting culturally with the ghetto, a young black may avoid compromising his public presentation of self, but *at the cost of further alienating law-abiding whites and blacks.*[14]

Anderson is very clear that it is joblessness, racism, and hopelessness that fuel the violence in these men. But depicting a vicious circle much like those I have been emphasizing, he notes that the violence in turn serves to confirm the negative stereotypes and negative attitudes that many whites hold toward them, thus again limiting their prospects and confronting them with rejection and disdain.

Richard Majors and Janet Billson describe a very similar phenomenon under the rubric of what they call "cool pose." A stance adopted by many black men to preserve their self-esteem and sense of masculinity in the face of oppressive circumstances and limited opportunities, cool pose is designed to convey to others that one is "calm, emotionless, fearless, aloof, and tough."[15] Like the stance described by Anderson, cool pose as a response to the deprivations and assaults of ghetto life is a solution that perpetuates the very problems it is intended to solve. Thus, for example, the "tough talk and aggressive posturing"[16] that must be manifested in order to face down the dangers these men regularly encounter, and to project an image of masculinity in the face of few mainstream options for success, "propels black males on a collision course with each other and with whites."[17]

Even more often, however, the consequence of these various patterns of behavior is not collision but avoidance. Born of exclusion and marginalization, the cool pose portrayed by Majors and Billson, or the "hardcore" or "street-oriented" manner described by Anderson, puts off and scares off whites and results in still further exclusion and marginalization.

Massey and Denton's approach to these behaviors especially highlights the role of isolation in both generating and maintaining them. They note that many of these behaviors—including not just the "tough" or threatening dimensions, but the "devaluing of work, schooling, and marriage" that so pervasively impede successful participation in the larger world of American society—are strongly reminiscent of earlier accounts of the "culture of poverty." They suggest, however, that we might better think of them as reflecting a "culture of segregation." While, as discussed in Chapter Four, I do not agree that the concept of a culture of poverty necessarily entails blaming the victim—it all depends on the purposes to which such an analysis is put—I do think that Massey and Denton's reconceptualization has several important advantages.

To begin with, conceptualizing a culture of segregation helps to highlight more clearly the role of the larger society in maintaining this state of affairs. The segregation of any group, after all, cannot be meaningfully discussed without reference to the group it is segregated *from*. Segregation is, by its very nature, a two-sided process, a process in which the dividing line itself highlights the impact of one group upon another. Responsibility for a culture deriving from segregation is thus more clearly seen to lie not just within the ghetto.

A second very important implication of Massey and Denton's reconceptualization is that some of the attitudes they describe are not necessarily limited to the poor. Because housing discrimination restricts the residential options of working-class and middle-class blacks, they often must live in much closer proximity to poor and deteriorating neighborhoods than do whites of similar income, and their children must go to schools where they encounter behavior and values that may differ quite considerably from what their hardworking parents are trying to instill. As Anderson and others have pointed out, in interacting with these tougher street kids they must often themselves learn to take on a hard-edged stance in order not to be victimized. Moreover, some of the dynamics I have been discussing in the last few chapters can lead the children of more privileged or successful black families to view youngsters from the inner city as more genuinely "black" and to seek to emulate them in certain respects. In Anderson's words, "Many less alienated young blacks have assumed a street-oriented demeanor as a way of expressing their blackness while really embracing a much more moderate way of life. . . . These decent people are trying hard to be part of the mainstream culture, but the racism, real and perceived, that they encounter helps to legitimate the oppositional culture."[18]

Here we encounter another of the ironies that pervade the interactions—and the separations—between the races. Whites, troubled by certain values and behavior patterns that they perceive among blacks, attempt to keep blacks at arms length. What they accomplish thereby is to further isolate and concentrate black communities, thus contributing to the perpetuation of those very values. And blacks, troubled and angered by their isolation, respond to that isolation in ways that increase its likelihood of continuing.

How Residential Segregation Multiplies Problematic Influences

Addressing housing segregation is certainly not the only point of entry in attempting to break this cycle. Indeed, it is a central point of this entire book that efforts to intervene at *any* single point are likely to be unsuccessful on their own. But I believe that Massey and Denton are correct in identifying housing segregation as an unusually important and powerful factor in our racial impasse. A child or youth at a critical choice point is likely to be influenced by the choices made by those around him. Like most of us, he is most likely to go where the prevailing winds take him. If the neighborhood makes the prevailing wind one of crime, drugs, or alienation from mainstream values and aspirations, that may well be the life choice he too makes. But this same youth, from the very same family, might have gone in a different direction were his context different.

As we view these choices retrospectively, they may appear "inevitable" given the individual's family background, poverty and deprivation, etc. But the same individual configuration can yield quite different results when the vulnerable are not so tightly clustered that the only influence upon their behavior is each other.[19]

Although in a general way there is widespread recognition that growing up in a "bad neighborhood" or being subject to "bad influences" can have a significant impact on how young people turn out, that knowledge is often compartmentalized, and problematic behavior among inner-city residents tends to be viewed in terms of character defects or family characteristics. In essence, we have created environments that bring out the worst in people, and then use the behavior we have elicited as justification for the existence of those environments.

Further compounding the impact of a segregated environment is the way the community in which one lives magnifies individual handicaps or advantages in finding jobs, especially good jobs. A high percentage of jobs are found through personal and word-of-mouth networks. Consequently, when those with whom an individual regularly interacts do not have jobs, it becomes harder for him or her to find one as well. This is a function not just of the psychological impact of discouragement and lack of role models, but of the concrete fact that people growing up in neighborhoods where unemployment is higher than average are less likely to have contact with people able to point them to job opportunities. Their nonparticipation in the labor market, moreover, in turn contributes further to depressing the prospects of still others in the neighborhood, as one more link in the chain that connects people to jobs and participation in the economy is severed.[20]

Enforcing Fair Housing Laws: Essential But Complex

The evidence is massive that discrimination in housing remains widespread and persistent and that it has a powerful negative effect on the black community and, ultimately, on the prosperity and tranquility of our entire nation. How best to address this problem, however, raises difficult questions. In certain respects, the model of legislation and enforcement that achieved such substantial success in other spheres of civil rights still holds considerable promise. The Fair Housing Act long lacked the teeth of other aspects of civil rights legislation, and even since 1988, when new, tougher enforcement provisions were added, it has not been as vigorously enforced.[21] Clearly, greater effort to strengthen and enforce such legislation is called for, and can be expected to make at least some

useful contribution to diminishing the stubborn persistence of segregation in housing.

Enforcement of these laws alone, however, is unlikely to be sufficient. For one thing, enforcement, and even detection, of discrimination is expensive and easier to evade than in other realms. Signs
announcing that a rest room or drinking fountain was for "whites
only," or schools officially designated as white or black, left no ambiguity. And although enforcement of nondiscrimination laws in
employment encountered somewhat more difficulty—employers
could "officially" offer equal opportunity but "just happen" to hire
mostly whites, or could find "in their best business judgment" that
the white applicants were better suited—efforts in this realm were
able to gain major momentum by concentrating on large employers,
where the numbers were sufficient to detect statistically improbable
differentials in the percentages of blacks and whites hired for equivalent jobs. The impact of enforcement could then in turn spread
through smaller firms.[22] In contrast, the housing market is characterized by a very large number of individual transactions, and subterfuges such as saying a house was just sold or an apartment just
rented, or only showing potential black buyers or renters homes in
certain areas, are widespread.

This is not to suggest that there are no points of leverage—large
real estate agents, along with landlords and developers, provide
potential targets for intervention. But often the enforcement of fair
housing laws requires black and white testers, matched in the economic status they present, who pretend to seek homes in the same
area and can document that they are shown homes in different neighborhoods or that the white is offered a place after the black has been
told it is taken. Such efforts are expensive and, because the home
market is not dominated by a few giant corporations, they must be
replicated again and again to achieve widespread compliance.[23]

Does Attitude Matter?

Even more fundamentally, focusing on antidiscrimination statutes
alone does not address the biases, hostilities, and fears that make it
so difficult for us to live together. Achieving a situation in which
people live side by side only because they are *forced* to is likely to be
a Pyrrhic victory. Without addressing the underlying attitudes that

fuel white resistance to integrated housing, we place a burden on fair housing laws alone that they cannot bear.

To many—on the right *and* the left—such concern with attitudes may appear hopelessly utopian or naive. On the right, the objection is likely to be embodied in a variation of the idea that "you can't legislate morality"—a topic I will take up shortly below—combined with the view that people have the right to associate with whomever they wish, and it is none of our business what those preferences are. From the left, a focus on feelings or attitudes may appear wrongheaded for a different reason. Many on the left—both black and white—emphasize that blacks aren't asking that whites *like* them; they simply want justice, the right to live wherever they choose and can afford. If they wish to live in neighborhoods where whites live, it is not that they particularly crave contact with white people, but simply that the political and economic realities are such that those are the neighborhoods in which schools and public facilities are generously funded, in contrast to the ways in which society skimps on such facilities for black neighborhoods.

Both sides are surely right that we can neither legislate, nor even plan for, how people will feel about each other. All that legislation and law enforcement can do is ensure equal access to participation in the economy and freedom from harassment or intimidation on the basis of race or ethnicity. But surely it behooves us to consider whether the ways we go about securing equal access contribute to healing or to greater conflict and hostility.[24] Moreover, if we truly wish to make fair housing laws work, we must conceptualize our approach in ways that take into account the will to enforce them. In both regards, it pays to ask ourselves *why it is* that, as Massey and Denton put it, "When the legislative agenda turned to housing, . . . the momentum on civil rights stalled."

Viewed from a reverse angle, Massey and Denton's point can be reframed to ask why civil rights legislation worked so much better in reducing discrimination in employment or in access to public accommodations than in the realm of housing. It is not that there was no resistance in the former realms. There was a great deal, and indeed there still is. Blacks now have legal access to all stores open to the public, for example, but it is widely reported that small shopkeepers who keep their doors locked do not always buzz in black potential customers. And in many stores, large and small, black shoppers are often either trailed or ignored in ways that make them uncomfortable and that compromise their experience of equal access. When it comes to work, there are also ways in which the changes have been less than total and in which residues of earlier hiring practices and work atmospheres remain. But in both employment and public facilities, for all the imperfections, the changes have been of historic scope. A Rip Van Winkle who awoke from a forty-year nap would find much of today's America unrecognizable; but by and large, our housing arrangements would hardly cause him to bat an eyelash.

Part of why our success has been so much more limited with regard to housing, I believe, is that in certain respects we have learned the wrong lesson from the successes in the 1950s and 1960s in overturning Jim Crow laws in the South. Or at the very least, we have overgeneralized from those successes. One of the contentions by defenders of segregation in that era was that "you can't legislate morality." This was in part a moral claim, rooted in the view—ironically consistent with much so-called postmodern rhetoric now largely centered on the left—that one community's view of right and wrong should not be imposed on another community that holds a different view. But it was also a practical claim, a warning that legislation that is not consonant with the values of a community will not succeed, that people will not obey such laws and will inevitably find ways to subvert them.

From the perspective of several decades later, it now appears that it *is* possible to "legislate morality." That is, a set of legal initiatives, bolstered by the enforcement of the federal government, not only achieved compliance with civil rights legislation and judicial decisions but, in a relatively short time, brought about changes in people's view of what is right and proper. Today there are rather few voices in the South who would contend (one suspects even privately) that it is proper to require blacks to drink at different fountains, ride in the back of the bus, or eat at separate lunch counters.

But it is essential as well to bear in mind that the people of the South did not impose these legislative and judicial remedies on themselves. It was very largely the fact that the South was out of step with the rest of the country—and that the larger majority outside of the South was prepared to impose its differing views of what was appropriate and acceptable *on* the South—that enabled the dismantling of Jim Crow to succeed, and even to take root in people's hearts and minds.

Now, to be sure, the vigorous opposition to the South's racial attitudes on the part of Northerners was in good part a process of moral purification by people whose own racial attitudes were more complex and conflicted than they acknowledged. It is a common psychological operation to purge the self of troubling, conflicted attitudes and emotions by attributing them to someone else. As I shall elaborate shortly, this hidden psychological complexity caused considerable mischief when the civil rights struggle was taken out of a regional context and made a national issue. But initially, this projecting of the conflicted racial feelings of many whites throughout the country onto a single region served to give special vigor and impetus to the effort to bring to an end abuses that were most harsh and overt in the South. The moral force of the entire nation, backed up by the military force of the federal government, provided a steadfastness that enabled remarkable changes to be accomplished quite rapidly.

In essence, the South, as a discrete and perceptually separable region, was split off from the country's experience of itself and became the representative of aspects of our feelings that we aimed to cast out. In struggling against those feelings in ourselves, projected onto the South as "other," we found the resolve to produce fundamental changes in an entrenched system of inequality. But when the rest of the population was required to take into account *their own* behavior and attitudes, and to address the less overt but quite substantial degree to which they too supported a segregated and unequal state of affairs, the success was less complete. Whereas Jim Crow laws have been virtually eliminated, de facto segregation in housing and schooling—the two most *personal* areas in the civil rights agenda—remain widespread, not only in the South but throughout the country.

The fate of efforts to rectify de facto school segregation via busing provides a good illustration of how the conflicted feelings of the majority of Americans block further steps toward a truly integrated society. In approaching the closely related aim of overcoming *residential* segregation, the problems encountered with busing provide an important object lesson. It is useful to remind ourselves that most of the white Northerners who opposed busing were *not* supporters of officially segregated schools. Moreover, I believe it oversimplifies matters to assume that their declared opposition to segregation in principle was merely hypocrisy. Hypocrisy there was, to be sure, but that is not the whole story.

Many opponents of busing, like most of us in most realms of our lives, were in conflict. They believed in equal access to education and in the impermissibility of officially designating schools as black or white. But those beliefs sat side by side with quite different feelings, including socially regressive stereotypes and prejudices, as well as concerns about their own children or about being invaded or coerced.

It is not that some of these were their "real" feelings and others just a socially acceptable cover. They were *all* real feelings. What aspect of their complex and often conflicted set of attitudes was brought to the fore depended, as for all of us in almost every context, not only on the specific issue but on how it was framed.

This is a very important point for those working to achieve social change, because it means that we should not simply write off people as opponents, but rather think about how to reach the side of them that is inclined toward change. One tragedy of busing was that, for so many people, it brought to the fore their fears and their narrowest vision of their self-interest. But that does not mean that there was not another side to many opponents of busing, or that, even today, it is not possible to formulate progressive programs to which they can respond. One key in doing so is to elicit their active participation, to help people find ways to shape programs that feel fair to their own children at the same time as they address the inequities that the vast majority of our citizens know are there.

Magnet Neighborhoods?

One possibility for developing integrated housing on a foundation of enthusiasm rather than coercion is to create "magnet neighborhoods" in a way that roughly parallels what have come to be called magnet schools. Magnet schools are schools that offer some form of special enrichment such that parents and children from diverse neighborhoods will be drawn to them voluntarily. "Magnet neighborhoods," funded to make desirable amenities uniquely affordable, and designed to assure a genuine ethnic and racial mix, have the similar possibility of bringing blacks and whites together not because they are forced but because both have *chosen* the overall advantages the total package provides.[25]

Given the realities of current racial feelings, it would be necessary to make the advantages of such neighborhoods quite considerable to attract a significant proportion of whites. In current projects aiming at integration, such as Starrett City in New York or Atrium Village in Chicago, the demand by blacks is so much higher than it is by whites that there is, ironically, a racial quota for precisely the aim of maintaining integrated housing. Black and white applicants in these projects are put on separate waiting lists, and because so many more blacks desire to live in these settings than whites, the waiting list is much longer for blacks, who must wait until a designated "black" unit becomes vacant.[26]

If designed properly, magnet neighborhoods should *not* have to engage in quotas or, indeed, be established on an explicitly racial basis at all. Once a municipality announced its intention to construct a magnet neighborhood—and backed this intention up by funding it generously enough that it provided substantially more for the price than exclusively white neighborhoods were providing—it could apportion the right to purchase in the neighborhood on a strictly lottery basis. Racial and ethnic mixing would occur not by administrative fiat but by the combination of individual choice and random eligibility; the proportions from different ethnic groups winning the right to purchase homes in the newly constructed neighborhood would likely replicate those of the city at large.[27]

Such a program could readily be structured so as to provide housing opportunities for poor families as well as middle-income and even upper-middle-class families. The proportion of poor families (that is, of smaller or less luxurious units at lower prices) would be designed to incorporate what we currently know about the dynamics of who influences whom in neighborhoods. That is, in line with the discussion earlier in this chapter, planners of the development would, on the basis of available research, attempt to achieve a proportion of poor families such that the direction of influence was from stable and successful families to families that were struggling, rather than vice versa.[28] Avoiding the dynamic resulting from high concentrations of people in straitened circumstances would be a high priority.[29]

In such a community, where the influence of middle-class and solid working-class families would be so substantial, the danger of poor and minority families feeling isolated even if they live next door is important to address. The development of a separate isolated subculture within the community would be destructive of its very aims, and efforts to prevent this from happening would be essential. In part, this would be a task for the schools. One important entice-ment such a neighborhood could provide would be schools funded to offer programs that can enhance the learning of the gifted while providing enrichment for those whose backgrounds to that point have impeded their progress. Since the poor children would be not the kids "over there" in another neighborhood, but kids living liter-ally next door, residents of such a community would likely have a greater stake in and willingness to explore programs that bound children and youths together in cooperation and shared values.

Children who were well above grade level might be enlisted to work closely with kids who were further behind. Approached prop-erly, such an arrangement would greatly enrich the educational experience of the more advanced children—one learns material in much greater depth through teaching it—while at the same time helping to pull up the slower children. Where feasible, once some of the initially slower kids progressed, they could in turn be enlisted to help in teaching those in grades below them, so that they too could experience the teacher role and not be only recipients of help.

Group projects in which the success of all depends on the suc-cess of each could further be a backbone of the schooling and social-ization in the community. A scheme called the "jigsaw classroom," in which children learn in groups in which each child receives a dif-ferent portion of the total information needed and children can only master the necessary material by listening to and encouraging the learning of others, has been found to increase positive feelings across racial and ethnic groups and to enhance the learning of minority children without ill effects for the others.[30]

Further drawing together children coming from different eco-nomic levels and racial and ethnic backgrounds might be another amenity offered as part of the inducement package—attractive parks and facilities, along with supervised recreational programs. Enlist-ing children and teenagers in supervised programs would diminish the prospects for kids at all economic levels getting into trouble, as well as providing opportunities to knit them together and create a greater sense of community. Sports leagues in which integrated teams from a number of such communities competed could provide further opportunities for cross-racial and cross-ethnic identifications by community members.

Turning to the fear of crime more directly, one might imagine a provision in which, for all families entering the community, the first three years' payments were treated as "rent with an option to buy." By contract, the rent payments made to that point would be applied toward the down payment on the purchase price—and the only grounds for denying purchasers the option to buy in this way would be being convicted of a crime. Such an arrangement would contribute to crime control in several ways, yet protect residents' rights in important respects as well. On the one hand, it would provide still another incentive for residents of the neighborhood to steer clear of criminal activity and shady associates, and for parents to watch their children closely: The chance to purchase a home in such an area at the special prices that would be offered might be a once-in-a-lifetime opportunity, and people would not lightly let it slip away, especially since the money they had *already* paid in rent, which would effectively become theirs as it was applied to their down payment, would be completely lost.[31]

At the same time, the political and moral dilemmas encountered in dealing with disruptive residents of public housing projects would not hold in this circumstance. People who are denied the option to purchase, and the application toward the purchase price of rent already paid, are not being thrown out of a home of last resort; they are losing a very special and unusual benefit, for which they were eligible only by good luck, but to which they have no inherent right. Moreover, they will not have been cheated out of the money they paid in rent: they got a place to live for the money just as any renter gets; they simply did not get the extra bonus of "getting it back" in the form of a down payment.

The Continuing Need to Enforce Fair Housing Laws and the Equally Crucial Need to Supplement Them

Magnet neighborhoods offer the advantages of a potentially more successful experience of integration to at least some citizens, and by serving as a model showing that integration *can* work, they can perhaps help increase the likelihood of success in other more "ordinary" realms. But it should be clear that a magnet neighborhood strategy can by no means be a solution in itself. By the very logic of their creation, magnet neighborhoods cannot become the norm. For then they would offer no special benefits over and above what the housing market generally provides, and thus would not be a magnet. Only in Lake Wobegone can every neighborhood be above average.

Thus any viable strategy to overcome the residential segregation that is so pervasive in our society must still rely substantially on the enforcement of fair housing laws. But fair housing laws alone will not do the job, and to understand why we simply have to ask ourselves why enforcement of such laws has been so difficult and so tepid. People are especially protective of their homes and neighborhoods, and approaches that have worked in more public spheres of our society's life will not necessarily work well in this realm.

We are confronted with different problems in attempting integration of middle-class neighborhoods and in addressing the isolation of the black poor. In the former realm, the influence of racism, prejudice, and stereotyping is more thoroughly exposed. When black college graduates are steered away from certain neighborhoods or when whites evoke resentment in their neighbors by selling their home to a black who can afford the price, we may see most palpably how thin are some of the rationalizations that justify what really are unthinking prejudices.

But even here, the interconnectedness of the problems that plague and divide us—a central theme of this book—is evident, and this interconnectedness challenges simple dichotomies. Beyond the contention that blacks moving into a neighborhood lower the property values—a phenomenon, it should be clear, that is strictly about the behavior of other *whites* (who are, after all, the people now less willing to pay the same price to live in the neighborhood)—the primary "justification" for white resistance to integration at the middle-class level is that "we can't tell the difference between middle-class blacks and a more dangerous element." That is, once black faces are in evidence on the block, some whites no longer feel safe. They cannot know if the black youth walking down the street is a friend of the son of the black doctor down the block or a potential mugger or burglar who now feels more comfortable entering a neighborhood he once avoided because he would stand out.

Here once again—aided by the magnifying effects of prejudice and stereotyping—we see the impact of perceptions of the inner-city poor on the way all blacks are perceived. White racism and prejudice on the one hand, and the culture of segregation on the other, are the dual foundations of our impasse, reinforcing both each other and the entire structure of inequality with which we must cope.

It is thus essential, even for the successful integration of the black and white middle class, but especially in attempting to change the circumstances and prospects of those who are most trapped in the segregated neighborhoods we call ghettoes, to address simultaneously both segregation and the *culture* of segregation. Whites as much as blacks have a stake in breaking this cycle whereby the one reproduces the other. The pain is felt most intensely by those kept behind the invisible walls that maintain a segregated society, but the loss of economic productivity, the increased fear of crime, and the larger sense of a society that has failed to live up to its own ideals impact on all of us. Indeed, even the "property values" whites wish to maintain can be seen, from another angle, as the *excessively* high price whites pay for housing because the vicious circles of segregation, poverty, and the behavior they produce lead whites to feel they must seek an almost exclusively white neighborhood and to pay a premium for doing so.

In addressing the ways in which segregation and the cultural and behavioral consequences it produces perpetuate each other, it is important to be clear that this circle intersects with others that are just as crucial. The patterns Massey and Denton labeled as the "culture of segregation" derive not just from unequal access to housing, but from poor schools, real and perceived blocks to employment opportunity, the temptations and dangers of drugs and crime, and a host of other factors that make many black neighborhoods not only separate but unequal.

The Fair Housing Act of 1968 was originally written as part of a larger body of legislation and a larger set of programs to bring African Americans into the mainstream and to address poverty among all groups of our society. These days it is fashionable to discredit the War on Poverty and the Great Society programs as ineffective or even as exacerbating the problems they were designed to address. Certainly there were errors, whether resulting from foolishness, ideological blinders, or simply the inevitable inferiority of foresight to hindsight. We have learned from the errors, and must continue to learn. But the present atmosphere of wholesale rejection of the role of government-sponsored social programs is a blueprint for continuing racial strife. The ghettoes will not heal themselves, and the market's cures go to those who can pay.

Successful efforts at promoting housing integration cannot be divorced from investment in schools, health care, drug treatment, employment counseling, youth and community centers, jobs programs, affordable access to public universities, quality day care, or earned income tax credits to assure that everyone who works earns a living wage.[32] Without investment in the lives of those who are so persistently kept apart, keeping them apart still longer will look like the only solution to those who are outside the confines of the ghetto.

But in a nation where suburbanization has so triumphed that the ghetto too is increasingly being suburbanized, with poor black enclaves located somewhere within most suburban counties, exemption from the costs of a segregated society is increasingly difficult to assure. Crime and fear are no longer a problem of the inner city alone. Mall parking lots, for example, have become a locale in which, not much different from city streets, people look over their shoulders and listen for footsteps.

Single-family suburban homes, with multiple entrances and ground-level windows are potentially a far more vulnerable target than high-rise city apartments. The enormous number of guns sold in this country—most, as the NRA will leap to tell you, sold not to criminals but to people who feel a need to protect themselves—attests to the sense of vulnerability that segregation and suburbanization have failed to quell.

Without investing in the programs needed to change the culture of segregation—by overcoming not only segregation but the despair and nihilism that accompany and exacerbate it—we cannot remain a safe and prosperous nation. The thicker we build the walls, the greater is the pressure that builds up within.

Beyond Affirmative Action

Toward a Resolution of Our Divisions

Central to almost all of the vicious circles discussed in this book is an either-or way of thinking that impedes the resolution of conflicting perspectives and perpetuates alienation and division. The debate over affirmative action is an example *par excellence* of this narrowly adversarial mode of discourse. Affirmative action policies, designed to help us address the inequalities in environment and preparation that make competition for jobs and college admissions skewed and factitious, have in certain ways ended up contributing to the forces that maintain those inequalities. Both the substantive assumptions of some affirmative action proponents and the reactions evoked in the general public by the sometimes problematic arguments of both supporters and opponents have contributed to diminishing support for needed programs to combat the very inequalities that have made affirmative action necessary.

My aim in this chapter is to get underneath some of the obscuring rhetoric and to place the affirmative action debate in a larger context that takes account of the ironies and vicious circles that have been the focus of this book. I do not believe we have reached a point where affirmative action programs can be terminated. But I wish to offer three caveats to supporters of affirmative action which I believe can contribute to making it a less divisive issue and a more sharply focused tool for achieving social justice.

First it is essential that we recognize that there can be genuinely *principled* opposition to affirmative action. It is certainly true that negative attitudes about affirmative action can reflect prejudice, bigotry, and narrow self-interest. As a psychologist, I am especially aware of how purportedly principled stands can mask feelings and attitudes that are much less acceptable to express in public or even to acknowledge to oneself.[1] Opposition to affirmative action, however, can issue from fidelity to values that are far from dishonorable, indeed from values that are widely shared by affirmative action's supporters. Attention to the sincerely held principles that guide some of those who seriously question affirmative action can have a useful impact on how we structure affirmative action efforts.

This brings us to the second of my caveats. Both supporters *and* opponents often tend to hold too global a conception of affirmative action—as something one is either "for" or "against." Affirmative action, however, is not a single policy or idea, but a name that has been given to a *set* of ideas, some of which are quite different from others. Indeed, I will suggest later in this chapter that it may be time for us to retire the *term* "affirmative action" altogether, and employ a more differentiated vocabulary to address the policies needed to attain equality as a reality. "Affirmative action" has become a buzz phrase that generates more heat than light.

Third, *whatever* we mean by affirmative action, *the entire package* of programs and strategies is insufficient. Affirmative action alone cannot solve our problems. Indeed, affirmative action *alone* is likely to exacerbate them. In recent years, advocates for racial equality have focused their efforts on maintaining affirmative action policies as if succeeding in implementing these policies were virtually identical with achieving justice itself. This preponderant focus on affirmative action has in large measure reflected our society's hesitancy to invest the resources necessary to achieve more genuine equality. But, in one more ironic circle, it has also *contributed* to that hesitancy. Affirmative action policies pursued in isolation from efforts to enable the disadvantaged to develop the necessary skills to compete effectively—attempts, that is, to *override* deficiencies rather than to remedy them—have fueled resentments. In turn, those resentments have fed back to reduce public support for the very programs that could enable disadvantaged minority applicants to compete *without* such an emphasis on affirmative action.

A Crucial Distinction

Much of the rancor and mutual misunderstanding that character-izes the debate over affirmative action derives from failing to make a crucial distinction. Although discrimination—especially covert dis-crimination—has by no means disappeared in American life, in many arenas, especially in university admissions and faculty hiring, blacks now do have at least equal opportunity when they apply for a posi-tion for which they have credentials and experience equal to those of white applicants. Indeed, given the same qualifications, they may well even have an edge. This is the part of the picture most readily seen by whites, as well as by black conservatives, and minimized by affirmative action activists.

On the other hand, there is very considerable inequality of opportunity when one considers the likelihood that a given African American, especially a poor black male from a poor neighborhood, *will get to develop* equivalent skills and qualifications. Growing up in a neighborhood plagued by poverty, violence, drugs, and the perva-sive presence of men and women who cannot find work, attending schools that are underfunded and poorly functioning, or having to cope with constantly being perceived through a filter of distressing and disparaging stereotypes makes it very difficult to obtain the proper qualifications.

Depending on which of these two perspectives on our current circumstances one takes, one's attitude toward affirmative action is likely to be very different. From the first view, affirmative action seems no longer necessary and even unfair, an instance of "reverse discrimination." From the second, affirmative action is a way of deal-ing with pervasive and systemic unfairness that still exists in our society to a very substantial degree.*

Affirmative action has become such a contentious and emotion-ally loaded issue in large measure because advocates (pro or con) often leave out or brush aside the half of the picture that does not fit their narrowly conceived purposes. Proponents of affirmative action frequently fail to acknowledge that qualified blacks *are* sought after.

---

* These two perspectives, of course, do not exhaust the rationales for supporting or oppos-ing affirmative action. I shall have occasion later to discuss other perspectives and other rationales. But these two perceptions do capture a fundamental difference in focus that is very much at the heart of the debate.

Opponents frequently ignore the continuing circumstances that make a mockery of the idea of a level playing field.

The basic sense of fairness of most Americans is not compatible with a competition in which some start out so much less advantaged than others. Most whites recognize that they would not want their children to grow up in the circumstances they know greet many black children virtually from the day they are born. This difference in the typical daily reality of black and white children is the moral foundation for affirmative action efforts, and it remains a basis for a potential political consensus around such efforts. But notwithstanding this potential, remedies that are perceived as replacing one form of unfairness with another will be rejected.

Origins of Affirmative Action: Taking "Color Blindness" Seriously

The first use of the term "affirmative action" in connection with national policy regarding racial inequalities appears to have been in an executive order by President John Kennedy, which stated that contractors doing business with the government must "take affirmative action to ensure that applicants are employed, and employees are treated during their employment, without regard to their race, creed, color, or national origin."[2] Note here that there is no call for preferences for blacks, only for vigorous ("affirmative") efforts to ensure that preferences do *not* go to whites.

In some respects, the policy implied by this version of affirmative action is no longer controversial. Absence of discrimination by race—the "color blind" society—is now professed to be the national consensus. It is endorsed even by those conservatives who, the historical record shows, fought the idea tooth and nail when it struggled to emerge as the law of the land.

But in fact, even this meaning of affirmative action—vigorous efforts to ensure nondiscrimination—is fraught with complexities and controversy. Given the numerous and subtle ways in which discrimination and bias can persist behind an official policy of equal opportunity, it is not long before any serious ("affirmative") effort to ensure nondiscrimination comes upon the specter of "goals" or "quotas." Noble sentiments not backed by checks and enforcements remain just that—noble sentiments.

It is not difficult to understand why quotas would be controversial, and it behooves supporters of affirmative action to appreciate the sincerity and legitimacy of many Americans' aversion to that concept. Although the aim of affirmative action quotas today is primarily one of inclusion, quotas have a long history of being associated with *exclusion*. Throughout our history, quotas have served to keep universities and prestigious occupations from being "flooded" with members of whatever groups were currently viewed as undesirable (especially if they had the temerity to have achieved sufficiently to merit inclusion by non-rationed selection criteria).

Today's "quotas" are intended to serve a different purpose, and opponents of affirmative action are at times disingenuous in their seeming failure to grasp this point. But the historically rooted connotations of the term are powerful, and it is unfair to dismiss concerns about quotas simply as racism. Moreover, notwithstanding the ultimate advantage to the entire national community in achieving an economy in which previously excluded groups are enabled to contribute their talents, in the short run there do remain "zero sum" features to affirmative action quotas. If we reserve spaces for members of one group in a competition for limited berths, we reduce the spaces for others.

Given the complexities and difficulties introduced by the concept of quotas, why then do I introduce the term in this section—that is, in discussing the least controversial aspect of affirmative action, the affirmation of the ideal of a color blind society? Why spoil a nice picnic by inviting ants that might not even have showed up? Why not at least wait to introduce this difficult topic until the discussion below of more controversial versions of affirmative action? At least here, why not stand on the rhetorically higher ground of "goals" rather than "quotas"?

To begin with the latter question, I do believe that at times it is appropriate to describe what occurs under affirmative action efforts as goals rather than quotas. "Quota" is a term that often implies a rigidly fixed number that will be filled regardless of qualifications. Goals, in contrast, imply no such predetermined outcome, only an effort or intent that may be modified in response to the actual qualities of the applicants that are recruited and evaluated. But although this distinction is real, and corresponds to genuine differences in the way different organizations approach affirmative action efforts, it is important to acknowledge that the two shade into each other.

"Goals" is often a euphemism for quotas or, at the very least, quotas approached flexibly.

More directly to the point of why I am introducing the topic of goals or quotas here, I do so because in fact any sincere effort to ensure that we do proceed in a color-blind fashion requires some means of enforcement, and effective enforcement without some kind of numerical tally to keep track of what is actually happening is virtually impossible.

Numerical tallies, of course, are not infallible. But they are an indispensible tool in evaluating whether covert bias has been operating. If, in a region where twenty-five percent of the work force is African American, ninety-five out of the last one hundred people hired "just happened" to be white, it seems appropriate to place the burden of proof on the company doing the hiring. It is *possible* that the company made a good faith effort to find qualified African Americans and simply could not. But with such numbers, a healthy degree of skepticism is warranted.

Indeed, much of what affirmative action amounts to (especially affirmative action of the variety I am discussing thus far) is a matter of who bears the burden of proof. It certainly must be acknowledged that requiring the company to bear the burden of proof may lead management to institute numerical goals or quotas themselves as a defensive effort, in order to protect themselves against potential claims of discrimination. They may hire minority workers who are less qualified than white applicants simply to avoid the hassle of defending a lawsuit—even one they could win, but only after lengthy and expensive legal proceedings.

If there are problems with placing the burden of proof on the company accused of discriminating, however, there are even worse problems in placing the burden of proof on the people who contend they have been discriminated against. The costs are significant for a corporation, but they are virtually insurmountable for an individual. Moreover, the person who believes he or she has been the victim of discrimination does not have access to the documents detailing the company's decision-making process. It entails still further expense to obtain those, and one can never be sure if everything relevant has really been submitted. The company, in contrast, does not have to engage in an adversarial process to gain access to its own records, and it can be sure that every shred of documentation in its favor will be fully presented at trial or negotiations. Indeed, American University economist Barbara Bergmann, in a strongly argued defense of affirmative action, has argued that even when the burden of proof is on the company, the difficulties facing individuals who believe they have been discriminated against are daunting in the extreme.[3]

Is Affirmative Action Still Needed?

The attentive reader may wonder if my discussion of the need for numerical tallies to ensure the absence of discrimination contradicts the comment I made at the beginning of this chapter that in many situations blacks already have at least an equal chance to be selected for a job if they have comparable qualifications to a white applicant. If that is the case, why the need to keep checking so carefully? The answer is that it is precisely continuing affirmative action efforts—at the very least the sort that entail statistical checks of the rates of hiring and promotion of minority employees—that *enable* qualified blacks to have a chance. Opponents of affirmative action regard the opportunities now available for minorities as evidence that affirmative action is no longer necessary. But it is not at all clear that those opportunities would still be available without our continuing to check that significant imbalances or disproportions do not reemerge.

Disparities in how applicants are judged, and hence in hiring or admissions figures, need not derive from intentional discrimination. They may arise from unconscious biases and assumptions that lead evaluators to expect minority applicants to be less qualified and to perceive them in accordance with those expectations. Most hiring decisions involve consideration of *multiple* criteria (education, experience, reports of performance in previous jobs, assessed ability to work independently, to work cooperatively with others, to take charge of subordinates, etc.). In deciding among applicants, it is relatively unusual for one to be head and shoulders above the others on *all* criteria. Usually, some have stronger credentials on one, some on another, and the evaluator must weigh the overall picture and decide who is most qualified.

Social psychological research has shown that evaluators can exhibit bias toward choosing applicants from groups they are more familiar or comfortable with by unwittingly changing their subjective weightings of which criterion is most important from one appli-

cant to another. They are simply more "struck" by the independence
issue with one applicant, by the cooperation issue with another, by
the importance of an advanced degree with a third, by on-the-job
experience with a fourth, never quite realizing that in each instance
they are giving greater weight to those factors on which the individual from the mainstream group excels and downplaying those in
which the member of the excluded group does.[4] They thus can sincerely believe that they are merely choosing the individual who has
stood out, and it can be difficult to persuade them to question what
they have "seen with their own eyes." For this and other reasons, we
have still not arrived at the day when we can comfortably assume
that *even without the continuing pressure of affirmative action programs,*
African Americans and members of other previously excluded
groups will be viewed as equally attractive prospects.

From Choosing Fairly to Reaching Out

Thus far I have focused on the least controversial facet of affirmative action—the attempt to ensure that either overt or subtle discrimination does not go undetected. But the term affirmative action
has taken on quite a few other meanings since JFK's enunciation
of the "affirmative" effort to be nondiscriminatory. Some of these too
have entered the national consensus, but a number of them remain
controversial. Perhaps the most immediate extension of the original
meaning of affirmative action (indeed, perhaps an interpretation
inherent in the original articulation of the concept) is the effort
not just to eliminate discrimination against those minority applicants who come through the door but to actively *seek out* qualified
minorities.

   To some degree, this approach already breaches the border of
giving minorities a special break. It is *they* who are being sought out,
not just qualified individuals in general. But this approach has
tended to fall on the "acceptable" side of the border for two reasons.
First, there is a general recognition that previous discrimination has
discouraged blacks from even applying for many jobs, and thus an
outreach effort is needed. Second, what differentiates a broadly
acceptable outreach effort from the more intensely controversial versions of affirmative action to be discussed next is that the former

confines itself to seeking out minority applicants whose qualifications manifestly match those of other applicants, and does not imply
that they will get a break in how the qualifications themselves are
judged. Thus, they would not be displacing a white applicant who,
by previously agreed upon standards, had stronger credentials.

"Compensatory" Versions of Affirmative Action and "Equality of Results"

We enter a realm of greater controversy when affirmative action is
framed as a matter of "compensation" for injustice. There are a number of versions of this rationale for affirmative action that are often
lumped together by opponents, but in fact they differ quite considerably. They all imply in some way that we must *make up for* some
type of unfairness that would persist if no compensatory effort were
made, but as we shall see, they differ in whether they emphasize
compensating for what happened in the past or for circumstances
that still persist, as well as in how they view instances in which, by
traditional criteria, black and white applicants appear to have quite
different qualifications.

A compensatory dimension was introduced very early in the formulation of what came to be known as affirmative action. Not long
after John Kennedy introduced the term to our political discourse,
Lyndon Johnson, in a commencement address at Howard University in 1965, suggested that although the triumphs of the civil rights
movement were significant and real, "freedom is not enough. You do
not take a person who, for years, has been hobbled by chains and lib-
erate him, bring him to the starting line of a race and then say, 'You
are free to compete with all the others' and still justly believe you
have been completely fair."[5]

In essence, the version of affirmative action that derives from
JFK's 1961 Executive Order proceeds on the assumption that black
job applicants are equal in qualifications to white applicants, and that
all we need to do is vigorously ensure that applicants with equal
qualifications receive equal treatment regardless of race. The rationale issuing from LBJ's Howard University speech is quite different.
It clearly implies that our national task is *not* just a matter of ensur-
ing that black applicants whose credentials are equal to those of

whites have equal opportunity to get the job. Rather, we must deal with the reality that—for reasons that cast shame on our nation and its history, not on the applicant per se—many black applicants do not come to the race with the same qualifications.

This reformulation of the meaning of affirmative action opened a floodgate of controversy that still has not subsided. Especially serving as a lightning rod was Johnson's statement that "We seek not just equality as a right and a theory but equality as a fact and equality as a result."[6] The phrase "equality as a result" had unfortunate ambiguities, and has by now taken on a life of its own as an element of our political rhetoric. It has been a source of much genuine confusion and perhaps even more dishonest demagoguery. In some respects, it can seem to imply little more than a commitment to the ideal embodied in President Kennedy's version of affirmative action, now relatively uncontroversial: we must move past sanctimonious declarations to programs that will be *effective*, that will bring us to equality not just as a piously expressed ideal but as a reality; that is, as a *result*.

For opponents of affirmative action, however, equality as a result (or its currently more common variant, "equality of result") implies something quite different. It means that beneficiaries of affirmative action do not have to work hard or accomplish anything; they will simply be handed a job or admission to a university on the basis of the color of their skin. It is their membership in a group, not their qualities as individuals, that determines the outcome.

In this connection, it is interesting to note the words that precede the controversial phrase about equality as a result in President Johnson's speech: "It is not enough just to open the gates of opportunity. All our citizens must have the ability to walk through those gates." Enabling each citizen to develop "the ability to walk" through the gates of opportunity is quite different from asking that they be *carried* through the gate. Those who appropriate the term "equality as a result" as a buzz phrase for the political purpose of denouncing affirmative action imply it is the second meaning that is the result that is sought. This is particularly ironic because it is often those who most oppose affirmative action who also most strongly oppose the programs that could *enable* everyone to walk through those gates without the need for further assistance.

The distorting rhetoric of affirmative action opponents, however, has unfortunately been matched at times by a different set of obfuscations on the part of affirmative action supporters. As I have discussed throughout this book, advocates for racial equality have often been hesitant to acknowledge the full toll of injustice and inequality on the skills and motivations that many African Americans bring to the competition for jobs and university admissions. As a consequence, over time some versions of affirmative action did begin to converge toward a kind of equality of results that amounted to apportionment by race rather than eliminating differences in qualifications. These include, in different ways, affirmative action rationales that stress compensation for past injustices (as opposed to compensation for the *continuing* impediments that confront many African Americans) and rationales that emphasize diversity as a central ordering feature or that challenge the usual criteria for hiring or university admissions as culturally biased or Eurocentric.

One significant cost of these strategies is that they all attempt to finesse significant differences in qualifications that whites can see with their own eyes (and that even the most liberal whites tend to acknowledge in private, sometimes in tones of embarrassment, sometimes of frustration over what they can see but feel they cannot say). The result is that an element of dishonesty—and even covert condescension—is introduced that poisons the atmosphere of race relations and impedes the likelihood of resolving our differences and of developing effective programs to finally put the stigmata of our history behind us. Indeed, in another of the ironic circles that have been a central concern of this book, the perceived condescension in turn deepens the reluctance to acknowledge deficits, keeping us locked in a pattern in which the fundamental issues cannot be effectively addressed.

Compensation for Past Injustices?

One way of introducing a compensatory version of affirmative action without acknowledging deficits is to root the rationale in the injustices of *the past*. How pivotal this idea is among today's advocates of affirmative action is difficult to determine. But it is clearly an affirmative action rationale widely cited by *opponents* of affirmative action policies. The reason for this is not difficult to discern: this way of conceptualizing affirmative action most readily lends itself to the view that affirmative action is a policy that victimizes innocent whites.

The question of what responsibility "whites" have for what "whites" did in this country is one fraught with complexities and contradictions. Even white Southerners who are the direct descendants of people who several generations ago were slave owners may feel it is unjustified to hold them responsible for acts committed before they were born. And in a society of immigrants such as ours, where millions of whites can say that not even their ancestors had anything to do with slavery, indeed that at the time of slavery on these shores, their ancestors were oppressed people themselves in a continent across the ocean, the sense of bearing responsibility for what occurred simply because they are "white" is likely to seem far-fetched, even offensive.

Basing affirmative action efforts on the rationale of making up for the past is, of all rationales for affirmative action, the one most likely (and in some respects, most justifiably) to be perceived as "reverse discrimination" by whites. It lends itself easily to the view that innocent whites must now give up their jobs to blacks with lower qualifications in order to make up for what *other* whites did to *other* blacks a long time ago. It is thus important to be clear that confronting the surplus resistance that such a rationale evokes is *unnecessary*, and unnecessary precisely because the impact of past injustices is so pervasively evident *in the present*. Grounding affirmative action in the inequities of the present establishes much the same moral foundation with fewer of the pitfalls.

Diversity as an End and a Value in Itself

Another approach to conceptualizing affirmative action in a way that does an end run around the issue of deficits is to argue that *diversity* is a value in itself, that being racially or ethnically different is a qualification in its own right. Here again, there are elements to this approach that are valid and helpful, but as a foundation for affirmative action efforts, it suffers from a lack of candor.

Diversity is indeed a legitimate value in a number of ways and in a number of settings. Given the tensions between the police force and minority communities, for example, a police force that did not have significant minority representation would be highly problematic. In an educational setting, students clearly learn something by interacting with people of diverse backgrounds. Education is designed to make us less parochial, and direct contact with people who are different serves that end. Thus, selecting students in part for their diversity can genuinely further the aims of the educational community.

But diversity is nonetheless a weak, and at times misleading, rationale for apportioning scarce slots. "Diversity" is often a euphemism, a way of increasing the proportion of minority students on campus without having to address the question of whether they are equally qualified or whether they are being given a break. Ostensibly, they are being chosen because, like the star student, star athlete, or outstanding musician, they add something unique and valuable that the college needs. But the rationale of diversity—so pleasingly positive but less than fully honest—obscures the issue of lesser academic or professional qualifications. As a consequence, it diverts us from addressing the *sources* of the academic deficiencies (for example, in the public schools, in the neighborhoods our society neglects, and in the antiacademic culture that develops in those neighborhoods as a consequence of that neglect).

The emphasis on diversity is not, of course, the primary reason these sources remain unaddressed. But in clouding our perception of the full impact of our inequalities, in papering over genuine differences in readiness to do academic work that are the product of those inequalities and reinterpreting them as differences in cultural orientation or point of view, the diversity rationale unwittingly bolsters our society's tendency to put off dealing with the more fundamental inequities that lie behind differential college admission rates or employment statistics.

Indeed, because emphasizing "diversity" as the grounds for affirmative action leaves the more fundamental sequelae of inequality unaddressed, it actually undermines the effective impact of diversity itself. Precisely because the diversity rationale places a fig leaf over differences in developed academic abilities that are hard to disguise for very long, it creates fertile ground for the separatist inclinations discussed in Chapter Nine. Consequently, one finds on many campuses that minority students isolate themselves, living separately, eating separately, and generally avoiding interactions that might reveal the unacknowledged deficiencies. When this happens, students do not have the experience of significant informal exchange that promotes learning from each other. All they learn from each other is how daunting is the gap between them.

A Better Rationale: Affirmative Action and Unfulfilled Potential

In contrast to the foregoing rationales for affirmative action, which all seem to me in one way or another to subtly accept a form of second-class citizenship for African Americans, the soundest basis for conceptualizing compensatory affirmative action, in my view, remains some version of the rationale President Johnson offered in his Howard University speech: It is indeed "not enough just to open the gates of opportunity. All our citizens must have the ability to walk through those gates."

Such a rationale has several advantages that some more recent versions of affirmative action have relinquished. To begin with, rather than presenting a vision of reality that clashes sharply with the direct experience of those who question affirmative action, it grounds its case for affirmative action in the very observations that lie at the center of their opposition—black applicants for jobs or university admissions often do *not* have the same credentials, skills, or qualifications. If a national consensus around some form of affirmative action is to be maintained, it will be essential that considerable numbers of people who now count themselves as opponents modify their views on the matter. This will not happen if their fundamental perceptions are simply swept aside.

A rationale for affirmative action grounded in the idea that many African Americans have not had the same opportunity as whites to develop their skills is not about racial spoils or group entitlements. It is a frank acknowledgement that years, indeed centuries, of injustice have taken a heavy toll and that *true* fairness, *honest* concern with merit, must take this into account.

It is far more likely that a black baby born today will be born into poverty than a white baby; that his neighborhood growing up will be a dangerous place; that his living quarters will be cramped, and room and quiet to study will be difficult to find; that the school he attends will have poor facilities, demoralized teachers, and frightening events a regular feature of daily life. Such circumstances, encountered by innocent children from the very beginning of their lives, make it extremely difficult for them to attain the same scores and develop the same skills and credentials as a child growing up in a comfortable middle-class suburb.

Fairminded consideration of these differences in life circumstances should make it clear that affirmative action, conceived in this way, is not appropriately characterized as "reverse discrimination." Most whites, if they grew up in the circumstances of most blacks, *would not have attained* the scores or the skills they bring to the competition. Whites have a leg up in the race—have a leg up *today*—and adjusting the criteria to remove that extra advantage is not the same as penalizing them. As Richard Kahlenberg has put it in *The Remedy*, one of the most thoughtful and influential recent books on affirmative action, "A poor applicant from the inner city who scores 1000 on the SAT surely has more potential than a wealthy student with private tutors who scores 1050."[7] "Going by the scores" is not always the fairest way to make a decision.

The leg up whites have is most obvious if one compares the majority of whites to the black residents of the inner city, but it holds in important ways as well even if the comparison is made with middle-class blacks. Andrew Hacker describes asking his white students at Queens College how much they would have to be paid to compensate for having to live the next fifty years with black skin. Most of them "seemed to feel it would not be out of place to ask for $50 million, or $1 million for each coming black year."[8]

Such a thought experiment, of course, "proves" nothing. But it does reflect a recognition on the part of whites of how much harder it is to be black in America—a recognition that they sometimes disregard when addressing the issue of affirmative action. Middle-class blacks, of course, do not have to cope with the poverty and devastation that confronts so many in the inner city. But, as detailed in previous chapters, they share with their poorer bretheren a number of impediments that comparably situated whites do not encounter. These include the pervasive impact of stereotypes, even at the highest levels of social and economic achievement,[9] the not unrelated difficulties many successful African Americans have in attaining the same choice of housing available to their white peers, and the consequent greater likelihood that middle-class black children will attend schools and encounter neighborhood influences that are substantially different from those of middle-class white children. It is thus not surprising that African Americans' scores on exams such as the SATs tend to be lower than those of whites from families of the same income level.[10] Relying solely on "objective" or "race-neutral" indicators that do not take into account the powerful impact of race ignores a significant "objective" reality of American life.

Implementing Affirmative Action: From Taking Account of Race to *Moving beyond* Race

In thinking about *how* to address the consequences of vastly unequal circumstances, and how to *move us past* this state of affairs, the question of implementation is crucial. In a much quoted comment, Supreme Court Justice Lewis Powell stated that "In order to get beyond racism we must first take account of race."[11] In certain ways this is clearly true. At the very least, we cannot even assess if racial discrimination is occurring if we do not keep some track of the differential fortunes of blacks and whites. If we are completely color-blind, we are also blind to others not being so. But for most Americans, moving *beyond* taking account of race remains an ideal, and *how* we "take account of race" is crucial.

Powell's remarks were made in the context of the case of *Bakke v. University of California*, in which Allan Bakke, an applicant to the medical school at the University of California at Davis, sued because he was denied admission and black applicants with lower scores were accepted. Powell's rationale for upholding the university's affirmative action policy introduced the idea of "diversity" to the Court's lexicon. In his own view, this attention to race was a step on the path toward its own dissolution. The aim was a society in which race no longer mattered. But diversity as the vehicle for taking us to that promised land has turned out to be highly problematic. As Richard Kahlenberg has described, many contemporary advocates of diversity no longer view attention to race as a temporary necessity pointing us toward the day when it is no longer required. Rather,

> [they] argue that the color-blind ideal was wrong all along. Race does matter, and it always will, because race is not just skin color but a substantive cultural characteristic of such great importance that it ought to be a significant factor in the distribution of bene-

fits and burdens. In the new way of thinking, to deny the central and fundamental importance of race is itself a form of racism, and race consciousness is a good thing, in both the short run and the long run.[12]

This, Kahlenberg notes, is a striking departure from the views which for so long had characterized the heart of the civil rights movement.

What has happened to the idea of diversity, introduced by Justice Powell twenty years ago as a temporary expedient for the purpose of speeding us along on the path toward a color-blind society, should alert us to the snares and complexities that await us in devising policy to address our inequalities. Part of the difficulty is that we have lost track of the larger vision within which affirmative action efforts were inititated. Affirmative action made sense as a *secondary* and *supplemental* effort within the larger context of the Great Society programs which were introduced along with it. But the main burden of change must lie with programs that can develop a degree of genuine equality that will make affirmative action unnecessary.

We are clearly not yet at the point where we have achieved that goal. The playing field remains far from level. Thus, we are charged with the task of developing an approach to affirmative action that is capable of increasing opportunities for those who have been disadvantaged without fostering a spurious sense that whites are the new victim class. In this connection, wherever we are able to accomplish the aims of affirmative action without explicitly making race a criterion, we are likely to achieve better and more stable results.

One approach that illustrates, far better than the diversity rationale, how *taking account* of race can potentially move us toward *getting beyond* race is attention to what has been called "disparate impact."* In the landmark case *Griggs v. Duke Power Company*, the Supreme Court ruled that tests and other criteria that had a disparate impact on blacks and whites were unacceptable unless there was a strict business necessity. The advantage of a "disparate impact" approach is that, properly implemented, it points us *away* from making an exception for blacks or holding them to a different standard. Rather, it requires us to find standards to which *all* applicants can be held and to consider critically whether any criterion

---

* As we will see, however, this approach to transcending our preoccupation with race by first focusing on race is also not without hazards.

that would largely exclude blacks is in fact essential. In particular, it directs us to reconsider the easy or "intuitively obvious" assessment criteria (high school diploma, college degree, grades, exam scores) and to devise instead criteria that are more directly related to the task for which the individual is being hired.

Thus, for example, in a case in which black firefighters successfully sued several cities in New York State for using hiring and promotion standards "which have a disparate impact on Blacks and which are neither demonstrably valid nor job-related," the resolution of the suit entailed developing measures which *were* relevant to job performance *and* did not impact blacks differentially. These included a variety of very specific tests of physical strength and endurance in which applicants performed actions very closely tied to the actual job of a firefighter—for example, moving and mounting a twenty-four-foot extension ladder, pulling a section of hose weighing fifty-two pounds from the ground to the roof of a tower, and climbing a seventy-foot ladder (to ensure that the applicant does not have a fear of heights).[13]

Disparate impact conceptualizations are not without potential problems. The danger is that they can be a basis for sweeping under the rug real differences in developed skills which, even if not related to the performance of a specific job narrowly defined, do reflect real handicaps that have arisen from the impact of pervasive stereotyping, educational inequities, and the personal and cultural defenses developed to cope with them. Success in restricting job decision criteria to narrowly job-related grounds may advance the cause of African Americans in the short run but at the same time contribute to covering over the continuing neglect in their schools and neighborhoods that in the long run keeps African Americans in a secondary position.

Notwithstanding these concerns, the disparate impact criterion does offer a way to address the continuing disparity in who appears qualified to be hired without resorting to outright preferences or adjustments to actually attained scores. It thus, in principle, provides an opening to achieve greater parity in hiring without arousing the intense resentments that can be stirred by preferences or by tactics such as "race norming" (adjusting the scores of blacks and other minorities so as to compare them to scores of their own group only rather than to the overall scores achieved by all test takers).[14] Pursued wisely, disparate impact analyses can enable black and white applicants to compete as equals on criteria that are scored the same for both and that are manifestly related to the job at hand.

Achieving greater racial balance without specific preferences or overriding grades or scores could be achieved in other ways as well. In setting criteria for jobs or university admissions, for example, attention to "merit" does not require us to line up everyone's scores from one to 999. We could as readily set as a criterion the score level actually necessary to perform the job or handle the course work competently, and then choose randomly from among all the applicants who scored above that criterion.[15] If the choice within the pool of qualified applicants was made in completely random fashion, without consideration of race, then the chances of white or Asian applicants in the pool of finalists would be just as great as those of black applicants. But setting the criterion with regard to who is *qualified,* as opposed to who has the *very highest* score, would at the same time provide some counterweight to the differences in scores that current inequities have produced.

There are probably some circumstances in which the effort to find the "absolute best"—to the degree we are capable of this— would continue to be important. Stephen Carter, author of *Reflections of an Affirmative Action Baby,* has suggested surgeons and Supreme Court Justices as examples.[16] But for most purposes, setting a reasonable criterion for what it would take to be genuinely qualified to be in the pool would ensure sufficient quality control. There might be some loss of "efficiency" if we did not assign the absolutely most qualified individual, but merely *a* qualified person, but there would be offsetting gains in social harmony.[17] And indeed, there would at times be overall *gains* in efficiency, as segments of the population who ordinarily do not get to develop their full capacities were brought into the mix. In this connection, it is interesting to note the finding that among Harvard graduates, those who achieved most after graduation were students from blue-collar backgrounds with lower SATs.[18]

Class-Based Affirmative Action

Still another way of addressing the inequalities that continue to exist without enshrining race as a criterion is to construct affirma-

tive action efforts on the basis of class rather than race or ethnicity.
Not only is this fairer—many poor and working class whites *also*
have lower SAT scores and lack other credentials for reasons having to do with their relative position in society—but it also is a policy that is much more likely to generate sufficient support to be
maintained.[19] At the same time, class-based programs also do have
the effect of providing substantial assistance to the racial and ethnic groups who have suffered most from discrimination and economic deprivation, because that very deprivation would mean that
under a class-based system they would disproportionately qualify—
even *without* consideration of race or ethnicity. As Richard Kahlenberg has put it,

> Where opponents of affirmative action call for a color blindness
> that ignores history, and proponents offer the prospect of unend-
> ing color consciousness, class preferences are at once color-blind
> and remedial, disproportionately benefitting those who have
> suffered most under our nation's history of discrimination. . . .
> In short, class preferences are a way to remedy the historic racial
> wrongs of our country without resorting to 'the disease as
> cure.'"[20]

In general, Kahlenberg's emphasis on class rather than race or
ethnicity seems to me useful and constructive. But in viewing all of
our inequities through the lens of class, he seems to see African
Americans from middle-class or professional families primarily as
among the privileged. While it is undeniable that the life circumstances of middle-class blacks differ substantially from those of the
inner-city poor—and that in certain important respects the black
middle class has advantages not available to poor whites—race is a
significant enough social and psychological factor in our society that
class alone is insufficient to characterize the fault lines in the fragile
structure of equal opportunity. Class is indeed of crucial importance,
but *along with* race, not instead of race.

As we saw in Chapter Five, even African Americans from families with rather comfortable incomes show a decrement in SAT
scores and other measures usually used to apportion the most desirable positions in our society. We saw the explanation for these differences in such factors as the stereotype anxiety studied by Claude
Steele and the very substantial differences in the neighborhoods and

schools available to middle-class whites and middle-class blacks. As a consequence of these differences, programs that go beyond the usual criteria in assessing the abilities or potential of even "privileged" African Americans seem to me still appropriate.[*]

A New Vocabulary?

Whatever mix of programs we finally decide is best, we are likely to sharpen our thinking if we introduce a new vocabulary. Affirmative action, as we have seen, is a term that covers a variety of approaches to overcoming the consequences of long-standing and still persisting inequities. Some of these programs contribute significantly to making us a more just and well-functioning society. Some contribute instead to maintaining our divisions and rubbing salt into our wounds. The multiplicity of meanings, intentions, and practices that have accrued to the account of "affirmative action," and the often intense emotional connotations that the term evokes, serve to introduce considerable confusion into our dialogue. If we really wish to *think* about our problems, rather than fighting over slogans, it may be time for us to retire the term "affirmative action" altogether. Instead of asking ourselves if we should continue or phase out a conglomerate entity called affirmative action, we could consider the more differentiated and meaningful question of *which* of the specific programs and principles—each under a separate and more communicative name—should be continued, which modified, and which eliminated.

Affirmative Action in a Larger Context: Addressing the Vicious Circles at the Heart of Our Difficulties

Whatever decisions we make about terminology, the primary implication of the analysis offered in this book is that affirmative action should be but a part of our strategy in battling the continuing legacy of slavery, segregation, and discrimination. We have seen over and

---

[*] I am not addressing here the question of whether special considerations might also hold for other groups, such as Latinos or women. Although matters of discrimination, prejudice, and the impact of old-boy networks apply more generally, our nation's history of slavery and legally sanctioned segregation points to distinctive issues in considering the claims of African Americans.

over that the persistence of our problems derives from the way in which so many problematic influences interlock and reinforce each other. Each element in the circle of baleful influences feeds back to strengthen the others:

Housing segregation and poverty breed crime and a larger "culture of segregation." In turn, both crime and the behaviors associated with that culture maintain the forces that yield further segregation and poverty. The impact of pervasive stereotyping impairs school performance, which further strengthens the stereotype. Defensive efforts to maintain self-esteem in the face of these stressful events lead to disparagement of intellectual achievement as "acting white," and the consequence is further failure, alienation, and isolation, and thus still further defiant and defensive refusal to "act white." Children and youths confronted with violence and danger act tough and aggressive to avoid being victimized and thereby contribute to perpetuating the violence. Poverty and stress lead to family breakdown, which leads to further poverty and stress.

Whites, afraid they will be accused of being racist and experiencing blacks as "oversensitive," are awkward and avoidant in their interactions with blacks. In turn, the middle-class blacks with whom they are most likely to come into contact, finding that even when they have "made it" they are not fully accepted, become wary and embittered. But the discomfort this mistrust and resentment engenders for whites seems to confirm their wariness and prompts still further awkwardness and detachment, starting the cycle again.

Racism and indifference lead to underfunding of inner-city schools, and the failure thereby produced maintains racist stereotypes and further hesitation to "throw good money after bad." White defenses against guilt over our enormous disparities lead to hesitance to acknowledge their severity and consequences, thereby permitting the disparities to continue, as well as the need to maintain the same defenses against the guilt. Reluctance by conservatives to invest the resources needed to make affirmative action no longer necessary leads to excessive emphasis on affirmative action by liberals as the only remedy; and the excesses resulting from this overemphasis create self-righteous anger among affirmative action opponents that results in still further reluctance to invest the necessary resources and still further need to resort to affirmative action as the only remedy.

The list goes on and on, as each of these circular patterns intersects with the others, tightening the weave with every turn until the fabric of our troubles seems virtually seamless. Can we do anything about this painfully repetitive process? There is a danger that attending to how intertwined and self-justifying these patterns are can simply add to discouragement or immobility, proving to some that racism is inevitable and to others that investing in programs to break a cycle that can't be broken is a waste of money and effort. Such reactions, of course, are but one more constituent of the larger circle, one more set of self-fulfilling prophecies in which the assumption shapes the result.

I do not share in the pessimism these responses embody. To begin with, the dynamic I have just been describing is not the only one at work. One can point instead to a variety of signs that things are getting better, that race relations are improving, the most manifest forms of racism diminishing, and the economic circumstances of a large segment of the African American community improving substantially.[21] Accounts of this facet of our reality must not serve as posters for complacency; it should be evident from the description of persisting vicious circles immediately above that I believe there is still an *enormous* amount we need to do. But appreciation that the dynamics of change and the circular dynamics that impede change are operating simultaneously can enable us to keep working to strengthen the former even in the face of the frustrating persistence of the latter.[22] At times, to be sure, it can feel like we are dancing in quicksand; every step we take to extricate ourselves from the mire seems to sink us in more deeply. But it is important to see that there is in fact potential solid ground. There are many steps we can take that will *not* be futile.

It is the current fashion to deride social programs as utopian and wasteful, and even at times as contributing not to the well-being of those they are intended to help but rather to trapping them further in poverty and despair. In fact, however, there is substantial evidence that, properly implemented and sufficiently funded, social programs can make a very substantial difference. In recent years, several important books have documented the success of creative programs to address disadvantage.[23] In large measure, those successes reflect at least an implicit understanding of the ironies and vicious circles I have been addressing and of the ways that problems typically approached in piecemeal fashion are in fact linked and mutually reinforcing.

The programs that can move us beyond our present impasse are not limited to the actions of government. A variety of privately run programs, funded either by foundation grants and individual and corporate donations or by a partnership of public and private sources, have done extremely creative and valuable work in helping people turn around their lives. Programs like those of the Rheedlen Centers[24] and STRIVE[25] are exemplars of what we can achieve. A number of church-run programs have similarly shown impressive effectiveness in reaching young people in troubled neighborhoods, and have at times been insufficiently appreciated or respected by progressive thinkers.[26]

But, ultimately, the scale of our persisting problems is such that without a substantial role for public funding and broad government initiatives we are unlikely to reach the point where the ramifications of our history of racial injustice are finally behind us. There is a widespread sense today that we can no longer afford the kinds of social programs that characterized Lyndon Johnson's Great Society initiatives; that, in the present parlance, "the era of big government is over." This perception is rooted in still another set of circles and ironies that I have discussed in detail elsewhere: the workings of our economy include, as an unfortunate side effect, a frequent inability for us to notice—and hence to enjoy—how much we have.[27] To answer the question of whether we can afford the kinds of social programs we felt comfortable committing ourselves to in the 1960s, it is useful to compare our economic circumstances now to those in that decade of perceived affluence and readiness to fund ambitious government efforts to overcome poverty and social inequity.

In the early years of the Johnson Administration, when we thought we *could* afford social programs, the average per capita disposable income in this country was barely more than half what it is today, even correcting for inflation.[28] When Lyndon Johnson took office, only 14 percent of American homes had air conditioning, 7 percent had dishwashers, and 21 percent had clothes dryers. Today, almost 70 percent have air conditioning, 45 percent have dishwashers, and over 70 percent have dryers.[29] In 1963, 22 percent of American households had two or more cars. Today, the number is close to 35 percent. In 1970 (the earliest year for which I could find a figure), 36 percent of the new homes built were under 1,200 square feet. By 1996, only 9 percent were that small. Conversely, in 1970 only about a fifth of the homes built were over 2,000 square feet. By 1996, almost half were.[30] Moreover, in addition to these indicators of vast improvement in the economic circumstances of most Americans, many American homes have still other amenities that did not even exist in 1965 or that were available only in very primitive form or to very few—computers, microwave ovens, VCRs, compact disc players, etc. The increase in our nation's wealth has in fact been enormous, and the fact that many Americans do not feel as affluent now as their counterparts did in the 1960s, when our incomes and stores of material goods were much, much less, is a social contradiction of enormous consequence. I have attempted to explain that contradiction in *The Poverty of Affluence*. Here I wish simply to make clear that the problem is not that we cannot afford programs to address our peristing inequalities. We could spend twice as much as we did on the Great Society programs and *still* have more left over for each of us to buy what we want than our parents had in the affluent 1960s.[31]

The centrality of affirmative action in our society's efforts to achieve social justice is in large measure a consequence of our failure to grasp this point. So long as we tell ourselves that we can no longer afford the kinds of social programs we could several decades ago, we will be committing ourselves to affirmative action as a safety valve against social unrest. But in surreptitiously using affirmative action in this manner, we turn a potentially valuable tool in the effort to achieve racial harmony and equity into a blunt instrument of dubious benefit.

Ultimately, both left and right share an interest in reaching a point where compensatory efforts like affirmative action are no longer needed. But some on the right pretend we are already there, and some on the left act as if that day will never come. We have painted ourselves into a corner as a society, largely turning our back on efforts to address the fundamental sources of our continuing inequalities and confining ourselves to arguing over how to *manage* those inequalities rather than eliminating them. At this point in our history, affirmative action remains a necessary element in a larger strategy. If it is employed, however, as a substitute for programs to address the deeper sources of our persisting disparities, it is likely to contribute to perpetuating the vicious circles that plague us rather than to resolving them.

Breaking the Cycle of Poverty and Disadvantage

Head Starts, Handicaps, and the Importance of Ongoing Life Circumstances

A widely acknowledged key to breaking the cycle of poverty and disadvantage is to start early, before problematic patterns have become entrenched. But efforts to correct for problematic early experiences are often based on a faulty understanding of *why* those experiences can be so pivotal or of *how* the impact of early experiences is perpetuated. As a consequence, compensatory programs are often not as effective as they might be. There is a widespread view that the special impact of early experiences derives from their capacity to carve deeply into pristine minds, leaving a lasting imprint. In this view, once an inclination or perception is "internalized," it becomes a permanent fixture in the individual's psyche that later experiences are virtually unable to modify. What that view leaves out is the crucial role of the ongoing environment in which the child continues to live. In large measure, early tendencies frequently persist because the environment that generated them persists as well.

When this crucial role of the ongoing environment is not sufficiently taken into account—and when the vicious circles that contribute so powerfully to perpetuating that environment are not addressed—programs intended to overcome our inequalities are likely to be poorly conceived. Moreover, they are likely to be prematurely labeled as failures by those who are skeptical that social programs can do much to reduce our inequalities.

A case in point is Project Head Start. Of all the interventions that have been developed to break the cycle of poverty, Head Start is perhaps the most extensively implemented and widely supported. In principle, the Head Start approach seems eminently reasonable. If children enter school already handicapped by earlier experiences and heading toward a repetitive cycle of deprivations, stereotypes, negative expectations, and failures, it makes sense to try to interrupt the process as early as possible. And indeed, there is evidence that early intervention programs *can* make a significant difference in the lives of disadvantaged youngsters and in their performance in school. A number of comprehensive studies have shown that children who participate in Head Start show significant and rapid gains in cognitive test scores and in measures of social and emotional development.[1] However, some of those gains, especially in measured IQ scores,[2] seem to fade over time. After several years, the children who participated in Head Start no longer show the same advantages over their peers who did not participate.[3]

This dissipation of Head Start's effects over time has been a key element in the opposition in some quarters to funding such programs. In fact, however, the results of Project Head Start have very different lessons to teach us. To begin with, it is important to note that not all such programs fail to sustain their effects. The Perry Preschool Program, conducted in the 1960s and 1970s in a low-income black neighborhood in Ypsilanti, Michigan, bore many similarities to Head Start. Years later, the young adults who had attended the program as preschoolers had gone further in school, earned higher incomes, been arrested less, and had fewer drug problems, fewer teenage pregnancies, and more stable marriages than did a control group of their peers who did not attend the program. Estimates of the ultimate savings in public outlays (considering such costs as welfare, special education, and criminal justice expenses, and taking into account the taxes paid by these more successful individuals) suggested that every dollar spent on the project was ultimately repaid at a ratio of more than seven to one.[4]

Critics of Head Start, however, contend that the Perry findings are not relevant to considering the impact of Head Start because the Perry program was a much better-funded, higher-quality program.[5] Indeed, the Perry program did spend twice as much per child as Head Start does, which permitted higher paid, better-trained staff and smaller class size. But the critics' argument in response to the striking success of the Perry program seems rather odd. Given the clear evidence that a well-funded, well-conducted program can make a substantial positive impact on the lives of vulnerable youth *and*, over the long run, also save money, the reasonable conclusion would seem to be that Head Start is insufficiently supported and should be funded at a higher level.

When a business is not sufficiently capitalized, whatever money *was* invested is very much at risk. Investing a sufficient amount, on the other hand, even if initially more costly, may yield considerable gain. It should not surprise us that similar contingencies hold for social programs. Insufficent amounts spent, even if in the abstract they seem like "a lot," may seem to suggest that the enterprise cannot make a go of it and that the money was wasted. But spending enough to accomplish the task well will lead to a quite different conclusion.[6]

A second lesson of the tendency for the gains of Head Start programs to dissipate over time is even more fundamental and even more germane to the key point of this chapter. As Head Start was ultimately implemented, it was rooted in a highly problematic, if widespread, view of psychological development. In essence, Head Start attempted to give these young children enough "good stuff" in their early years to serve as an innoculation against the deprivations and stresses they would encounter in the environments in which they would continue to live. Head Start alone could do little or nothing about those environments, and once the children had "graduated" from Head Start, they were largely on their own in dealing with life in impoverished schools and neighborhoods.[7]

This approach did not necessarily reflect the views of the psychologists and other experts in human development and early childhood education who originally conceived the program.[8] Rather, it resulted from the compromises that were necessary to steer the program through the political process and achieve Congressional funding. Not coincidentally, the view of psychological development implicit in Head Start as finally implemented suggested that intervening in the cycle of poverty and poor school performance could be done relatively cheaply[*]: Little needed to be done about the circum-

---

[*] To be sure, billions have been spent on Head Start. But many more billions would need to be spent to achieve the changes in the children's overall context necessary to create a

stances the children would assuredly encounter as they grew up in our nation's most abandoned neighborhoods; that would all take care of itself if the children only received a proper "head start" in their run through the gauntlet.[9]

Thus, insufficiently funded, and addressing the needs of four-year-olds without considering the environments in which they would live as eight-year-olds or twelve-year-olds, the program as implemented could serve, for those so inclined, as another demonstration that "social programs don't work." In contrast, early intervention programs that *have* included later follow-through have yielded more long-lasting results, and programs of longer duration and greater intensity have achieved what programs implemented as a cost-cutting compromise have not.[10]

There is little that should be surprising in the finding that many of Head Start's gains did not persist after several years of post–Head Start neglect. The more suprising finding is that the Perry program noted above, which also did not include programmatic follow-through, did show sustained gains. It suggests that if a program is implemented with sufficient money, effort, and attention to quality, remarkable results can be obtained.[11] However, attempting to change the life course of children by helping them out at age three, four, or five, but leaving virtually untouched the circumstances they will encounter a few years later—hoping that the change in the children will be sufficient to change those later powerful circumstances or to cushion the children sufficiently against them—is a high-risk enterprise. It is possible at times to reach one's destination even by swimming upstream against a powerful current; but it is not usually the recommended route.

The Public Schools: A Reverse Head Start Program?

The next institutional context encountered by most Head Start graduates that is designed to help them enter the social and economic mainstream is the school. In principle, public schools are the great equalizer in American society. Regardless of where the child may begin, public education is supposed to put him or her on an even foot-

genuinely level playing field. Such money would be well spent, and as noted earlier, even a sound economic investment; but it was not forthcoming.

ing with everyone else, imparting the knowledge and skills that are the key to upward mobility. Many readers of this book, no doubt, are testimony to the success of our schools in accomplishing this task.

But for many African American children—as well as other children from backgrounds outside the white middle class—school is not an experience that promotes overcoming their handicaps and sense of stigmatization, but a place where those experiences are perpetuated and confirmed. In part, this state of affairs reflects the "savage inequalities" that Jonathan Kozol has particularly vividly illustrated in his book of that title.[12] Overcrowded classrooms, crumbling buildings, sometimes even an absence of texbooks in poor inner-city neighborhoods convey to students what society thinks of them and their prospects. In contrast, pleasant, well-equipped suburban schools, with ample computers and sports facilities convey to their students a quite different message about how they are valued. Far from minimizing our differences, the state of our schools at this point in our history both reflects and exacerbates them.

In essence, our society has chosen to invest the least resources where the need is greatest. In one inner-city high school in the Bronx, the *New York Times* reported, the blackboards were "so badly cracked that teachers are afraid to let students write on them for fear they'll cut themselves," and students must shower after school to wash from their hair the plaster that has fallen from the walls and ceiling.[13]

Many inner-city schools virtually depend on truancy and dropouts, because when everyone shows up there are not enough chairs in the room! Books are similarly in short supply. Kozol writes that in much of the predominantly black Detroit school system, there is only one set of books for every three elementary school classes; only starting in the sixth grade does every student have his or her own textbook. In the high schools, students are taught word processing—but without word processors! Funds for computers are not available.[14]

In Illinois, Kozol reports, annual spending for a child's education in the poorest districts is $2,100; in the richest it is $10,000.[15] The results are predictable. In the eighteen Chicago high schools in the highest poverty areas, a total of 6,700 children enter the ninth grade each year. Only three hundred of them both graduate and read above the national average.[16] None but the most blatantly racist fringe is likely to conclude that this enormous failure rate simply reflects the basic intellectual equipment these kids bring to school. Clearly, the schools have failed these children.

Faced with such palpable signs of the contempt in which they are held, it is remarkable that some of the students in our poorest school districts do go on to learn and to strive, and hardly a surprise that so many of them do not. Yet, rather than the low scores of students in poorly funded inner-city schools being viewed as a compelling indication that greater funding is needed, those scores often end up serving as a rationale for maintaining the very inequities that generate them: "These kids can't learn; the reading scores show it again and again. So what's the point of pouring good money after bad in a futile effort to bring them up to standard? Better to spend the money on kids who *can* learn!" We have here, of course, another vicious circle. Students in poorly funded schools do poorly, and this becomes a justification for continuing to maintain the circumstances that keep their performance subpar.

The argument that it is pointless to put more money into trying to educate inner-city children is usually not framed in the grossly genetic terms of a Charles Murray. Often, it is cast as a claim that what matters is not money spent on schools but the influence of parents; bad parenting and bad parental values, not crumbling or overcrowded or poorly equipped schools, are the source of inner-city kids' poor performance. The *Wall Street Journal*, not ordinarily associated with the view that money is not all that important, suddenly becomes the scourge of Mammon when it comes to poor kids' education: "Money doesn't buy better education. . . . Increasing teachers' salaries doesn't mean better schooling. . . . Big budgets don't boost achievement. . . . Cash alone can't do the trick." What *does* matter? "It's parental influence that counts."[17]

It is certainly true that parental influences make a difference in children's performance at school. Indeed, some of the most successful and progressive efforts, such as the school development approach of Yale psychiatrist James Comer, place parental involvement in the school process at the very heart of successful schooling for the disadvantaged.[18] But for those who are spending very substantial sums for their children's own educations—either in highly expensive private schools or in generously funded suburban school districts—to prattle about how little money matters in the quality of education children receive is the height of disingenuousness.

Schools and Self-Fulfilling Prophecies

Self-fulfilling prophecies regarding poor minority children affect not just the funding of their schools or the physical facilities they encounter. They can affect the way their teachers regard them as well.

In 1968, Robert Rosenthal, a social psychologist at Harvard, published a book along with Lenore Jacobson, an elementary school principal, that was destined to cause an enormous stir. The book, *Pygmalion in the Classroom*, expanded upon work Rosenthal had done earlier on the ways in which social science experimenters unwittingly communicated their expectations to the subjects of their research, who in turn frequently fulfilled those expectations without either party realizing the role those communicated expectations had played in influencing the subjects' behavior. *Pygmalion* extended the investigation of expectancy effects from researchers and subjects to teachers and students. When teachers were led to think that certain students in their class had been identified as "late bloomers," who could be expected to show unusual intellectual gains in the course of that school year, those students in fact did better when tested at the end of the year. In reality, however, the students so designated were chosen completely randomly. The only thing that really differentiated them from the other children was the expectation induced in their teachers.[19]

Rosenthal and Jacobson's findings were not without controversy.[20] Questions arose, for example, about how readily the findings could be replicated. On that score, a series of quantitative reviews of all the studies done on the phenomenon established firmly that expectancies could have a significant impact on teachers' evaluations of students, on grades and performance on objective tests, and even on measures of IQ (supposedly, in the view of those who regard IQ tests most concretely, a measure reflecting immutable properties of the individual being assessed).[21] When teachers hold differential expectancies regarding the abilities and performance of black and white students, these expectancies can similarly be presumed to play a role in the students' experience of school, and very likely in their performance as well.[22]

The criticism of experiments like the *Pygmalion* study that has perhaps the most relevance to the emphasis in this book on vicious circles is that the expectations in the *Pygmalion* experiment were artificially induced: the teachers were told the students had achieved a certain score on a mythical test that supposedly evaluated their pace of intellectual development. In the typical classroom, however, expectations do not arise from such arbitrary or random foundations. Their sources are multiple and varied, and they include the actual experiences the teacher has had with the child or with children the teacher takes to be like the child.[23] Thus, expectations may not ordinarily *distort* in the way they did in the *Pygmalion* study; rather than being arbitrary, they may be largely an accurate and realistic reflection of previous experience.[24]

But while such an argument has substantial merit as a corrective to overly one-sided interpretations of expectancy effects, it is essential to avoid falling into an equally one-sided alternative: teacher expectations are not influencing the kids; the kids' performance is shaping teachers' expectations. As I have stressed throughout this book, interpersonal reality is much messier than such either-or conceptualizations would suggest. The shaping and influence is almost always mutual. But often so too is the inclination to deny this mutuality and to see the responsibility for the pattern as lying in only one direction.

Such tendencies were amply evident in my classes on racial and ethnic stereotypes. Many of the African American students, based in part on their own experiences in public schools, contended that the teachers don't really teach, have little respect for the abilities of black kids, and basically give up on them. White students were initially hesitant to question this description, but once the class "warmed up," and it became clear that there was a safe environment for expressing more genuinely held views, there would always be some who offered a quite contrasting view, based on their own experiences as student teachers, or on the accounts of friends or relatives who were teachers. In this view, young teachers generally come into inner-city schools very ready to teach, and even skeptical of the cynical things they do indeed hear older teachers say. But they then get burned out by the bitter experience of trying to teach and finding either that the kids don't learn or that, at an older age, they are actively hostile to the entire enterprise.

Must we dismiss one or the other of these reported experiences? More likely, the two experiences are in continuous interaction, each reflecting a real (if partial) truth and each contributing to the perpetuation and amplification of its opposite number. Thus, although many African American children, despite all the obstacles and impediments they encounter, enter school with enthusiasm and eagerness to learn, they *also* enter with expectations derived from the experience of earlier cohorts in the same setting. Older brothers and sisters, parents, and others in the neighborhood have often had experiences with school that were painful, discouraging, or infuriating. The feelings associated with those experiences can't help but be communicated and make the expectations of African American children different, by and large, from those of white children. Notwithstanding the positive affect and anticipation that they also bring—and that a good teacher or good school will find a way to contact and amplify—they often come as well with a wariness, an anxiety, a potential dawning proclivity to disidentify that is likely to be greater than for a white child.[25] Put differently, it is not only the teachers who have expectations that may end up being fulfilled; the children do too.

When the children's conflicting inclinations are met by a school setting that includes teachers who genuinely expect the kids to learn and the resources to translate those expectations into effective action, it can be the side of these children that is eager to learn that is most strongly elicited, and as patience and effort breed success, that side can be further strengthened. Indeed, there is evidence that positive expectations by teachers can be *especially* facilitative for African American children and for children from lower socioeconomic levels.[26]

But all too often, the wrong side of *both* the teachers and the students is brought out by their interactions with each other. Whatever the complexities that actually account for the kids' difficulties—from factors within the school, such as overly large classes, to the broad range of discouraging and debilitating circumstances the children encounter in their marginalized neighborhoods—the experience of teaching in an inner-city school is often an immediate experience of seeing kids fail. New teachers entering the system may be rapidly trained by those already there to expect the same failure they have experienced (and, unwittingly, thereby to contribute to it). In some instances this may be conveyed quite explicitly by more experienced teachers who have become (or who always were) cynical about the abilities of minority children. But most of the time, the "training" is probably unintentional, an unconscious "leaking" of attitudes of which the senior teacher herself may be unaware. In either case, the attitudes that evolve may turn out to be "confirmed"—not because the kids can't learn, but because the circumstances that have hampered their ability continue to operate and because the teacher's expectations become one more of those circumstances.[27]

Once again, however, it is important to remind ourselves that this picture, which can seem to convey an airtight system into which no intervention is possible, is a picture of what happens *if we do not* intervene. The prospects look quite different if we do.

Children's Fates Are Not Sealed in the Earliest Years

The range of factors contributing to the difficulties that poor African American children encounter in school is daunting and can readily lead to a paralyzing—and in important respects unfounded—pessimism. Even before they are born, these children face a greater likelihood of parental crack addiction, poor prenatal care, and poor maternal nutrition. They are more likely to be raised by a single parent, to encounter stereotypes that disparage their intellectual abilities, and to go to schools that are underfunded and demoralized.[28] As they grow older, they are likely to encounter a peer culture that discourages intellectual achievement and views hard work and success in school as "acting white."[29] While all these factors are important to note in combatting racist explanations of the lower grades and test scores of African American children, they also can contribute to a discouraging picture of these children's prospects or even be taken as still further rationale for doing nothing. The cards sometimes seem so stacked against these children that even people of goodwill may be tempted to give up in despair.

More recently, still other factors have been discovered that, on the one hand, add further to our understanding of why leaping to genetic explanations of the poor school performance of these children is so indicative of bias, but, on the other hand, may induce still further pessimism. There is evidence that differences in early experiences of stimulation have significant impact on the development of the brain itself, and that there are consistent differences in such stimulation related to social class. In one study, observing interactions between parents and children in the first two and a half years of life, children of professional parents heard an average of 2,100 words an hour, whereas children of working-class parents heard only 1,200, and children of parents on welfare heard 600. The study also found large differences in the *quality* of the interactions between groups. Children of professional parents received positive feedback twice as often as children of working-class parents and five times as often as children from welfare families. When the children were tested at age three, these differences corresponded to differences in measures of the children's cognitive and language development.[30]

Such findings do seem to me both important and troubling. They point to still one more way in which the cards are stacked against the children of the poor. But they also lend themselves to a fallaciously pessimistic interpretation which, if it discourages us from intervening because "there is nothing we can do, the game is already over for these kids," can become a self-fulfilling prophecy. Reporting the views of Dr. Betty Hart, for example, who conducted this research, a *New York Times* article states that "by age two, the differences among children were so great that those left behind could never catch up."[31]

Here, once again, what is left out is the effect of the child's ongoing environment. Children who are with parents who talk to them a lot and give a lot of positive feedback at age one or two are likely to continue to experience such a home environment at age six or eight. They are also, for reasons of class, likely to attend a much better equipped and more nurturant school.

My point is not that the early experience is irrelevant, or that children who start out behind do not encounter a handicap that would likely, at least for a time, leave them less able to take advantage of later opportunities even if they *were* the same. Rather, it is that since the later opportunities almost never *are* really the same, it is almost impossible to sort out what is due to a permanent or quasi-permananent effect of the early experience and what to the continuing difference in the life experiences they encounter. To state that the less advantaged children "could never catch up" even if their environment were to change is going way beyond the available data.

Advances in our ability to measure brain activity associated with crucial cognitive functions or to trace the actual connections formed in the brain when learning occurs are of enormous value in treating neurological disorders; but this new knowledge may actually contribute to misleading us in evaluating research on the impact of early experiences. The concreteness and "hard science" feel of finding differences in children's brains tend to evoke images of something primal and immutable. But finding that differences in early stimulation are related to differences in neuronal growth and in the establishment of neural connections and networks should really be unsurprising. It merely tells us something we already know—that, as embodied creatures, our experiences are both dependent upon and registered in actual neural events and structures. It is indeed a significant advance to be able to measure and detect the changes at that level, and I admire the elegance of research that does so. But because the vast majority of children whose brains show the signs of their early experience will not encounter a radically different environment in the years that follow, even *continuing* differences in their brains tell us absolutely nothing about whether the effects of the early experience are inherently permanent.

A good illustration of how our assumptions can mislead us about the impact of early experiences is offered in an illuminating series of studies by Harvard developmental psychologist Jerome Kagan. Studying cognitive development of children in the U. S. and in rural villages in Guatemala, Kagan found that early levels of functioning that would have serious negative implications for the later development of American children were not associated with later difficulties for the Guatemalan children.[32]

The Guatemalan children showed at an early age what looked, from an American perspective, like considerable impairment. Moreover, that seeming impairment was precisely what would be expected from prevailing American views of what is required for successful early development. The Guatemalan children spent the first year of life in a small, dark, windowless hut, they rarely were taken outside where they could encounter other stimulation, and they had few toys or other stimulating objects and few interactions with adults. Very little time was spent speaking to them by any of their caretakers. However, although the Guatemalan children were considerably behind American children as infants and toddlers, when they were tested again at a later age, they no longer showed any ill effects. On a variety of culture-free measures of cognitive development, their level of functioning at that point was equal to that of middle-class American children.

In understanding why these children did not show the lasting impairment that American children reared similarly tend to show, several considerations are relevant, and they bear significantly on how we must understand the school performance of black children in America and the appropriate foundations of programs to overcome our present inequalities. First, the upbringing of the Guatemalan children was considered "normal" in the context of their culture. No stigma was attached to either their circumstances or their actual functioning. The culture of the Guatemalan villages in which these children were raised does not emphasize stimulation in the earliest years because its view of normal child development is that children do not show much responsiveness in the early years but develop very rapidly later in childhood. Thus these "slow" children (by American standards) are regarded as perfectly fit rather than as impaired. When they reach the age at which the culture expects rapid development, the villagers begin to respond to them differently, both stimulating them more and conveying the expectation that they will now greatly accelerate their learning and responsiveness. And sure enough, that is just what happens. In essence, they were not impaired but simply on a different timetable.

In contrast, American children reared in the way Kagan's Guatemalan children were reared are an exception, and they are likely to come from families that are dysfunctional or severely deprived and marginalized. Unlike the Guatemalan families, who, at the point when their culture indicates that children need more stimulation, are capable of providing it and ready to do so, American families who provide little stimulation to their infants are likely to *continue* to provide little stimulation as the child grows older. The environment remains the same, and hence the child's impaired development is likely to continue as well.

Also very important, American children who get off to a slow start are viewed as impaired, and *they begin to be treated as impaired*. That is, not only do they continue to encounter the same environment at home, but they are treated differently from other children at school and in other settings where a corrective experience might occur.

In the United States, for a multitude of reasons, significant numbers of African American children encounter circumstances growing up that do not elicit their full potential. But unlike the Guatemalan children in Kagan's study, the expectations for them do not change as they grow older. They are likely to encounter the same deprivations and the same expectations again and again unless some unusual intervention occurs. The early deprivation is associated with later impairment not simply as a consequence of a direct lasting impact of that experience, but because the early deprivation is but the first occurrence of what is likely to be a *lifelong series* of deprivations, affecting their development continuously and repeatedly. When this does *not* occur, as in the Guatemalan example, the seemingly inexorable consequences of the early experience become less evident. But because American children who are brought up in such circumstances are likely to continue to encounter essentially the same circumstances—and particularly for African Americans, to encounter continuing expectations of inferiority—the early experience looks more decisive and permanent.

We *can* reverse many of the consequences of inequity and deprivation, but in order to do so, we must address ourselves not only to training the children and imparting skills, but to the environment they will continue to encounter through their growing-up years and beyond. If we see the problem as only "in them," we will, unfortunately, often see this vision confirmed, as we attempt to improve children's chances in the morning, while permitting these efforts to be undermined in the afternoon.

14

Beyond Black and White

We have seen many instances throughout this book of circular patterns that perpetuate themselves through their own consequences. Head Start, for example, is funded sufficiently to create the feeling that we have spent "a lot," but not sufficiently to really have the full benefits kick in. Moreover, it is implemented in isolation from (and often instead of) other efforts to address the larger and the later context of the children's lives, and so its achievements do not appear enduring. For those so inclined, this result then conveys the message that "we have tried, but the problems are so intractible that further spending is just throwing good money after bad."

Similarly, because schools are funded by local municipalities rather than nationally or statewide, they are funded at levels that are dramatically lower for poor children than for the majority. When those poor children do not thrive under these difficult circumstances, this is taken as further evidence that it is perfectly appropriate to provide "vastly superior course offerings"[1] to the children of the well off, because they are the only ones who can benefit from such offerings.

From a different angle, we may recall the culture of opposition described by John Ogbu, Massey and Denton's observations on the culture of segregation, Majors and Billson's accounts of "cool pose," or Elijah Anderson's descriptions of the "hardcore" and "street-oriented" behavior generated in our inner cities by alienation and

despair. Circularity is evident in the way these attitudes and behaviors, fueled by the very real discrimination and contempt these
young people face, end up frightening and repelling those outside
the ghetto culture, thus eliciting still further discrimination and contempt. There is similar circularity in the way initially less alienated
young African Americans may be drawn into participating in these
patterns in order to survive in the harsh world they inhabit, and
then end up contributing to and extending that very harshness.

We may also include among the tragic circles Claude Steele's
depictions of the ways in which African American children, in the
face of disparaging stereotypes about their intellectual capacities,
"disidentify" with school and with the realm of intellectual endeavor
altogether, only to—falsely but powerfully—"confirm" those very
stereotypes, not only to whites but to themselves. We may, relatedly,
factor in the sad disabling forces that are set into motion when intellectual pursuits and attentive behavior in school are viewed as "acting white" or marking one as an "oreo" or "wannabe."

Compounding the tragic circularity still further are observations such as those reported by psychologist Vonnie McLoyd in a
review in the journal *Child Development* of research on "The Impact
of Economic Hardship on Black Families and Children":

> Numerous studies of both black and white adults, employing both
> interview and observational methods, report that mothers who
> are poor, as compared to their advantaged counterparts, are more
> likely to use power-assertive techniques in disciplinary encoun-
> ters and are generally less supportive of their children. They value
> obedience more, are less likely to use reasoning, and more likely
> to use physical punishment as a means of disciplining and con-
> trolling the child. Lower-class parents are more likely to issue
> commands without explanation, less likely to consult the child
> about his or her wishes, and less likely to reward the child verbally
> for behaving in desirable ways. Poverty also has been associated
> with diminished expression of affection and lesser responsiveness
> to the socioemotional needs explicitly expressed by the child.[2]

As McLoyd notes, such behavior is scarcely surprising, given the
stresses these parents are under. But the terrible result is that such
modes of child-rearing increase significantly the likelihood that their
children too will confront poverty and deprivation when *they* grow

up. (Recall the research cited in Chapter Thirteen about the consequences for children's development of parents talking more or less frequently and in more or less supportive and explanatory a manner.) Moreover, as a consequence of confronting the same stresses as their parents did, they will in turn be likely to rear their own children in similar fashion, keeping the circle going still again.

Understanding the daunting and disturbing extent of these circles can lead us in either of two directions. It can become still another element in the interlocking set of circles itself, in which the conviction that nothing can be done assures that nothing effective *is* done. Or it can, by the very way it confronts us with the complex and interconnecting nature of our problems, point us toward investing sufficient resources so that our efforts are truly effective.

"There's Nothing We Can Do": Not Bitter Truth, but Self-Fulfilling Prophecy

Lisbeth Schorr, reviewing a variety of successful programs to address poverty and disadvantage, finds a common denominator in the programs that have been most effective: those programs work best that offer intensive, comprehensive, and *integrated* services. When the programs are linked, and staff members are able to address the full range of the family's or child's needs rather than providing a single narrowly defined service, the impact of all of the various components is activated and magnified.[3]

Schorr's conclusions, on the basis of intensive examination of which programs work and which do not, are quite consistent with the vicious-circle analysis advocated in this book. The fabric of our racial difficulties is a seamless whole. We may, for certain purposes, choose to focus on a particular element—on crime or jobs or welfare or education—but if we follow the thread of any one of these, it is not long before we find ourselves, if we are willing to see, face to face with the others. Crime rates are related to unemployment rates; whether one is employed or not depends significantly on education; the education one receives depends very largely on the neighborhood one has grown up in; the neighborhood one grows up in depends on one's family's income and economic resources; and on and on and on.

The solution is unlikely to be found in efforts that focus exclusively on one sector. Although there have indeed been some remarkable inner-city schools that have achieved great success,[4] our efforts are greatly handicapped if we do not link efforts to educate inner-city kids—who are often taught to be cynical both by older peers and by bitter experience—with efforts to demonstrate concretely, through *other* programs simultaneously, that if they work hard in school they will truly be able to get good jobs, live in safe and pleasant neighborhoods, and be treated with respect.

Synergy is the nemesis that generates and perpetuates our seemingly most intractible social problems. So many baleful influences intertwine and reinforce each other that our problems seem to have an almost unbearable resiliency. Single-pronged strategies, attempting to address any of the problems in isolation, may end up convincing us that our problems are unsolvable.

But synergy is also a potential ally in attempting to overcome those problems. Lisbeth Schorr's observations regarding the greater effectiveness of programs directed toward several dimensions of our problems at once dovetail with considerations advanced by Jonathan Crane, an innovative researcher at the University of Illinois's Institute of Government and Public Affairs. Crane has shown how feedback processes similar to those discussed in this book can produce epidemic-like accelerations of social problems and neighborhood decay.[5] But he has also shown how strategies in which resources are intensively concentrated in a community can achieve results that would not have been anticipated judging from less intense and comprehensive interventions of the same sort.[6] In attempting to reverse the effects of interlocking forces of disintegration and neglect, our efforts often need to reach a critical mass before their real power and impact are manifested.

In many neighborhoods across America, years of neglect have brought them to a "tipping point" that yields an accelerating harvest of social problems and isolation.[7] Programs to address the highly intertwined influences that have maintained our troubles and divisions must be of sufficient scale and comprehensiveness that they bring us to a *new* tipping point, one that accelerates change in a more salutary direction and enables a more positive self-sustaining dynamic to become the norm.

Race *in the Mind* of America

Much of this book has focused on poverty and the inner cities, because that is where the need is most acute for intervention to break the cycles that perpetuate our past in our present. But the pains and inequalities associated with race in our society affect everyone. Middle-class blacks may be better off economically (may be a "privileged class," to use Ellis Cose's painfully ironic phrase), but they experience almost daily the sting of discrimination and disregard. Indeed, research shows that it is not the black poor but economically or professionally successful blacks who are most likely to describe themselves as victims of discrimination and who report the most alienation and disaffection from the American Dream.[8]

This experience is important for our nation to address in its own right, as one more sign that we have not fully transcended the injustices that are so deeply woven into our history. But it is also important because another implication of the interlocking circles I have been stressing is that gaining ground in our efforts to change the circumstances, values, and behavior patterns of the black poor is not independent of the experience of the black middle class. It is largely the middle class that supplies the leaders of the African American community, and it is the middle class who articulate many of the ideas that shape the consciousness of all African Americans. Moreover, if better-off African Americans report mostly pain and continued disrespect, there is little reason for the black poor to believe that they can really transcend their circumstances or achieve a state of dignity through hard work and study.

The experience of the black middle class highlights the crucial importance of the subjectively experienced dimensions of our persisting divisions. Righting the economic inequalities, the differentials in access to quality education, housing, medical care, and jobs is certainly a crucial task. But so too is the healing of the deeper wounds that persist even when "the numbers" look better. So-called hard indicators by no means exhaust the crucial determinants of human behavior or experience.

Among the most serious obstacles we face in achieving a more just and harmonious society is the idea of race itself. Much of the alienation and sense of otherness that divides blacks from whites in

America can be traced to this idea, an idea that is strikingly lacking in biological substance or validity.[9] Orlando Patterson, in an important recent book, has suggested we eliminate altogether the use of the term "race," as well as the terms "black" and "white," when discussing our social divisions, referring instead to Afro-American and Euro-American ethnic groups.[10] In large measure I agree with Patterson's view of the problematic implications of these terms. I have employed them in this book, however, because what I offer here is primarily a psychological analysis, and these *ideas* and *images* have shaped—and continue to shape—people's experiences and behavior.

The concept of race itself is an element in the vicious circles with which this book is concerned. It heightens the tendency toward stereotyping and leads us to exaggerate our differentness from each other. Race, as the title of this book implies, is not an objective reality but something "in the mind of America"—though America, of course, is not alone in this manner of thinking. The mental images and ideas that guide our perceptions often need to have only the barest relation to reality to remain compelling to us. Much of the viciousness of the vicious circles I have been describing lies in their capacity to persuade us, over and over, that the shadowy preconceptions with which we approach other people are bright and fast realities.

Like a river whose course divides the landscape and provides a rationale for human beings to create boundaries, the idea of race has defined the social territory we inhabit. Where we live, whom we marry, whom we care about, and what our prospects are in life all have been profoundly shaped by the divisions that derive from this idea. Over the years, the seemingly inexorable flow of racial feelings has cut a deep gorge in the social terrain. My aim in this book has been to lay the foundations for a bridge across that gorge. It will take money to build that bridge; but most of all it will take understanding that the divide we seek to traverse is not the handiwork of nature but itself a human construction.

Notes

Chapter One

1. Compare, for example, Joseph Breuer and Sigmund Freud, Studies on Hysteria, in *The Standard Edition of the Psychological Works of Sigmund Freud*, Vol. 2, London: Hogarth, 1955; Charles Brenner, *An Elementary Textbook of Psychoanalysis*, New York: Anchor, 1957; and Otto Kernberg, *Object Relations Theory and Clinical Psychoanalysis*, New York: Jason Aronson, 1976.

2. Elsewhere, I have compared these hypothesized remnants of early childhood to the woolly mammoths occasionally found buried in the Arctic ice. These psychological formations are assumed to be, much like the woolly mammoths, preserved in their original form. In the psychological case, rather than the preservation being due to a deep freeze, it is viewed as the result of a process which splits the wish or image or fantasy off into a realm of the psyche that is inaccessible to the influence of new perceptions. Hence, I have labeled these conceptualizations "woolly mammoth" theories. (See, for example, my book *Psychoanalysis, Behavior Therapy, and the Relational World*, Washington, D.C.: American Psychological Association, 1997.) It will be apparent that the vicious circle conceptualization of the same phenomena is quite different.

3. See in this connection Paul L. Wachtel, *Action and Insight*, New York: Guilford, 1987; *Psychoanalysis, Behavior Therapy, and the Relational World*, Washington, DC: American Psychological Association, 1997; and C. H. Zeanah, T. F. Anders, R. Seifer, & D. N. Stern, Implications of research on infant development for psychodynamic theory and practice, *Journal of the American Academy of Child and Adolescent Psychiatry*, 1989, 28, 657–668.

4. For example, since a person caught in this sort of trap develops a sense of self that centers on being "nice," and since the social roles she fills with others have a similar emphasis, anger *continues* to be threatening, and hence, as just described, it continues to be *generated*. Moreover, because so many life experiences in living this way are infuriating (even if—or, in a sense, especially because—they are not acknowledged to be), and because this way of life causes the individual to avoid the experiences whereby we learn to express anger in a modulated way, the anger that is being defended against feels "primitive" and "explosive," and thus must be further defended against—with predictable results.

   For a detailed examination of how vicious circle patterns work in individual neuroses, and how a vicious circle perspective contrasts with more linear accounts of the direct effects of early childhood experiences, see Paul L. Wachtel, *Psychoanaly-*

sis, Behavior Therapy, and the Relational World, Washington, DC: American Psychological Association, 1997. *Therapeutic Communication,* New York: Guilford, 1993, and *Action and Insight,* New York: Guilford, 1987; as well as David Shapiro, *Neurotic Styles* New York: Basic Books, 1965 and Karen Horney, *New Ways in Psychoanalysis,* New York: Norton, 1939, and *Our Inner Conflicts,* New York: Norton, 1950.

5. The impact of stereotype anxiety will be discussed in more detail in Chapter Five.

6. Quoted in Studs Turkel, *Race,* New York: Doubleday, 1992, p. 11 (emphasis added). See also, Regarding the construction of the identity of "white" and its social function, Noel Ignatiev, *How the Irish Became White,* New York: Verso, 1995.

7. Dinesh D'Souza, *The End of Racism,* New York: Free Press, 1995.

8 See, for example, Andrew Hacker, *Two Nations,* New York: Ballantine, 1992.

9. Blacks constitute slightly under 13 percent of the population, but they represent 44.8 percent of those arrested for murder, rape, aggravated assault, and robbery. See Michael Tonry, *Malign Neglect: Race, Crime, and Punishment in America,* New York: Oxford University Press, 1995, p. 128.

10. *Statistical Abstract of the United States,* Table 584, p. 376.

11. Holly Sklar, "Young and guilty by stereotype." *Z Magazine,* July/Aug. 1993, Vol. 6, No. 7/8, pp. 52–61. See also, Bob Herbert, "The Soap Opera Machine," *The New York Times,* November 9, 1994, p. A27. Herbert discusses complaints by whites in the previously mostly white working-class neighborhood of South Boston that efforts to promote integration in the neighborhood had increased crime. In fact, he reports, crime rates *fell* by 18 percent since blacks began moving in. Whites in South Boston, he reports, were eight times more likely to be victimized by a white person than by an African American or a Latino. Herbert also quotes James Alan Fox, dean of Northeastern University's College of Criminal Justice, who stated that the difference between black and white crime rates overall, which is indeed substantial, is entirely attributable to differences in socioenomic factors. "When blacks and whites of similar incomes from the same neighborhood are compared . . . the discrepancy at which whites and blacks commit crime disappears."

12. Liberals and conservatives may see different implications in this differential opportunity, but they tend to agree that the differential itself is the main source of the differing black and white rates of white-collar offenses.

13. *Sourcebook of Criminal Justice Statistics,* U.S. Department of Justice, Bureau of Justice Statistics, 1992, pp. 434 (Table 4.9) and 600 (Table 6.46)

14. The assumption that a book about race is a book about blacks is itself a symptom of the unfortunate state we are in. It reflects the view, sometimes explicit and sometimes so far from consciousness that some who hold it would be embarrassed to realize it, that the "race problem" in this country is essentially a "black problem," that blacks are the problem, not whites. It should be apparent as the reader proceeds that this is most decidely not my own view.

Chapter Two

1. On another occasion, a white participant pointed out that blacks are not a minority in South Africa and asked, "Does that mean that by definition South African whites can't be racist?" The black participant then amended her claim, saying that *any* oppressed group, even if a majority, could not be racist; only the oppressor could. This then led to a discussion about whether whites were in fact oppressors in Amer-

ican society (everyone in the group was in agreement about South Africa). Here the debate was not so much about definitions (though the contention about that remained) as about the facts. Was it so cut and dried that whites are oppressors and blacks oppressed? Not surprisingly, there were significant differences between whites and blacks with regard to this question.

2. *The MacNeil-Lehrer NewsHour*, Thursday, June 11, 1992. Transcript provided by WNET and WETA. Page 14.

3. See, among many examples, "Are you a racist?", by Peter Noel, *Village Voice*, February 11, 1992, pp. 34–35

4. James M. Jones, Racism in black and white, in P. Katz & D. Taylor (Eds.), *Eliminating Racism: Profiles in Controversy*, New York: Plenum, 1986, p. 129. Emphasis added.

5. Robert Miles, *Racism*, London: Routledge, 1989, p. 50.

6. Stokely Carmichael and Charles V. Hamilton, *Black Power*, New York: Vintage, 1967.

7. Carmichael & Hamilton, *Black Power*, p. 5.

8. Many of these extensions of the meaning of racism are reviewed in Miles and depicted by him as an instance of "conceptual inflation." See also R. Blauner, *Racial Oppression in America*, New York: Harper & Row, 1972; D. Wellman, *Portraits of White Racism*, Cambridge: Cambridge University Press; and S. Steinberg, *The Ethnic Myth*, Boston: Beacon, 1989.

9. A great deal of evidence demonstrating the powerful effects of parental income and social class on children's prospects is reviewed by Richard Kahlenberg in *The Remedy: Class, Race, and Affirmative Action*, New York: Basic Books, 1997. See especially pages 86–94.

10. I assume that something similar happens when a plane crash is announced on the news in other countries as well. The phenomenon I am describing is by no means uniquely American.

Chapter Three

1. Neil McLaughlin, Beyond "Race vs. Class": The Politics of William Julius Wilson, *Dissent*, Summer 1993, p. 361.

2. Gunnar Myrdal, *An American Dilemma: The Negro Problem and American Democracy*, New York: Harper, 1944.

3. See, for example, the discussion of Edward Banfield in Chapter Four.

4. Carmichael and Hamilton, *Black Power*, p. 23.

5. See Lee Rainwater & William Yancey, *The Moynihan Report and the Politics of Controversy*, Cambridge, MA: MIT Press, 1967.

6. Reprinted in Rainwater & Yancy, p. 411 (emphasis added).

7. Rainwater & Yancy, p. 214.

8. Quoted in Rainwater & Yancy, p. 429.

9 Quoted in Rainwater & Yancy, p. 202.

10. Rainwater & Yancy, p. 13 (emphasis added).

11. Quoted in Rainwater & Yancy, p. 212 (emphasis added).

12. Moynihan did, in fact, note explicitly in a number of places in the report the differences between middle-class and lower-class blacks, but the frequent appearance of terms like "the breakdown of the Negro family" was, not surprisingly, a more prepotent stimulus for many readers.

13. Quoted in Rainwater & Yancy, p. 25.

14. *The Negro Family: The Case for National Action*, Washington, DC: Office of Policy Planning and Research, United States Department of Labor, March, 1965 [Henceforth to be referred to in these notes as "The Moynihan Report"], Preamble.

15. The Moynihan Report, p. 47.

16. Rainwater & Yancy, p. 263.

17. The Moynihan Report, p. 5.

18. The Moynihan Report, p. 47 (emphasis added). In fairness, it must be added that the sentence immediately following states, "The cycle can be broken only if these distortions are set right." As I discuss in more detail below, it seems to me that there is ample evidence that Moynihan was *not* absolving white society of responsibility for the circumstances he was describing or implying that there was nothing that could be done. But his efforts to muster support for programs that *could* intervene in the cycle were undermined by a failure to appreciate the problematic aspects of a preponderant emphasis on the family. I might add here that Moynihan's later unfortunate comment advocating "benign neglect" in racial issues seems to me not an uncovering of his "true" intentions all along but rather, to a significant degree, a response to the emotional reactions his report evoked (as well as to events intervening in the ensuing years). Moynihan's "benign neglect" memo is not a response I endorse or admire, but I do not think it reflects the mindset with which the report was written.

19. As I will discuss in Chapter Thirteen, the problem does not lie in positing a powerful shaping role for early experiences, but in *how* that role is understood to operate. The effects are not direct and linear, but rather mediated by countless later experiences whose probability is skewed by the earlier experience. See Wachtel, 1987, 1997, op. cit., for a more detailed discussion.

20. For further discussion of how the impact of early experiences is often overestimated or misunderstood, and of how later experiences can modify their effects, see Michael Lewis, *Altering Fate: Why the Past Does Not Predict the Future*, New York; Guilford, 1997; A. M. Clarke & A. D. B. Clarke (Eds.), *Early experience: Myth and evidence*, New York: Free Press, 1976; C. H. Zeanah, T. F. Anders, R. Seifer, & D. N. Stern, Implications of research on infant development for psychodynamic theory and practice, *Journal of the American Academy of Child and Adolescent Psychiatry*, 1989, 28, 657–668; .Paul L. Wachtel, *Action and Insight*, New York: Guilford, 1987; Paul L. Wachtel, *Psychoanalysis, Behavior Therapy, and the Relational World*, Washington, DC: American Psychological Association, 1997.

21. I do not mean here to endorse a "Lord of the Flies" view of childhood. Children are certainly capable of loving and responsible behavior, and participation in the peer group is an essential part of how human beings come to form attachments and learn loyalty, collaboration, and respect for others. But when the pressures of the peer group become too prominent among the forces shaping the child's socialization, the more unfortunate aspects of a world ruled by twelve-year-olds or sixteen-year-olds come to the fore.

22. It is important to note that similar processes can occur in white middle-class homes as well. An economy in which parents feel they must work long hours to maintain their standard of living, and a suburban landscape essentially *designed* to permit children to roam free outside the home, have led to at least somewhat similar processes in the suburbs, with a corresponding sense that parents have "lost control" of their children. Our preoccupation with "family values" reflects this sense of loss

of control on the part of middle-class parents as much as it does a reaction to the behavior patterns of the inner city.

23. See, for example, Stephen Steinberg, *The Ethnic Myth*, Boston: Beacon, 1989, p. 120.

24. Moynihan Report, Introduction and summary page (no page number).

25. Moynihan Report, p. 44.

26. Moynihan apparently decided consciously to play down specific policy recommendations in the report, focusing instead on a basic examination of the nature of the crisis we faced. According to Rainwater and Yancy, he did this "for fear that all of the attention would go to the recommended programs rather than to the definition of the problem and also that there would be premature budget estimates of the cost of the recommended programs" (p. 28). This was, I believe, a faulty decision that contributed to the negative reception the report received; it made it easier for those with different agendas than Moynihan to claim that the report's primary implication was that things were out of hand and nothing could be done until blacks reformed themselves. Yet even in the version that did appear, it requires a perverse reading— whether by black militants or white conservatives—to see it as anything other than a document urging us to take action and pointing toward concrete steps that could and should be taken to *break* the cycle he described.

27. See, for example, p. 47 of the Report.

28. Moynihan Report, p. 3.

29. Rainwater & Yancy, p. 24.

30. Rainwater & Yancy, p. 29.

31. Gerald D. Jaynes and Robin M. Williams, Jr., *A Common Destiny: Blacks and American Society*, Washington, DC: National Academy Press, 1989. In a section summarizing the data and conclusions, the authors state that "a majority of black children under eighteen live in families that include their mothers but not their fathers; in contrast, four of every five white children live with both parents." (p. 25)

32. See, for example, William Julius Wilson, *The Truly Disadvantaged*, Chicago: University of Chicago Press, 1987.

Chapter Four

1. Douglas G. Glasgow, *The Black Underclass*, New York: Vintage, 1981, p. 154.

2. See, for example, in addition to Glasgow, William Ryan, *Blaming the Victim*, op. cit.; Stephen Steinberg, op. cit; Michael B. Katz, *The Undeserving Poor*, New York: Pantheon, 1989; Eleanor Leacock (Ed.), *The Culture of Poverty: A Critique*, New York: Simon & Schuster, 1971; Bill E. Lawson (Ed.), *The Underclass Question*, Philadelphia: Temple University Press, 1992 (especially chapters by Tommy Lott and Leonard Harris).

3. See, for example, John U. Ogbu, Immigrant and involuntary minorities in comparative perspective, in M. Gibson & J. Ogbu, *Minority Status and Schooling*, New York: Garland, 1991; and Douglas Massey & Nancy Denton, *American Apartheid: Segregation and the Making of the Underclass*, Cambridge, MA: Harvard University Press, 1993.

4. Hylan Lewis, Culture of poverty? What does it matter?, in E. Leacock (Ed.), *The Culture of Poverty: A Critique*, New York: Simon & Schuster, 1971, p. 347 (emphasis added).

5. See, for example, Ellis Cose, *The Rage of a Privileged Class*, Joe R. Feagin and Melvin P. Sikes, *Living with Racism: The Black Middle Class Experience*, Boston: Beacon Press,

1994; and A. J. Franklin, The Invisibility Syndrome, *The Family Therapy Networker*, July/August, 1993, p. 34.

6. Not all poor people, however, are characterized by a culture of poverty. Lewis notes examples throughout the world of populations that are poor but have not developed a culture of poverty, and he estimates that only twenty percent of the American poor show such an adapation.

7. Lewis, p. 69

8. Ryan, *Blaming the Victim*, p. 25.

Other critics were less colorful, but often no less condemning and single-minded in their views. Among the most influential was anthropologist Charles Valentine, whose book, *Culture and Poverty: Critique and Counter-Proposals* (Chicago: University of Chicago Press, 1968), offered a series of obfuscations and misrepresentations in academic garb that seemed to lend substance to the effort to tar both the concept of a culture of poverty and Oscar Lewis himself. Lewis (accurately, I believe) characterized Valentine's book as "tendentious, self-righteous, pedestrian, and downright irresponsible in its distortions of the views of others," and he and other scholars pointed out numerous distortions and shortcomings in Valentine's work. Valentine was much praised, however, by those who saw the culture of poverty idea as a devious threat to the interests and reputations of the poor, and the chilling effect of his and other attacks on the concept and those who dared to employ it was considerable. (Lewis's comment appears in the journal *Current Anthropology*, 1969, 10, No. 2–3, p. 189. Other reviews exposing the distortions and fatuities in Valentine's work appear in that same issue, along with comments by Valentine and by writers who were highly supportive of Valentine's work. For many years, Valentine was perhaps the most cited writer in the effort to discredit the idea.)

9. Michael B. Katz, *The Undeserving Poor*, New York: Pantheon, p. 43.

10. Charles Murray's *Losing Ground* (New York: Basic Books, 1984), which argued that federal programs to aid the poor are counterproductive, is a prime and influential example of the narrowly economic understandings of human behavior that Katz says gained ascendancy as a consequence of the absence of an alternative organizing concept when cultural influences were ruled out of liberal discourse. Murray portrays welfare clients as engaging in a kind of street arbitrage, cannily calculating costs and benefits and deciding that teenage motherhood was a good investment, with dividends coming in the form of welfare checks.

11. William Julius Wilson, *The Truly Disadvantaged*, Chicago: University of Chicago Press, 1987, p. 6.

12. Edward Banfield, *The Unheavenly City Revisited*, Boston: Little Brown, 1974, p. 56

13. Banfield, p. 53.

14. Banfield, p. 54.

15. Banfield, p. 143.

16. Banfield, p. 167.

17. Banfield, p. 159 (emphasis added).

18. Banfield, p. 235.

19. Among opponents of the culture of poverty concept, this crucial point is often denied. One source of supposed evidence for that denial is the observations of Elliot Liebow in his classic book, *Tally's Corner* (Boston: Little, Brown, 1967). Liebow does vividly portray the enormous impact of external circumstances of injustice and

blocked opportunity on the black street corner men he studied, and he raises important and probing question both about the depth of expressed values that seem to differ from those of the mainstream and about the ways that cultural explanations can mask the impact of each generation's meeting the same external circumstances. But his vision is far more complex than that of writers who cite him simply to debunk the idea of the culture of poverty (for example, Ryan in *Blaming the Victim* and Steinberg in *The Ethnic Myth*). What Liebow really objects to is not a vicious circle conception, which he explicitly endorses (p. 225), but the idea that the circle is "puncture proof" and the use of cultural and circle conceptions as an excuse to evade acknowledging injustice and taking responsibility for creating a more equitable distribution of incomes and opportunities. In this and in many other respects, Liebow's views are very much in accord with my own.

20. Such conclusions, of course, are likely to be assisted by political demagogues eager to articulate and magnify this perception.

21. Charles Murray and Richard Herrnstein, *The Bell Curve*, New York: Free Press, 1994.

22. Valentine, op. cit., p. 134. It should be noted that by referring to "perceived" opportunities Valentine craftily provides himself an out. Taken in context, the meaning Valentine intends in the passage quoted is clear: offer the poor opportunities and they *will* perceive them *and* act on them. But stating that resignation and fatalism will give way when there is a change in "perceived" opportunities effectively begs the question. If change is not apparent when new opportunities are offered, Valentine can say that this doesn't contradict his notion at all: they simply didn't *perceive* the opportunities. But a crucial point of the culture of poverty theory he trashes is that opportunities are *not* readily perceived; the *reason* the culture of poverty is so problematic is that it *impedes* perception of opportunities. Valentine clearly knows this, but he couches his argument in a form that offers him an out in case resignation and fatalism do not change as "readily" as he implies.

Valentine is disingenuous in a second way as well. Though few readers will detect any real tone of tentativeness in his assault on the culture of poverty concept, he adopts the stance of the disinterested observer merely listing potential "alternatives" to the culture of poverty theory he is attacking. If his predictions are not borne out, he can point to this nominal evenhandedness to disavow any real commitment to the "alternatives" he was merely spinning out as hypotheticals.

23. Valentine, op. cit., p. 69.

24. See, for example, Glasgow, *The Black Underclass*, op. cit.; Ryan, *Blaming the Victim*, op. cit.; Janet E. Helms, Why is there no study of cultural equivalence in standardized cognitive ability testing?, *American Psychologist*, 1992, 47, 1083–1101; A. W. Boykin, The academic performance of Afro-American children, in J. T. Spence (Ed.), *Achievement and Achievement Motives*, (pp. 322–371), San Francisco: Freeman, 1983; James M. Jones, *Prejudice and Racism*, New York: McGraw-Hill, 1997.

Chapter Five

1. See, for example, Andrew Hacker, *Two Nations: Black and White, Separate, Hostile, Unequal*, New York: Ballantine, 1992. Other references documenting and bearing on these differences are cited throughout this chapter at the appropriate points.

2. Various dictionaries differ in their definitions of the term racism, but virtually all of

them converge on this meaning as fundamental. See R. Mills, *Racism* (op. cit.) for a comprehensive review of the origins and meanings of the words racism and racist.

3. See, for example, Robert Sternberg, *The Triarchic Mind: A New Theory of Human Intelligence*, New York: Viking Press, 1988; and Sternberg and R. K. Wagner, The g-ocentric view of intelligence and job performance is wrong, *Current Directions in Psychological Science*, 1993, 2, 1–5; Howard Gardner, *Multiple Intelligences*, New York: Basic Books, 1993; Daniel Goleman, *Emotional Intelligence*, New York: Bantam, 1995.

4. Herrnstein & Murray, p. 527.

5. Claude S. Fischer, Michael Hout, Martin Sanchez Jankowski, Samuel R. Lucas, Ann Swidler, & Kim Voss, *Inequality by Design: Cracking the Bell Curve Myth*. Princeton: Princeton University Press, 1996, p. 172.

6. Alan Ryan, Apocalypse Now?, *The New York Review of Books*, Nov. 17, 1994, p. 11.

7. Thomas Sowell, Ethnicity and IQ, *The American Spectator*, February 1995, p. 34.

8. Sowell, p. 33.

9. Related by George Albee in a talk to the Ph.D. program in Clinical Psychology at City College, March 28, 1995.

10. See, for example, Lisa A. Suzuki & Richard R. Valencia, Race-Ethnicity and Measured Intelligence, *American Psychologist*, 1997, 52, 1103–1114.

11. For good discussions of these differences, rooted in data but offering more than merely numbers, see the National Research Council Volume, *A Common Destiny: Blacks and American Society* (Gerald David Jaynes and Robin M. Williams, Jr., editors), Washington, DC: National Academy Press, 1989; Andrew Hacker, *Two Nations*, New York: Ballantine Books, 1993; Douglas Massey and Nancy Denton, *American Apartheit*, Cambridge, MA: Harvard University Press, 1995; David K. Shipler, *A Country of Strangers*, New York: Knopf, 1997.

12. See Melvin L. Oliver and Thomas M. Shapiro, *Black Wealth/White Wealth* (New York: Routledge, 1997) for a comprehensive examination of this issue. Two statistics cited by Richard Kahlenberg (*The Remedy: Class, Race, and Affirmative Action*, New York: Basic Books, 1997, p. 168) are also relevant here: (1) One in three white households receive some financial inheritance, but only one in ten black households do; (2) Less than a third of white middle-class mothers came from working-class backgrounds, but fully *eighty-two percent* of black middle-class mothers did. Kahlenberg notes that this differential in class origins of black and white middle-class mothers provides much of the explanation for the differential IQ test performance of their children. The class background of the children's mothers was a good predictor of their IQ scores.

13. See Chapter Eleven.

14. Douglas Massey & Nancy Denton, *American Apartheid: Segregation and the Making of the Underclass*, Cambridge, MA: Harvard University Press, 1993, p. 153.

15. At lower socioeconomic levels, the differences in environment between blacks and whites of supposedly the same SES is perhaps even more dramatic. In one study, poor blacks were found to be *six times* as likely as poor whites to live in areas of high poverty concentration. (See Loic J. D. Wacquant and William Julius Wilson, "Poverty, Joblessness and the Social Transformation of the Inner City," in J. Cottingham and D. Ellwood (Eds.), *Welfare Policy for the 1990s*. Wilson's book, *The Truly Disadvantaged* provides enormous documentation of the impact of what Wilson calls "concentration effects" and of the very large differences in the degree to which poor blacks and poor whites live in areas of concentrated poverty. See also, Massey

& Denton, *American Apartheid*, and Gerald D. Jaynes and Robin M. Williams, Jr. (Eds.), *A Common Destiny: Blacks and American Society*, especially pp. 283–287.

16. For a good summary of Steele's research, see Claude M. Steele, A Threat in the Air: How Stereotypes Shape Intellectual Identity and Performance, *American Psychologist*, 1997, 52, 613–629.

17. Claude M. Steele & Joshua Aronson, Stereotype threat and the intellectual performance of African Americans, *Journal of Personality and Social Psychology*, 1995, 69, 797–811.

18. See, for example, Charles Spielberger and Peter R. Vagg (Eds.), *Test Anxiety: Theory, Assessment, and Treatment*, Washington, DC: Taylor & Francis, 1995.

19. Steele's demonstrations of the powerful effects of stereotype anxiety on performance, it should be noted, are not limited to African Americans. He has shown similar effects resulting from stereotypes regarding women and mathematical ability.

20. Claude M. Steele & Joshua Aronson, Stereotype threat and the intellectual-test performance of African Americans, *Journal of Personality and Social Psychology*, 1995, 69, 797–811. See also the work of Terrell and Terrell and their colleagues regarding cultural mistrust, which is closely related to issues of disidentification, achievement, and academic versus nonacademic goals and choices (e.g., F. Terrell, S. L. Terrell, and F. Miller, Level of mistrust as a function of educational and occupational expectations among black students, *Adolescence*, 1993, 28, 573–578; F. Terrell, S. L. Terrell, and J. Taylor, Effects of race of examiner and cultural mistrust on the WAIS performance of black students, *Journal of Consulting and Clinical Psychology*, 1981, 49, 750–751).

21. Jason W. Osborne, Academics, self-esteem, and race: a look at the underlying assumptions of the disidentification hypothesis, *Personality and Social Psychology Bulletin*, 1995, 21, 449–455; Osborne, Race and academic disidentification, *Journal of Educational Psychology*, 1997, 89, 728–735.

22. John U. Ogbu, Immigrant and involuntary minorities in comparative perspective, in M. Gibson & J. Ogbu, *Minority Status and Schooling*, New York: Garland, 1991, p. 14.

23. Gibson & Ogbu, p. 27.

24. Steele, p. 623; John Ogbu, The consequences of the American caste system, in U. Neisser, *The School Achievement of Minority Children: New Perspectives* (pp. 19–56). Hillsdale, NJ: Erlbaum, 1986.

25. Bob Herbert, *The New York Times*, October 26, 1994.

26. This observation should also remind us that the performance differentials shown by involuntary minorities are not only not reasonably attributable to genetics, they are not inherent in deep-seated features of their culture either. They reflect very specific adaptations that derive from the history of their coercive inclusion in the society and their subsequent caste-like status. These adaptations change when members of the group leave their locked-in circumstances and become ordinary "immigrants" in another society.

27. *The Bell Curve*, p. 117

28. Christopher Jencks has noted that most laymen, and even most social scientists, "interpret heritability statistics as if they set an upper bound on environmental influences rather than a lower bound." (Jencks, *Rethinking Social Policy*, Cambridge, MA: Harvard University Press, 1992, p. 107). Jencks demonstrates that heritability

estimates in fact indicate not a maximum role for the impact of environmental influences but an absolute minimum. Even when, say, sixty percent of the variation in a trait is explainable by inheritance, it is still possible for environmental factors to account for one hundred percent of the variation, and they *must* account for *at least* forty percent. To understand this seemingly counterintuitive truth, one must get past the simple idea that "environmental" and "genetic" are completely different and thus must add up to one hundred percent. If, for example, the environment treats children with the genes for African American skin color and facial features differently, then those genes will—"really" and strongly—be a factor in poorer performance, yet at the same time, if the environment were to change and people with those genes were *not* treated differently, the impact of those very same genes would reduce to zero.

29. David M. Cutler & Edward L. Glaeser, Are ghettos good or bad?, *Quarterly Journal of Economics*, 1997, 827–872.
30. See, for example, chapters Thirteen and Fourteen of this book, as well as Lisbeth Schorr's *Within Our Reach* and *Common Purpose* and Jonathan Crane's *Social Programs That Really Work*.
31. See Chapter Thirteen.
32. Herrnstein and Murray, p. 404.
33. Herrnstein and Murray, p. 405.
34. Letter to the editor, *The New Republic*, November 28, 1994, p. 5.
35. Herrnstein and Murray, p. 298.
36. Herrnstein and Murray, p. 298.
37. Herrnstein and Murray, p. 299 (emphasis in original).
38. Reynolds Farley, Residential Segregation in Urbanized Areas of the United States: 1970: An Analysis of Social Class and Racial Differences, *Demography*, 1977, 14, 497–518. Quote on page 514.
39. Herrnstein and Murray, p. 287.
40. Herrnstein and Murray,. p. 390.
41. For a sample of what I am referring to here, see Chapter 22 of *The Bell Curve*.
42. Daryl Michael Scott, *Contempt and Pity: Social Policy and the Image of the Damaged Black Psyche, 1880–1996*, Chapel Hill, NC: University of North Carolina Press, 1997, p. 17.
43. Janet E. Helms, Why is there no study of cultural equivalence in standardized cognitive ability testing?, *American Psychologist*, 1992, 47, 1083–1101.
44. Helms, pp. 1086–1087.
45. Helms, p. 1096.
46. Helms, p. 1094.
47. See Tables 1 and 2 in Helms.
48. See, for example, Helms, pages 1090 and 1097.
49. See again Tables 1 and 2 in Helms.
50. For competing views on these questions see Molefe Asante, *The Afrocentric Idea*, Philadelphia: Temple University Press, 1987; Martin Bernal, *Black Athena: The Afrocentric Roots of Classical Civilization*, New Brunswick, NJ: Rutgers University Press, 1987; Mary Lefkowitz, *Not Out of Africa: How Afrocentrism Became an Excuse to Teach Myth As History*, New York: Basic Books, 1996; Mary Lefkowitz and G. M. Rogers (Eds.), *Black Athena Revisited*, Chapel Hill, NC: University of North Carolina Press, 1996.

51. Paul L. Wachtel, *The Poverty of Affluence: A Psychological Portrait of the American Way of Life*, New York: Free Press, 1983.

Chapter Six

1. Recent research by C. Neil Macrae, Galen Bodenhausen, Alan Milne, and their colleagues provides experimental support for this phenomenon (C. N. Macrae, G. V. Bodenhausen, A. B. Milne, J. Jetten Out of Mind but Back in Sight: Stereotypes on the Rebound, *Journal of Personality and Social Psychology*, 1994, 67, 808–817; C. N. Macrae, G. V. Bodenhausen, A. B. Milne, & V. Wheelis, On resisting the temptation for simplification: Counterintentional effects of stereotype suppression on social memory, *Social Cognition*, 1996, 14, 1–20). See also, D. M. Wegner, Ironic processes of mental control, *Psychological Review*, 1994, 101, 34–52; D. M. Wegner & R. Erber, The hyperaccessibility of suppressed thoughts, *Journal of Personality and Social Psychology*, 1992, 63, 903–912; D. M. Wegner, D. J. Schneider, S. Carter, & L. White, Paradoxical effects of thought suppression, *Journal of Personality and Social Psychology*, 1987, 53, 5–13.

2. Cited in Joel Kovel, *White Racism: A Psychohistory*, New York: Columbia University Press, 1984, p. 92.

3. Gordon Allport, *The Nature of Prejudice*, Reading, MA: Addison-Wesley, 1954.

4. Quoted in David G. Myers, *Social Psychology*, 4th edition, New York: McGraw-Hill, 1993, p. 386.

5. Elliot Aronson, *The Social Animal*, New York: W. H. Freeman, 1992, p. 312.

6. Melvin J. Lerner, *The Belief in a Just World: A Fundamental Delusion*, New York: Plenum, 1980.

7. See J. T. Jost and M. R. Banaji, The Role of Stereotyping in System-Justification and the Production of False Consciousness, *British Journal of Social Psychology*, 1994, 33, 1–17; and John T. Jost, Negative Illusions: Conceptual Clarification and Psychological Evidence Concerning False Consciousness, *Political Psychology*, 1995, 16, 397–424. See also, J. Sidanius, The Pychology of Group Conflict and the Dynamics of Oppression: A Social Dominance Perspective, in S. Iyengar & W. J. McGuire (eds.), *Explorations in Political Psychology*, Durham, NC: Duke University Press, 1993, pp. 183–219.

8. See, for example, William Ickes, Black and white interaction, *Journal of Personality and Social Psychology*, 1984, 47, 330–341; Patricia G. Devine, S. R. Evett, and K. A. Vasquez-Suson, Exploring the interpersonal dynamics of intergroup contact, in R. M. Sorrentino and E. T. Higgins (Eds.), *Handbook of Motivation and Cognition: The Interpersonal Context* (Vol 3), New York: Guilford, 1997; P. G. Devine, M. J. Monteith, J. R. Zuwerink, and A. J. Elliot, Prejudice with and without compunction, *Journal of Personality and Social Psychology*, 1991, 60, 817–830; Walter G. Stephan and Cookie W. Stephan. Intergroup anxiety, *Journal of Social Issues*, 1985, 41, 157–175; W. G. Stephan and C. W. Stephan, *Intergroup Relations*, Dubuque, IA: Brown and Benchmark, 1995.

9. James M. Jones, *Prejudice and Racism*, New York: McGraw-Hill, 1997, p. 320.

10. See, for example, Paul L. Wachtel, *Psychoanalysis, Behavior Therapy, and the Relational World*, Washington, DC: APA Books, 1997.

11. See Jones, 1997, op. cit.; Stephan & Stephan, 1985, op. cit.; Norman Miller & Marilynn B. Brewer (Eds.), *Groups in Contact: The Psychology of Desegregation*, Orlando, FL: Academic Press, 1984; S. T. Fiske & J. B. Ruscher, Negative interdependence

and prejudice: Whence the affect?, in D. M. Mackie & D. L. Hamilton (Eds.), *Affect, Cognition, and Stereotyping: Interaction Processes in Group Perception*, New York: Academic Press, 1992; S. L. Gaertner, J. A. Mann, J. F. Dovidio, A. J. Murrell, & M. Pomare, How does cooperation reduce intergroup bias?, *Journal of Personality and Social Psychology*, 1990, 59, 692–704.

12. Neil Altman, *The Analyst in the Inner City*, Hillsdale, NJ: Analytic Press, 1986, p. 59.

13. Altman, p. 127.

14. Derrick Bell, *Faces At the Bottom of the Well*, p. ix.

15. Kovel, *White Racism*, op. cit.

16. Frantz Fanon, *Black Skin, White Masks*, New York: Grove Press, 1967, pp. 188–189.

17. Kovel, pp. 65–67.

18. Kovel, p. 32.

19. Kovel, p. 80–81.

20. A related idea is suggested by Elizabeth Young-Bruehl in her book *The Anatomy of Prejudices* (Cambridge, MA: Harvard University Press, 1996). Young-Bruehl views racism toward blacks as reflecting "hysterical prejudice," by which she means "a prejudice that a person uses unconsciously to appoint a group to act out in the world forbidden sexual and sexually aggressive desires that the person has repressed (p. 34).

21. Kovel, p. 81–82.

22. Kovel, pp. 44–46.

23. For further discussion of the ways in which overly concrete and literal derivations from Freud's biological speculations have been misleadingly presented as radical critiques, see Paul L. Wachtel, Are we prisoners of the past?: Rethinking Freud, in *Tikkun*, 2, July–August 1987, pp. 23–27, 90–92.

24. Quoted in Studs Turkel, *Race*, New York: Doubleday, 1992, p. 11.

25. See, for example, John Dollard, *Caste and Class in a Southern Town*, New Haven: Yale University Press, 1987; and Bruno Bettelheim and Morris Janowitz, *Social Change and Prejudice*, New York: Free Press, 1964.

26. W. G. Stephan & D. Rosenfeld, Effects of desegregation on racial attitudes, *Journal of Abnormal and Social Psychology*, 1978, pp. 36, 795–804.

27. See, for excample, Thomas Ashby Wills, Downward comparison principles in social psychology, *Psychological Bulletin*, 1981, 90, 245–271; Wills, Similarity and self-esteem in downward comparison, in J. M. Suls & T. A. Wills (Eds.), *Social Comparison: Contemporary Theory and Research*, Hillsdale, NJ: Erlbaum, 1991, pp. 51–78; Wills, Downward Comparison As a Coping Mechanism, in C. R. Snyder & C. E. Ford (Eds.), *Coping With Negative Life Events: Clinical and Social Psychological Perspectives*, pp. 243–267; Joanne V. Wood, Theory and Research Concerning Social Comparisons of Personal Attributes, *Psychological Bulletin*, 1989, 106, 231–248; Shelly Taylor & Marcia Lobel, Social Comparison Activity Under Threat: Downward Evaluation and Upward Contacts, *Psychological Review*, 1989, 96, 569–575; Brenda Major, Anne Marie Sciacchitano, & Janet Crocker, In-Group vs. Out-Group Comparisons and Self-Esteem, *Personality and Social Psychology Bulletin*, 1993, 19, 711–721.

See also earlier work on the relation between low self-esteem or diminished social status and the development or intensification of prejudice, for example, J. Harding, H. Proshansky, B. Kutner, & I. Chein, Prejudice and ethnic relations, in

G. Lindzey & E. Aronson (Eds.), *Handbook of Social Psychology* (Vol. 5), Reading, MA: Addison-Wesley, 1969; J. W. Smedley & J. A. Bayton, Evaluative race-class stereotypes by race and perceived class of subjects, *Journal of Personality and Social Psychology*, 1978, 36, 530–535; D. G. Taylor, P. B. Sheatsley, & A. M. Greeley, Attitudes toward racial integration, *Scientific American*, 1978, 238 (6), 42–49.

28. Carl Hovland and Robert Sears, Minor studies of aggression: Correlation of lynchings with economic indices, *Journal of Psychology*, 1940, 9, 301–310. See also Neal E. Miller and R. Bugelski, Minor studies in aggression: The influence of frustrations imposed by the in-group on attitudes expressed by the out-group, *Journal of Psychology*, 1948, 25, 437–442; N. E. Miller, Theory and experiment relating psychoanalytic displacement to stimulus-response generalization, *Journal of Abnormal and Social Psychology*, 1948, 43, 155–178; Miller, Liberalization of basic S-R concepts: Extension to conflict behavior, motivation, and social learning, in S. Koch (Ed.), *Psychology: A Study of a Science*, Vol. 2, New York: McGraw-Hill, 1959, pp. 196–292; R. R. Sears, J. W. M. Whiting, V. Nowlis, & P. S. Sears, Some child-rearing antecedents of aggression and dependency in young children, *Genetic Psychology Monographs*, 1953, 47, 135–234. For a dissenting view, see A. Bandura and R. H. Walters, *Social Learning and Personality Development*, New York: Holt, Rinehart and Winston, 1963.

29. cf., Robert Lifton, *The Protean Self*, New York: Basic Books, 1993.

30. See, for example, S. Solomon, J. Greenberg, and T. Pyszczynski, A terror management theory of social behavior: The psychological functions of self-esteem and cultural worldviews, in M. P. Zanna (Ed.), *Advances in Experimental Social Psychology*, Vol. 24, San Diego, CA: Academic Press, 1991, pp. 93–159; and J. Greenberg, T. Pyszczynski, S. Solomon, A. Rosenblatt, S. Kirkland, M. Veeder, and D. Lyon, Evidence for terror management theory II: The effects of mortality salience on reactions to those who threaten or bolster the cultural worldview, *Journal of Personality and Social Psychology*, 1990, 58, 308–318.

31. See, for example, Mark Zanna, On the nature of prejudice, *Canadian Psychologist*, 1994, 35, 11–23.

32. Theodor Adorno, Else Frenkel-Brunswick, Daniel Levinson, and Nevitt Sanford, *The Authoritarian Personality*, New York: Harper, 1950.

33. Robert Altemeyer, Reducing Prejudice in Right-Wing Authoritarians, in M. P. Zanna & J. M. Olson (Eds.), *The Psychology of Prejudice: The Ontario Symposium*, Vol. 7, Hillsdale, NJ: Erlbaum Asociates, 1994, pp. 131–148.

34. See Jim Sidanius, The pychology of group conflict and the dynamics of oppression: A social dominance perspective, in S. Iyengar & W. J. McGuire (eds.), *Explorations in Political Psychology*, Durham, NC: Duke University Press, 1993, pp. 183–219; J. Sidanius, F. Pratto, & L. Bobo, Racism, conservatism, affirmative action, and intellectual sophistication: A matter of conservatism or group dominance?, *Journal of Personality and Social Psychology*, 1996, 70, 476–490; F. Pratto, J. Sidanius, L. M. Stallworth, & B. F. Malle, Social dominance orientation: A personality variable predicting social and political attitudes, *Journal of Personality and Social Psychology*, 1994, 67, 741–763.

35. Emphasis on unconscious aspects of prejudice and stereotyping is not limited to psychoanalytic writers. Recent examinations of the unconscious operation of prejudice and stereotyping from a cognitive point of view have been offered by

Banaji and Greenwald. See, for example, A. G. Greenwald & M. R. Banaji, Implicit social cognition: Attitudes, self-esteem, and stereotypes, *Psychological Review*, 1995, 102, 4–27; and M. R. Banaji & A. G. Greenwald, Implicit stereotyping and unconscious prejudice, in M. P. Zanna & J. M. Olson (Eds.), *The Psychology of Prejudice: The Ontario Symposium*, Vol. 7, Hillsdale, NJ: Erlbaum Asociates, 1994, pp. 55–76. See also, Patricia G. Devine, Stereotyping and prejudice: Their automatic and controlled components, *Journal of Personality and Social Psychology*, 1989, 56, 5–18.

36. See, for example, J. B. McConahay, B. B. Hardee, & V. Batts, Has racism declined in America? It depends upon who is asking and what is asked, *Journal of Conflict Resolution*, 1981, 25, 563–579.

37. H. Sigall, H. & R. Page, Current stereotypes: A little fading, a little faking, *Journal of Personality and Social Psychology*, 1971, 18, 247–255.

38. Carl Word, Mark Zanna, & Joel Cooper, The nonverbal mediation of self-fulfilling prophecies in interracial interaction, *Journal of Experimental Social Psychology*, 1974, 10, 109–120.

39. Ibid. See also, Bargh and Chen, 1997 (op. cit.) for further interesting findings bearing on how activation of racial stereotypes and attitudes can lead to action that makes likely self-fulfilling prophecies and self-perpetuating mutual perceptions.

40. Samuel L. Gaertner & John F. Dovidio, The aversive form of racism, in J. F. Dovidio & S. L. Gaertner (Eds.), *Prejudice, Discrimination, and Racism*, Orlando: Academic Press, 1986, pp. 61–89. Quote is from p. 62.

41. Gaertner & Dovidio, p. 63. See also the interesting research of W. Ickes (Black and White Interaction, *Journal of Personality and Social Psychology*, 1984, 47, 330–341) and James M. Jones's discussion (p. 231) of more recent studies similarly stressing the discomfort and anxiety that may be experienced by whites who fear that they are, or that they will be perceived as being, prejudiced.

42. Gaertner & Dovidio, p. 73.

43. Gaertner & Dovidio, p. 74–75.

44. It is, of course, possible that the subjects could have consciously articulated from the beginning that they resented a black's being in a supervisory position, and that they *consciously* decided not to help him. The overall context of Gaertner and Dovidio's study makes this interpretation highly unlikely. In any event, it leaves standing the differential response to blacks and whites in authority, a reaction that is at odds with the repudiation of racial discrimination and stereotyping that is now consciously endorsed by most white Americans.

45. David O. Sears, Symbolic racism, in Phyllis A. Katz & Dalmas A. Taylor (Eds.), *Eliminating Racism: Profiles in Controversy*, New York: Plenum, 1988, pp. 53–84. Quote is from p. 53.

46. D. R. Kinder and D. O. Sears, Prejudice and politics: Symbolic racism versus racial threats to the good life, *Journal of Personality and Social Psychology*, 1981, 40, 414–431, p. 416.

47. Sears, op. cit.

48. John B. McConahay, Self-interest versus racial attitudes as correlates of anti-busing attitudes in Louisville: Is it the buses or the blacks?, *Journal of Politics*, 1982, 44, 692–720. Quote is from p. 705.

49. John B. McConahay, Modern racism, ambivalence, and the modern racism scale, in

J. F. Dovidio & S. L. Gaertner (Eds.), *Prejudice, Discrimination, and Racism*, Orlando: Academic Press, 1986, pp. 91–126. Quote is from p. 99.

50. Paul M. Sniderman, Thomas Piazza, Philip E. Tetlock, and Ann Kendrick, The new racism, *American Journal of Political Science*, 1991, 35, 423–447. Quote from p. 423.

51. Since the comparison was done by comparing groups of respondents who received different, but otherwise equivalent, descriptions, the respondents were not "tipped off" as they would have been if they had *each* been confronted with questions about equivalent black and white individuals.

52. Sniderman, et al, pp. 432–433.

53. Philip E. Tetlock, Political psychology or politicized psychology: Is the road to scientific Hell paved with good moral intentions?, *Political Psychology*, 1994, 15, 509–529.

54. For further complexities in evaluating the concept of modern racism and the scale used to measure it, see James M. Jones, *Prejudice and Racism*, New York: McGraw-Hill, 1997, especially pp. 156–157.

55. Lawrence Bobo, Group conflict, prejudice, and the paradox of contemporary racial attitudes, in Phyllis A. Katz and Dalmas A. Taylor (Eds.), *Eliminating Racism: Profiles in Controversy*, New York: Plenum, 1988, pp. 85–114. Quote on p. 88–89.

56. Thomas F. Pettigrew, Racial change and social policy, *Annals of the American Academy of Political and Social Science*, 1979, 441, 114–131 (p. 119).

57. See in this connection Paul L. Wachtel, *Therapeutic Communication*, New York: Guilford, 1993.

Chapter Seven

1. See, for example, J. Norcross & M. Goldfried, *Handbook of Psychotherapy Integration*, New York: Basic Books, 1992, p. 207; J. R. Anderson, *Cognitive Psychology and Its Implications*, Third Edition, New York: W. H. Freeman, 1990, p. 134; N. Cantor, From thought to behavior: "Having" and "doing" in the study of personality and cognition, *American Psychologist*, 1990, 45, 735–750 (p. 736).

2. As cognitive psychologist John Flavell has put it, in an authoritative presentation of Piaget's theory (John Flavell, *The Developmental Psychology of Jean Piaget*, Princeton, NJ: Van Nostrand, 1963):

   However necessary it may be to describe assimilation and accommodation separately and sequentially, they should be thought of as simultaneous and indissociable as they operate in living cognition. Adaptation is a unitary event, and assimilation and accommodation are merely abstractions from this unitary reality. As in the case of food ingestion, the cognitive incorporation of reality always implies both an assimilation *to* structure and an accommodation *of* structure. To assimilate an event it is necessary at the same time to accommodate to it and vice versa. . . . [T]he balance between the two . . . can and does vary. . . . Some cognitive acts show a relative preponderance of the assimilative component; others seem heavily weighted towards accommodation. However, "pure" assimilation and "pure" accommodation nowhere obtain in cognitive life (pp. 48–49).

3. For a more detailed examination of the social and psychological implications of the concepts of assimilation and accommodation, see Paul L. Wachtel, *Action and Insight* (New York: Guilford, 1987), especially Chapter Two.

4. Indeed, still further complicating matters is the likelihood that there is at least some truth in *both* interpretations of the transaction. Conflict is a pervasive fact of psychological life, and our motives and attitudes are rarely singular.

5. Recall here the study by Word, Zanna, and Cooper discussed in Chapter Six, as well as the work of Ickes, of Devine and her colleagues, and of Stephan and Stephan, all cited in Chapter Six. For a review of how these mutual "confirmations" operate more generally in almost all interpersonal transactions, creating misleading truths out of perceptual falsehoods, see Paul L. Wachtel, Cyclical processes in psychopathology, *Journal of Abnormal Psychology*, 1994, 103, 51–54.

6. See Paul L. Wachtel, *Therapeutic Communication*, New York: Guilford, 1993; and *Psychoanalysis, Behavior Therapy, and the Relational World*, Washington, DC: American Psychological Association, 1997.

7. Brent A. Staples, *Parallel Time: Growing Up in Black and White*, New York: Pantheon, 1994.

8. See, for example, Susan Fiske and Shelly Taylor, *Social Cognition*, New York: McGraw-Hill, 1992; and P. G. Devine, D. L. Hamilton, and T. M. Ostrom (Eds.), *Social Cognition: Impact on Social Psychology*, San Diego, CA: Academic Press, 1994.

9. Jerome S. Bruner, *Beyond the Information Given: Studies in the Psychology of Knowing*, New York: Norton, 1973.

10. David L. Hamilton & Robert K. Gifford, Illusory correlation in interpersonal perception: A cognitive basis of stereotypic judgments, *Journal of Experimental Social Psychology*, 1976, 12, 392–407.

11. In principle, of course, the tendency to see infrequent behaviors as more characteristic of a minority does not necessarily imply that they will be *undesirable* behaviors. In a domain where positive traits are rarer than negative ones, it should be the *positive* traits that are overattributed to the minority. Hamilton and Gifford argue, however, that by and large, people engage more often in behavior that is positively regarded by those around them than in behavior that is disapproved, and thus the most likely consequence is that it will be undesirable or disapproved behaviors that are misperceived as overrepresented in the minority.

   A subsequent study by L. Z. McArthur and S. A. Friedman (Illusory correlation in impression formation: Variations in the shared distinctiveness effect as a function of the distinctive person's age, race, and sex, *Journal of Personality and Social Psychology*, 1980, 39, 615–624) suggested that when actual socially significant categories were the basis of groupings rather than abstract concepts such as "Group A" and "Group B," there are specific biases that modify the effects of infrequency alone. The more infrequent *desirable* behaviors of whites and *undesirable* behaviors of blacks were more likely to be associated. This suggests that the "distinctiveness based" illusory correlations described by Hamilton and Gifford tend, in actual social situations, to interact with the "expectancy based" illusory correlations discussed next.

12. For a comprehensive review of the phenomenon, see B. Mullen & C. Johnson, Distinctiveness-based illusory correlations and stereotyping: A meta-analytic integration, *British Journal of Social Psychology*, 1990, 29, 11–28. For a discussion of the varying interpretations of the phenomenon, see K. Fiedler, The tricky nature of skewed frequency tables: An information loss account of distinctiveness-based illusory correlations, *Journal of Personality and Social Psychology*, 1991, 60, 24–36; E.

R. Smith, Illusory correlation in a simulated exemplar-based memory, *Journal of Experimental Social Psychology*, 1991, 27, 107–123; M. Schaller & A. Maass, Illusory correlation and social categorization: Toward an integation of motivational and cognitive factors in stereotype formation, *Journal of Personality and Social Psychology*, 1989, 56, 709–721.

13. See, for example, Galen V. Bodenhausen, Stereotypic biases in social decision making and memory: Testing process models of stereotype use, *Journal of Personality and Social Psychology*, 1988, 55, 726–737.

14. For more detail on each of these aspects of the impact of stereotypes, see D. L. Hamilton, S. J. Stroesner, and D. M. Driscoll, Social Cognition and the Study of Stereotyping, in P. G. Devine, D. L. Hamilton, and T. M. Ostrom (Eds.), *Social Cognition: Impact on Social Psychology*, San Diego, CA: Academic Press, 1994, pp. 291–321.

15. Birt L. Duncan, Differential social perception and attribution of intergroup violence: Testing the lower limits of stereotyping of blacks, *Journal of Personality and Social Psychology*, 1976, 34, 590–598.

16. See, for example, H. A. Sagar and J. W. Schofield, Racial and behavioral cues in black and white children's perceptions of ambiguously aggressive acts, *Journal of Personality and Social Psychology*, 1980, 39, 599–614.

17. Patricia G. Devine, Stereotyping and prejudice: Their automatic and controlled components, *Journal of Personality and Social Psychology*, 1989, 56, 5–18.

18. See, for example, Dinesh D'Souza, *The End of Racism.*

19. See, for example, David L. Hamilton & Tina K. Trolier, Stereotypes and stereotyping: An overview of the cognitive approach, in J. F. Dovidio & S. L. Gaertner (Eds.), *Prejudice, Discrimination, and Racism*, Orlando, FL: Academic Press, 1986, pp. 127–163.

20. Hamilton & Trolier, pp. 129–130.

21. See Shelly E. Taylor, A categorization approach to stereotyping, in D. L. Hamilton (Ed.), *Cognitive Processes in Stereotyping and Intergroup Behavior*, Hillsdale, NJ: Erlbaum, 1981, pp. 83–114; and Shelly E. Taylor & H. Falcone, Cognitive bases of stereotyping: The relationship between categorization and prejudice, *Personality and Social Psychology Bulletin*, 1982, 426–432.

22. Hamilton & Trolier, p. 131.

23. Schaller & Maass, op. cit., p. 710. See also the classic work of Henri Tajfel (e.g., Cognitive aspects of prejudice, *Journal of Social Issues*, 1969, 25, 79–97; and *Differentiation Between Social Groups: Studies in the Social Psychology of Intergroup Relations*. London: Academic Press, 1978) and Musafer Sherif (e.g., *In Common Predicament: Social Psychology of Intergroup Conflict and Cooperation*, Boston: Houghton Mifflin, 1966; and M. Sherif, O. J. Harvey, J. B. White, W. R. Hood, and C. W. Sherif, *Intergroup Conflict and Cooperation: The Robbers Cave Experiment*, Norman, OK: University of Oklahoma Press, 1961.

24. See, for example, P. W. Linville, P. Salovey, & G. W. Fischer, Stereotyping and perceived distribution of social characteristics: An application to ingroup-outgroup perception, in J. F. Dovidio & S. L. Gaertner (Eds.), *Prejudice, Discrimination and Racism*, Orlando, FL: Academic Press, 1986, pp. 165–208; P. W. Linville, G. W. Fischer, & P. Salovey, Perceived distribution of the characteristics of ingroup and outgroup members, *Journal of Personality and Social Psychology*, 1989, 57, 165–188; C.

M. Judd & B. Park, Outgroup homogeneity: Judgments of variability at the individual and group level, *Journal of Personality and Social Psychology*, 1988, 54, 778–788; C. M. Judd, C. S. Ryan, & B. Park, Accuracy in the judgment of in-group and out-group variability, *Journal of Personality and Social Psychology*, 1991, 61, 366–379; B. Park & C. M. Judd, Measures and models of perceived group variability, *Journal of Personality and Social Psychology*, 1990, 59, 173–191; C. M. Park & M. Rothbart, Perception of out-group homogeneity and levels of social categorization: Memory for the subordinate attributes of in-group and out-group membership, *Journal of Personality and Social Psychology*, 1982, 42, 1051–1068.

25. Hamilton & Trolier, p. 132–3.

26. See, for example, Hamilton & Trolier, op. cit. See also, with specific reference to racial and ethnic prejudice, Thomas F. Pettigrew, The ultimate attribution error: Extending Allport's cognitive analysis of prejudice, *Personality and Social Psychology Bulletin*, 1979, 5, 461–476.

27. See, for example, Christopher Jencks et al., *Inequality*, New York; Basic Books, 1972.

28. L. Ross, The intuitive psychologist and his shortcomings: Distortions in the attribution process, in L. Berkowitz (Ed.), *Advances in Experimental Social Psychology*, Vol. 10, New York: Academic Press, 1977, pp. 174–221.

29. James W. Vander Zanden, *Social Psychology*, New York: Random House, 1987, p. 482.

30. Leonard I. Pearlin, Group attachments and attitudes toward Negroes, *Social Forces*, 1954, 47–50.

31. James M. Fendrich, Perceived reference group support: Racial attitudes and overt behavior, *American Sociological Review*, 1967, 960–969.

32. R. C. Gardner, Stereotypes as consensual beliefs, in M. P. Zanna & J. M. Olson (Eds.), *The Psychology of Prejudice: The Ontario Symposium*, Vol. 7, Hillsdale, NJ: Erlbaum Asociates, 1993, pp. 3–4.

33. Ibid, p. 19.

34. James M. Jones, op. cit., p. 196.

35. See also, in this connection, C. Stangor, L. A. Sullivan, & T. E. Ford, Affective and cognitive determinants of prejudice, *Social Cognition*, 1991, 9, 359–380.

Chapter Eight

1. Paulette Moore Hines and Nancy Boyd-Franklin, Black families, in M. McGoldrick, J. K. Pearce, & J. Giordano (Eds.), *Ethnicity and Family Therapy*, New York; Guilford, 1982, p. 84.

2. Hines & Boyd-Franklin, p. 86.

3. Andrew Billingsley, *Climbing Jacob's Ladder: The Enduring Legacy of African-American Families*, New York: Simon & Schuster, 1992, p. 21. The exact proportions have changed slightly since Billingsley's summary, but the essential picture he describes remains the same.

4. Carol Stack, *All Our Kin: Strategies for Survival in a Black Community*, New York: Harper & Row, 1975.

5. Billingsley, p. 31. For further discussion of the strengths that black families bring to bear in addressing the stresses and challenges they confront, see also Nancy Boyd-Franklin, *Black Families in Therapy*, New York: Guilford, 1989; Robert Staples and Leanor B. Johnson, *Black Families at the Crossroads: Challenges and Prospects*, San Francisco: Jossey-Bass, 1993; Robert J. Taylor, James S. Jackson, and Linda M. Chat-

ters (Eds.), *Family Life in Black America*, Thousand Oaks, CA: Sage, 1997.

6. See, for example, Robert Boynton, The new intellectuals, *Atlantic Monthly*, March 1995, pp. 53–70; Jervis Anderson, The public intellectual, *The New Yorker*, January 17, 1994, pp. 39ff; Michael Alan Berube, Public academy, *The New Yorker*, January 9, 1995, pp. 73–80.

7. See, for example, Vonnie C. McLoyd, The impact of economic hardship on black families and children: Psychological distress, parenting, and socioemotional development, *Child Development*, 1990, 61, 311–346; Alvin F. Poussaint, The mental health status of black Americans, 1983, in Dorothy S. Ruiz (Ed.), *Handbook of Mental Health and Mental Disorder Among Black Americans*, New York: Greenwood Press, 1990, pp. 17–52; Joycelyn Landrum-Brown, Black mental health and racial oppression, in Dorothy S. Ruiz (Ed.), *Handbook of Mental Health and Mental Disorder Among Black Americans*, New York: Greenwood Press, 1990, pp. 11–13; G. Duncan & J. Brooks-Gunn, *The Consequences of Growing Up Poor*, New York: Russell Sage Foundation, 1997; Joy Osofsky, The effects of exposure to violence on young children, *American Psychologist*, 1995, 50, 782–788.

8. See, for example, David J. Garrow, On race, it's Thomas v. an old ideal, *New York Times*, July 2, 1995, Section 4, p. 1.

9. Reginald L. Jones (Ed.), *Black Psychology*, Third Edition, Berkeley: Cobb & Henry Publishers, 1991, p. 3.

10. Joseph L. White, Toward a black psychology, in *Reginald L. Jones*, Third Edition, p. 6.

11. Quoted in Richard Kluger, *Simple Justice*, New York: Knopf, 1975, p. 318.

12. See especially William Julius Wilson's *The Truly Disadvantaged* for a detailed examination of the implications of this ironic turn of events.

13. William E. Cross, Jr., *Shades of Black: Diversity in African-American Identity*, Philadelphia: Temple University Press, 1991, p. 148.

14. Ibid., p. 158–159.

15. Depicting the identity of individuals who have "not yet discovered their Blackness," black college students in Cross's influential 1976 study of the Negro-to-Black Conversion Experience stressed themes of "shame in relation to being a member of the Negro race, limited knowledge of Black History, the desire to be disassociated from the Negro race and striving for social acceptance on terms dictated by white society." (Cross, "Stereotypic and Non-Stereotypic Images Associated With the Negro-to-Black Conversion Experience: An Empirical Analysis," Doctoral Dissertation, Princeton University, 1976, p. 110.)

16. Cross, *Shades of Black*, p. 35.

17. Ibid., p. 17.

18. R. Kluger, *Simple Justice*, New York: Knopf, 1975. See, for example, p. 397.

19. Still another factor that must be taken into account in understanding the implications of the Clarks' studies is that they were conducted on rather young children, yet they were widely interpreted as bearing on the racial attitudes and self-esteem of black adults as well. In fact, in those analyses that separated out the very light-skinned black children, for whom (as per above) the stimuli were ambiguous, whatever tendency toward "self-rejection" might be seen as evident in the Clarks' data on six-year-olds has disappeared in their sample of seven-year-olds. See K. B. Clark and M. P. Clark, Emotional factors in racial identification and preference in Negro

children, *Journal of Negro Education*, 1950, 19, 341–350. See Table 9, p. 346.

20. Kenneth B. Clark & Mamie P. Clark, Skin color as a factor in racial identification of Negro pre-school children, *Journal of Social Psychology*, 1940, 11, 159–169. Quotation from p. 168.

21. See W. C. Banks, White preference in blacks: A paradigm in search of a phenomenon, *Psychological Bulletin*, 1976, 83, 1179–1186.

22. Several points are important to note in this regard. First, it is necesary to notice that the white tendency is being inappropriately employed as the standard in such interpretations. Deviations from the *white* tendency in these studies—to prefer one's own kind exclusively—are taken as inherently pathological. Second, not only is it highly questionable to take as a universal standard the inclinations of a particular group (in this case whites), but one might also view these data as at least raising questions about the appropriateness of *white* behavior. That is, is it really superior and desirable consistently to choose on the basis of race, or is it a healthier response to find race an *irrelevant* consideration? The black subjects, after all, did not "reject" their own kind; they simply did not as preponderantly choose it. Finally, the orientation of black children toward symbols of *both* white and black culture seems to reflect a bicultural orientation common among blacks, who live both in the larger, white-dominated society and in a separate culture of their own (see, for example, Cross, p. 58, and Gerald Early [Ed.], *Lure and Loathing*). This is at once a source of strength and a powerful stress, a matter that I shall have occasion to consider in more detail in the next chapter.

23. Cross, op. cit., p. 174.

24. Ibid., p. 35.

25. Ibid., p. 37.

26. Joseph L. White, Toward a black psychology, in Reginald L. Jones (Ed.), *Black Psychology*, Second Edition. New York: Harper & Row, 1981. Pp. 5–12. Quoted on page 5.

27. See Paul Wachtel, *Therapeutic Communication*, op. cit.

28. See, for example, Morris Rosenberg, Carmi Schooler, Carrie Schoenback, and Florence Rosenberg, Global self-esteem and specific self-esteem: Different concepts, different outcomes, *American Sociological Review*, 1995, 60, 141–156.

29. Cross, *Shades of Black*, op. cit.

30. Ibid.

31. People differ in the degree to which their self-esteem is dependent on the perceived status of the group to which they belong and in the degree to which group membership is central to their identity. See R. Luhtanen and J. Crocker, A collective self-esteem scale: Self-evaluation of one's social identity, *Personality and Social Psychology Bulletin*, 1992, 18, 302–318. See also, M. B. Brewer, The social self: On being the same and different at the same time, *Personality and Social Psychology Bulletin*, 1991, 17, 475–482.

32. Adelbert H. Jenkins, *Psychology and African Americans*, Boston: Allyn & Bacon, p. 33 (emphasis added).

33. Jennifer Crocker and Brenda Major, Social stigma and self-esteem: The self-protective properties of stigma, *Psychological Review*, 1989, 96, 608–630. See also, Thomas Ashby Wills, Downward comparison principles in social psychology, *Psychological Bulletin*, 1981, 90, 245–271; Wills, Similarity and self-esteem in down-

ward comparison, in J. M. Suls & T. A. Wills (Eds.), *Social Comparison: Contemporary Theory and Research* (pp. 51–78), Hillsdale, NJ: Erlbaum, 1991; Wills, Downward comparison as a coping mechanism, in C. R. Snyder & C. E. Ford (Eds.), *Coping With Negative Life Events: Clinical and Social Psychological Perspectives* (pp. 243–267), New York: Plenum Press, 1987; Joanne V. Wood, Theory and research concerning social comparisons of personal attributes, *Psychological Bulletin,* 1989, 106, 231–248; Shelly Taylor & Marcia Lobel, Social comparison activity under threat: Downward evaluation and upward contacts, *Psychological Review,* 1989, 96, 569–575; Brenda Major, Anne Marie Sciacchitano, & Janet Crocker, In-group vs. out-group comparisons and self-esteem, *Personality and Social Psychology Bulletin,* 1993, 19, 711–721.

34. Consider again in this regard the findings of Claude Steele on stereotype anxiety discussed in Chapter Five.

35. All quotes in this paragraph are from Cross, pp. 69–70.

36. It should go without saying that the reverse is also decidedly true: without addressing our society's fundamental economic and political inequalities, efforts to address self-doubts and the specific deficits associated with them are also doomed to fail.

37. See, for example, Charles D. Spielberger & Peter R. Vagg, *Test Anxiety: Theory, Assessment, and Treatment,* Washington, DC: Taylor & Francis, 1995; Marty Sapp, *Test Anxiety: Applied Research, Assessment, and Treatment,* Lanham, MD: University Press of America, 1993; Irwin G. Sarason & Barbara R. Sarason (Eds.), *Cognitive Interference: Theories, Methods, and Findings,* Mahwah, NJ: Erlbaum, 1996. See also Seymour Sarason's classic work, *Anxiety in Elementary School Children,* New York: Wiley, 1960, as well as the work of Claude Steele cited above (Steele, 1997; Steele & Aronson, 1995).

Chapter Nine

1. See, for example, Douglas Massey & Nancy Denton, *American Apartheid: Segregation and the Making of the Underclass,* Cambridge, MA: Harvard University Press, 1993.

   Authors such as Stephan and Abigail Thernstrom (*America in Black and White: One Nation Indivisible,* Cambridge, MA: Harvard University Press, 1997) challenge the characterization that we live in separate worlds, mainly by focusing on how much our separateness has diminished over time rather than on how much remains. But in many aspects of our national life, optimism does not entail seeing the cup as half full rather than half empty but rather rejoicing that it has any water at all. Studies, for example, that seem to indicate that many blacks and whites do have a single friend of the other race—and even those findings are methodologically suspect—do not exactly signal the end of racial divisions. I do not dispute that in certain respects things are improving. Indeed, it will be apparent to the reader that I regard characterizations of our society as irredeemably racist or unable to assimilate blacks into our national life as wrong and destructive. But there should be little question that we have a *very* long way to go before we are truly "one nation indivisible."

2. Gerald E. Early, *Lure and Loathing: Essays on Race, Identity, and the Ambivalence of Assimilation,* New York: Viking Penguin, 1993, p. xvii.

3. W. E. B. Du Bois, *The Souls of Black Folk* (1903), in *Three Negro Classics,* New York: Avon Books, 1965, pp. 214–215.

4. See, for example, Drew S. Days, III, Brown Blues: rethinking the integrative ideal, *Philosophy and Public Policy,* Vol. 17, No. 4 (Fall 1997), pp. 8–14. See also, Neil A.

Lewis, For black scholars wedded to prism of race, new and separate goals, *New York Times*, May 5, 1997, p. B9; and Peter Applebome, Schools see re-emergence of "Separate but Equal," *New York Times*, April 8, 1997, p. A10.

5. *Compact Edition of the Oxford English Dictionary*, Oxford: Oxford University Press, 1971.

6. The conflict is particularly vividly illustrated in Gerald Early's edited book, *Lure and Loathing: Essays on Race, Identity, and the Ambivalence of Assimilation* (New York: Penguin, 1993), in which twenty successful African American writers reflect on their growing up. The paths they chose span a wide range, but few of them did not encounter some degree of conflict along the way between their aspirations for success in the larger society and their identifications with fellow African Americans.

7. Henry Louis Gates, Jr., *Thirteen Ways of Looking at a Black Man*, New York: Random House, 1997, p. xvii, (emphasis in original).

8. Ibid. p. xviii.

9. Ibid., p. xvii (emphasis in original).

10. Ibid., p. xvii.

11. See, for example, Molefe Asante, *The Afrocentric Idea*, Philadelphia: Temple University Press, 1987; Wade Nobles, African Philosophy: Foundations of Black Psychology, in R. L. Jones (Ed.), *Black Psychology*, Berkeley: Cobb & Henry, 1991, pp. 47–64.

12. For a social psychological analysis of related themes, see Marilyn B. Brewer, The social self: On being the same and different at the same time, *Personality and Social Psychology Bulletin*, 1991, 17, 475–482.

13. Franklin's comments were reported in the June 1995 issue of *The APA Monitor* (p. 32). See Erin Burnette, "Black Males Retrieve a Noble Heritage."

14. James P. Comer & Alvin F. Poussaint, *Raising Black Children*, New York: Plume, 1992, p. 302–303.

15. Comer & Poussaint, p. 396.

16. See, for example, Geneva Smitherman, Talkin' and testifyin': Black English and the black experience, in R. L. Jones (Ed.), *Black Psychology*, Berkeley: Cobb & Henry, 1991, pp. 249–268. See also Philip A. Luedsdorff (Ed.), *Linguistic Perspectives in Black English*, Regensberg, Germany: Verlag Hans Carl, 1975; Robbins Burling, *English in Black and White*, New York: Holt, Rinehart & Winston, 1973; J.L. Dillard, *Black English*, New York: Random House, 1972; William Labov, *Language in the Inner City*, Philadelphia: University of Pennsylvania Press, 1997.

17. I am not entering here the still ongoing debates within the discipline of linguistics over this question. Every academic discipline has its abstruse, technical debates, and these often hinge not on the nature of the phenomenon but on conformity to definitions that are conventions of the discipline. Over time, the two not infrequently come to be confused.

18. A similar dynamic may be seen in England, where class accents have extraordinary power, and where individuals seeking upward mobility may feel phony taking on the accent of a higher class. Here too the problem arises because the imitation of the "right" way to pronounce a word has different implications if one is learning a new language than if one is imitating another (higher status) group's way of pronouncing one's own.

It is true that in America, too, individuals may struggle with how much to change their class or regional accents in order to get ahead. But it should be apparent that both the loyalty conflicts and the price that is paid if they do *not* change their way of speaking are much greater for African Americans.

19. See, for example, J. R. Kleugel and E. R. Smith, *Beliefs About Inequality: Americans' View of What Is and What Ought to Be*, New York: Aldine de Gruyteer, 1986; and J. Sidanius & F. Pratto, The inevitability of oppression and the dynamics of social dominance, in P. Sniderman & P. E. Tetlock (Eds.), *Prejudice, Politics, and Race in America Today*, Stanford, CA: Stanford University Press, 1995. See also, William Julius Wilson, *When Work Disappears*, New York; Knopf, 1996.

20. Jennifer Crocker and Brenda Major, Social stigma and self-esteem: The self-protective properties of stigma, *Psychological Review*, 1989, 96, 608–630. Quotation from p. 624.

21. Ogbu, 1986, op. cit., pp. 46–47.

22. Jason W. Osborne, 1995, op. cit.; Osborne, 1997, op. cit.

23. Steele, op. cit.; Steele & Aronson, op. cit.

24. Laurence Steinberg, Ethnicity and Achievement, *American Educator*, Summer 1996, p. 47.

25. Steele, 1997, op. cit. See also Ogbu, op. cit.

26. Clark, *Dark Ghetto*, p. 19–20. Clark's conclusions dovetail with a variety of more recent findings on self-esteem, self-protection, and avoidance among African Americans. See again, for example, Jennifer Crocker & Brenda Major, Social stigma and self-esteem: The self-protective properties of stigma, *Psychological Review*, 1989, 96, 608–630; Jason Osborne, Race and Academic Disidentification, *Journal of Educational Psychology*, 1997, 89, 728–735; Claude M. Steele & Joshua Aronson, Stereotype threat and the intellectual performance of African Americans, *Journal of Personality and Social Psychology*, 1995, 69, 797–811; and Claude M. Steele, A threat in the air: How stereotypes shape intellectual identity and performance, *American Psychologist*, 1997, 52, 613–629.

27. Douglas Massey & Nancy Denton, *American Apartheid: Segregation and the Making of the Underclass*, Cambridge, MA: Harvard University Press, 1993, pp. 167–168.

28. See again, for example, the discussion of Janet Helms's work in Chapter Five.

29. To be sure, that separation is not simply their own doing. As I will discuss in Chapter Eleven, white America meets them more than halfway in maintaining the boundaries that keep us separate.

30. Anderson J. Franklin, The invisibility syndrome, *The Family Therapy Networker*, July/August, 1993, p. 34.

31. See, for example, Hacker, *Two Nations*, pp. 141–146; and Laurence Steinberg, *Beyond the Classroom*, New York: Simon & Schuster, 1996.

32. Richard D. Kahlenberg, *The Remedy: Class, Race, and Affirmative Action*, New York: Basic Books, 1997, p. 66.

33. Kahlenberg, p. 67. See also a variety of other comparisons on pages 240–241.

34. Kahlenberg, p. 65.

Chapter Ten

1. Fox Butterfield, Crime fighting's about-face, *New York Times*, Sunday, January 19, 1997, Section 4, p. 1.

2. This is not to deny the very real impact of political and economic power exercised

to the detriment of those who have less of both. That impact is discussed throughout this book. But we will not get far with one-directional, one-dimensional accounts
in which the behavior induced by these injustices in its victims is erased from view
or in which its impact in perpetuating the injustices themselves is denied.

3. See, for example, Lynne Duke, Confronting violence: African American conferees
look inward, *Washington Post*, January 8, 1994, p. A1.

4. For further discussion of the impact of neighborhood violence on children, see J.
Garbarino, N. Dubrow, K. Kostelny, & C. Pardo, *Children in Danger: Coping With the
Consequence of Community Violence*, San Francisco: Jossey-Bass, 1992. See also, B.
Groves, B. Zuckerman, S. Marans, & D. Cohen, Silent victims: Children who wit-
ness violence, *Journal of the American Medical Association*, 1993, 269, 262–264; and
Joy D. Osofsly, The effects of exposure to violence on young children, *American Psy-
chologist*, 1995, 50, 782–788.

5. I certainly do not intend to suggest that violence is the only source of the test differences. Poverty, racism, and concrete matters of school funding clearly play an
enormous role. Middle-class kids not only can study without hearing gunfire; they
usually have a room to themselves while doing so. My point is simply that pervasive
crime is a significant compounding factor, adding to the sense of living in abandoned territory and of feeling unprotected and with diminished hope for the future.

6. Michael Tonry, *Malign Neglect: Race, Crime, and Punishment in America*, New York:
Oxford University Press, 1995, p. 128.

7. Randall Kennedy, *Race, Crime, and the Law*, New York: Pantheon, 1997, p. 22.

8. Whites too, of course, are part of the drug trade, but based on rates of arrest or
incarceration, a considerably smaller percentage of whites are street level dealers.
See, for example, Michael Tonry, *Malign Neglect: Race, Crime, and Punishment in
America*, New York: Oxford University Press, 1995

9. Dinesh D'Souza, in his book *The End of Racism*, does seem to make such a claim.
It should be apparent to the reader that my own views differ radically from
D'Souza's, which seem to me not only insensitive and morally obtuse, but at times
sophomoric.

10. Ellis Cose, *The Rage of a Privileged Class*, New York: Harper, 1993, pp. 12–13.

11. The distinction I am drawing here should not be taken to sanction prejudice toward
poorer and less educated blacks, most of whom *also* are not dangerous criminals.
Rather, I am describing the way the interactions of prejudices with (selectively perceived) realities make crime a factor that contributes to maintaining prejudices even
toward the individuals Cose is discussing.

12. Cose, p. 107.

13. See, for example, my *Action and Insight* or *Psychoanalysis, Behavior Therapy, and the
Relational World*.

14. See Paul L. Wachtel, *The Poverty of Affluence: A Psychological Portrait of the American Way of Life*, New York: Free Press, 1983.

15. *Hobbling a Generation: African-American Males in the Criminal Justice System of America's Cities: Baltimore, Maryland*, Washington, DC: National Center on Institutions
and Alternatives, 1992.

16. Bruce Wright, *Black Robes, White Justice: Why Our Legal System Doesn't Work for
Blacks*, New York: Lyle Stuart, 1987, p. 65.

17. Wright, p. 65.

18. The name of the attorney has been changed in order to protect my friend.

19. Jerome G. Miller, *Search and Destroy: African-American Males in the Criminal Justice System*, New York: Cambridge University Press, 1996, p. 126. Miller, it should be noted, views this example in a much more positive light than I do. Rather than seeing it as a faulty identification of law abiding blacks with those who victimize and stigmatize them, Miller sees these actions as a healthy rebellion against police injustice.

20. Jeffrey Rosen, One angry woman, *The New Yorker*, February 24 and March 3, 1997 (combined issue), pp. 54–64.

21. Ellis Cose (Ed.), *The Darden Dilemma*, New York: Harper Collins, 1997.

22. Ibid., pp. xiii–xiv

23. Ibid., pp. xiv–xv.

24. David Baldus, George Woodworth, and Charles A. Pulanski, Jr., *Equal Justice and the Death Penalty: A Legal and Empirical Analysis*, Boston: Northeastern University Press, 1990.

25. Marvin Wolfgang and Marc Reidel, Race, judicial discretion, and the death penalty," *Annals of the American Academy of Political and Social Science*, 1973, 407, 119–133. These results, it should be noted, held even after correcting for a host of variables that might account for the results on another basis.

26. Miller, p. 33

27. In further attempting to minimize the extent to which black street crime involves violence or the threat of violence, Miller cites other figures that move from the realm of minimization to outright distortion. As evidence for his claim that black defendants are routinely charged with more serious offenses than is merited, he cites a variety of figures that point to most arrests for aggravated assault ending up being reduced to misdemeanors and/or not resulting in felony convictions. In this, Miller conveniently ignores the role of plea bargaining in the way our system works. The reality is—and Miller assuredly knows this—that in many instances prosecutors know full well that a defendant has committed a particular crime but agree to charge him with a lesser offense because they are not sure, in the adversarial process that constitutes a trial, that a jury will convict on the basis of the evidence that can be presented in court.

    We do need to maintain high standards of evidence to ensure that innocent people are not convicted. But failure to garner such evidence, especially in light of many witnesses' fear of retaliation, should not be taken, outside the courtroom, as evidence that the person did *not* commit the crime. In hundreds of thousands of instances every year, plea bargaining entails *under*charging perpetrators, charging them with a lesser offense than they have actually committed. This may well be the price we must pay as a society to achieve a goal that Miller and I both affirm: to ensure that defendants are not convicted on the basis of racial stereotypes rather than convincing evidence. But it is disingenuous of Miller to take these figures—a product of the compromises necessary to meld often conflicting goals of protecting defendants and ascertaining truth—as indications that the initial charge was unfairly excessive.

28. Miller, p. 161.

29. Once again, it is important to distinguish the emphasis here on an element of reality behind white fears of black crime (offered in the service of finding more effective

means of addressing the deeper injustices and inequalities that continue to plague us) from the smug defense of the status quo by writers such as Dinesh D'Souza.

30. Hacker, *Two Nations*, p. 181.

31. *Hobbling a Generation: African-American Males in the District of Columbia's Criminal Justice System*, Washington, DC: National Center on Institutions and Alternatives, March 1992.

32. Miller, pp. 100–101.

33. Jane H. Lii, When the saviors are seen as sinners, *New York Times*, May 18, 1997, Section 13 ("The City"), p. 1.

34. Quoted in Jerome Miller, *Search and Destroy*, pp. 97–98.

35. See, for example, Tonry, *Malign Neglect* and Miller, *Search and Destroy*.

36. Tonry, op. cit.; Miller, op. cit.

37. Tonry, op. cit., p. 130.

38. Wilson, *The Truly Disadvantaged*.

39. Quoted in the *New York Times*, September 28, 1997, Section 4, Page 1.

40. See, for example, George L. Kelling and Catherine M. Coles, *Fixing Broken Windows: Restoring Order and Reducing Crime in Our Communities*, New York: Free Press, 1996.

41. See, for example, Malcolm Gladwell, The tipping point, *The New Yorker*, June 3, 1996, pp. 32–38; and Jonathan Crane, The epidemic theory of ghettos, *American Journal of Sociology*, 1991, 96, 1226–1259; and The epidemic theory of ghettos and its policy Implications, *Policy Forum*, 1992, Vol. 5, No. 3.

42. Kelling and Cole, pp. 149–150.

43. Kelling and Cole, p. 253.

44. Tonry, p. 135.

45. Tonry, p. 134.

46. See, for example, Tonry, pp. 31–39.

47. Tonry, p. 46.

48. See, for example, Miller, *Search and Destroy*, pp. 119–125; and Tonry, *Malign Neglect*, pp. 173–179.

49. See, for example, Tonry, pp. 173–179.

50. See the *New York Times*, September 17, 1994, p. A1.

51. Quoted in Miller, p. 220.

52. Elijah Anderson, The code of the streets, *The Atlantic Monthly*, March 1995. See also, Anderson, *Streetwise: Race, Class, and Change in an Urban Community*, Chicago: University of Chicago Press, 1990.

53. Richard G. Majors and Janet Billson, *Cool Pose: The Dilemmas of Black Manhood in America*, New York: Lexington Books, 1992.

Chapter Eleven

1. Reynolds Farley, Residential Segregation in Urbanized Areas of the United States: 1970: An analysis of social class and racial differences, *Demography*, 1977, 14, 497–518. Quote on page 514.

2. Reynolds Farley and Walter R. Allen, *The Color Line and the Quality of Life in America*, New York: Russell Sage Foundation, 1987, p. 141.

3. Farley & Allen, pp. 148, 150.

4. Roderick J. Harrison & Claudette E. Bennett, Racial and ethnic diversity, in

Reynolds Farley (Eds.), *State of the Union*, New York: Russell Sage, 1995, p. 162.

5. T. F. Pettigrew, New black-white patterns: How best to conceptualize them?, *American Sociological Review*, 1985, 11, pp. 329–346, 335.

6. Douglas Massey & Nancy Denton, *American Apartheid: Segregation and the Making of the Underclass*, Cambridge, MA: Harvard University Press, 1993, p. 11.

7. Ibid., p. 11.

8. Ibid., pp. 19–20.

9. Ibid., p. 30.

10. For a good summary of the evidence for the various forms of subtle and not so subtle coercion and racial steering noted briefly here, see Massey & Denton, especially pp. 96–109.

11. See, for example, Monte Williams, Blast hits car after man sells to blacks, *New York Times*, May 15, 1997, p. B12; Bob Herbert, Mounting a war on bias, *New York Times*, January 15, 1998, p. A21. See also Massey & Denton.

12. Massey & Denton, p. 8 (emphasis added).

13. See also, for example, Elijah Anderson, Elliot Liebow, Lee Rainwater, Kenneth Clark, Carol Stack, John Ogbu, Richard Majors & Janet Billson, and Terry Williams & William Kornblum.

14. Elijah Anderson, *Streetwise: Race, Class, and Change in an Urban Community*, Chicago: University of Chicago Press, 1990, pp. 177–178 (emphasis added).

15. Richard Majors and Janet M. Billson, *Cool Pose: The Dilemmas of Black Manhood in America*, New York: Lexington Books, 1992, p. 5.

16. Majors & Billson, p. 29.

17. Majors & Billson, p. 2.

18. Anderson, p. 94.

19. William Julius Wilson has written particulary persuasively and authoritatively about the impact of "concentration effects" on the behavior and attitudes of inner-city residents. See his *The Truly Disadvantaged* (University of Chicago Press, 1987). See also, Robert Havemen and Barbara Wolfe, *Succeeding Generations: On the Effects of Investments in Children* (New York: Russell Sage Foundation, 1994), whose research indicates that, controlling for all other factors, if children who grew up in a "bad" neighborhood were to grow up in a "good" neighborhood, the probability of their dropping out of school would decrease by more than fifty percent (p. 250).

20. Economists David Cutler and Edward Glaeser have recently estimated that reducing housing segregation by only thirteen percent would eliminate fully a third of the differences in economic outcomes between blacks and whites (David M. Cutler & Edward L. Glaeser, Are ghettos good or bad?, *Quarterly Journal of Economics*, 1997, 827–872).

21. See Massey & Denton, pp. 209–212.

22. As will be clear in Chapter Twelve, this does not mean that discrimination in employment has been eliminated, only that there has been greater success in reducing it than in the realm of housing.

23. Enforcement of antidiscrimination statutes, of course, also does not address the significant differences in income between blacks and whites. Notwithstanding the evidence cited above that income alone does not account for the degree of separation we experience, income differentials no doubt remain one significant contributor. Many blacks simply *cannot afford* to live in the neighborhoods where whites live.

24. Increased contact between groups can have the result of reducing or exacerbating stereotypes and prejudices. Substantial research on what has been called the "contact hypothesis"—the idea that contact between members of groups who have a history of hostility or prejudice with regard to each other can help to reduce those prejudices—has found that a number of conditions increase the likelihood of a positive result. Among those are a shared stake in a common outcome, more or less equal status of the individuals interacting, and contact that is pleasant and rewarding rather than involuntary and tense. See, for example, Y. Amir, Contact hypothesis in ethnic relations, *Psychological Bulletin*, 1969, 71, 319–342; Norman Miller & Marilynn B. Brewer (Eds.), *Groups in Contact: The Psychology of Desegregation*, Orlando, FL: Academic Press, 1984; M. Hewstone & R. Brown (Eds.), *Contact and Conflict in Intergroup Relations*, Oxford, England: Basil Blackwell, 1986; Mary R. Jackman & Marie Crane, "Some of my best friends are Black . . .": Interracial friendship and whites' racial attitudes, *Public Opinion Quarterly*, 1986, 50, 459–486; Lee Sigelman & Susan Welch, The contact hypothesis revisited: Black-white interaction and positive racial attitudes, *Social Forces*, 1993, 71, 781–795; Christopher G. Ellison & Daniel A. Powers, The Contact Hypothesis and Racial Attitudes Among Black Americans, *Social Science Quarterly*, 1994, 75, 387–400.

25. Magnet schools have been criticized as a subterfuge for providing enriched facilities to the well-off in the guise of providing wider opportunities for all. Whether in schools or in housing, care must be taken to set up such programs so that the magnets truly draw to them all poles of the community.

26. Massey & Denton, p. 226.

27. Even if not everyone who wanted a home in the new neighborhood could get one— if the project is done well, after all, there will be more people who apply than there are homes available—everyone would have an equal chance. The process of allotting homes would thus be truly "color blind," even as the aim of promoting integration in housing would be both clear and achieveable. Moreover, the lottery concept, if the homes and amenities in the area were made a very special bargain, would attract the support of a considerably larger constituency than the sheer number who would end up living there, since others in the municipality would have a stake during the construction process as "lottery" participants and *potential* residents. We have much evidence that people are willing to take a chance on lotteries even when their prospects of winning are slim; there is experienced "value," it appears, simply in being a participant who has *some* chance.

28. Jonathan Crane (The epidemic theory of ghettoes, *American Journal of Sociology*, 1991, 96, 1226–1259) has summarized research suggesting that the proportion of adults who hold positions of some responsibility is a key variable in maintaining the health and stability of a neighborhood. Thus, to assure the success of the project, both in attracting middle-class whites (who have the choice to go elsewhere, even if at higher cost with less amenities) and in maintaining the community as a well-functioning system that elicits the most prosocial side of its residents, the dominant influence in the neighborhood would have to be families where the adults work and where a reasonable percentage are people who have achieved positions of some responsibility.

It is worth noting, however, that it might well turn out that the percentage of poor people who could be integrated into such a community and still have it "work" might be substantially higher than it might first appear. Crane's research on what causes a neighborhood to go over a "tipping point," where social norms begin to deteriorate and crime and disorder begin to take over, suggests that a relatively small percentage of neighborhood residents who hold professional or managerial jobs serves to provide substantial inoculation against the spread of antisocial behavior in the neighborhood.

29. It is the poor most of all, of course, who need subsidized housing and an environment that will enable their children to escape the consequences of concentrated poverty. Magnet neighborhoods would provide concrete benefits for some families and would be a useful spur to innovation and overcoming stereotypes, but they must not be thought of as a *substitute* for enforcement of fair housing laws or for other efforts to make decent housing affordable for all families.

30. For the original work developing and assessing this approach, see, for example, N. Blaney, C. Stephan, D. Rosenfield, E. Aronson, & J. Sikes, Interdependence in the classroom: A field study, *Journal of Educational Psychology*, 1977, 69, 139–146; G. W. Lucker, D. Rosenfeld, J. Sikes, & E. Aronson, Performance in the interdependent classroom, *American Educational Research Journal*, 1976, 13, 115–123; E. Aronson & D. Bridgeman, Jigsaw groups and the desegregated classroom: In pursuit of common goals, *Personality and Social Psychology Bulletin*, 1979, 5, 438–445.

   For more recent developments and evaluations, see Elliot Aronson, Applying social psychology to desegregation and energy conservation, *Personality and Social Psychology Bulletin*, 1990, 16, 118–132; and Robert E. Slavin, *Cooperative Learning: Theory, Research and Practice*, Second Edition, Boston: Allyn & Bacon, 1995.

31. The rule would hold for all crimes of all residents, not as something specially directed at minorities or the poor. Middle-class white-collar criminals (or, for that matter, middle-class residents who commit murder, rape, assault, etc., as middle-class people also do, even if at a lower rate) would be subject to exactly the same sanctions.

32. MIT economist Paul Krugman notes that "The Earned Income Tax Credit raises incomes for many of the working poor by as much as 40 percent, at a taxpayer cost of about 0.4 percent of GDP—and most studies indicate that it not only raises incomes but encourages more people to work." (Krugman, "Superiority Complex," *The New Republic*, November 3, 1997, p. 21)

Chapter Twelve

1. See again Chapter Six in this regard.
2. Executive Order 10925, 1961. See Nicolaus Mills (Ed.), *Debating Affirmative Action*, New York: Dell, 1994, p. 5.
3. Barbara Bergmann, *In Defense of Affirmative Action*, New York: Basic Books, 1996. See expecially pp. 169–176.
4. See, for example, Susan Clayton & Faye Crosby, *Justice, Gender and Affirmative Action*, Ann Arbor: University of Michigan Press, 1992, pp. 73–78.
5. Mills, op. cit., p. 7.
6. Rainwater and Yancey, op. cit., p. 126.
7. Richard D. Kahlenberg, *The Remedy: Class, Race, and Affirmative Action*. New York: Basic Books, 1997, p. 100.
8. Hacker, *Two Nations*, p. 32.
9. See again the research of Claude Steele on stereotype anxiety discussed in Chapter Five.
10. Hacker, pp. 143–146.

11. *Bakke v. Regents of the University of California*, 1976.

12. Kahlenberg, p. 28.

13. I am grateful to Bertrand Pogrebin, one of the attorneys who devised this settlement, for calling it to my attention and providing me with a copy of the Consent Judgment.

14. This is a tactic that was widely used for a while, but has subsequently been viewed by the courts as unacceptable in most contexts.

15. See, for example, Lani Guinier, Beyond winner take all: Democracy's conversation, *The Nation*, January 23, 1995, pp. 85–88.

16. Stephen L. Carter, *Reflections of an Affirmative Action Baby*, New York: Basic Books, 1991.

17. For a discussion of why our notions of efficiency are often too narrow, and why maximizing output of goods is not necessarily a useful criterion for evaluating social policy, see my book, *The Poverty of Affluence* (New York: Free Press, 1983).

18. Kahlenberg, p. 100.

19. Indeed, as described by Richard Kahlenberg, class-based affirmative action efforts receive support even from some on the right who have been vociferous opponents of racially or ethnically based preferences. See, for example, p. 109, p. 173. William Julius Wilson (for example, in *The Declining Significance of Race, The Truly Disadvantaged*, and *When Work Disappears*) has argued more generally that programs designed to address the disadvantaged state of African Americans would receive greater support, and hence be more genuinely effective, if conceptualized in terms that provided benefits for Americans of all racial and ethnic groups. Notwithstanding the attacks Wilson's creative and clear-minded efforts have evoked, he in no way ignores the uniquely oppressive history of African Americans on these shores, but attempts to formulate policies that will actually accomplish the task of finally overcoming the results of that history.

20. Kahlenberg, p. xxvi.

21. See, in this connection, Stephan Thernstrom and Abigail Thernstrom, *America In Black and White: One Nation, Indivisible*, Cambridge, MA: 1997; Orlando Patterson, *The Ordeal of Integration*, Washington, DC: Civitas/Counterpoint, 1997; Paul M. Sniderman and Thomas Piazza, *The Scar of Race*, Cambridge, MA: Harvard University Press, 1993; and Paul M. Sniderman and Edward Carmines, *Reaching Beyond Race*, Cambridge, MA: Harvard University Press, 1997.

22. Orlando Patterson's account of progress in relations between Afro-Americans and Euro-Americans in his book, *The Ordeal of Integration*, is a good example of the kind of balanced and comprehensive vision to which I am referring.

23. See, for example, Lisbeth B. Schorr, *Within Our Reach: Breaking the Cycle of Disadvantage*, New York: Doubleday Anchor, 1988; and *Common Purpose: Strengthening Families and Neighborhoods to Rebuild America*, New York: Doubleday Anchor, 1997. See also, Jonathan Crane, *Social Programs That Work*, Sacramento, CA: Sage, in press, and a companion book edited by Crane, *Social Programs That Really Work*, Sacramento, CA: Sage, 1998.

24. See, for example, Bob Herbert, Take the A train, *New York Times*, September 27, 1996, and Men and jobs, *New York Times*, September 30, 1996; Felicia Lee, Where parents are learning to be parents, *New York Times*, March 14, 1993; and Geoffrey Canada, *Fist, Stick, Knife, Gun*, Boston: Beacon, 1997.

25. See Kay Hymowitz, Job training that works, *The Wall Street Journal*, February 18, 1997; "Urban league, STRIVE to train youth for jobs, *New York Amsterdam News*, July 4, 1992; Taylor Batten, Work program strives for change, *Boston Globe*, August 20, 1994; and Project STRIVE, *Model Program Briefs*, Drug Control Policy Group, United States Department of Housing and Urban Development.

26. See, for example, Joe Klein, In God they trust: Washington faces a new challenge: Should it let the churches take over the inner cities?, *The New Yorker*, June 16, 1997, pp. 40–48.

27. See my book, *The Poverty of Affluence* (New York: Free Press, 1983).

28. In 1992 dollars, the figures are $10,292 for 1965 and $19,158 for 1996, the most current year for which the numbers are presently available (*Statistical Abstract of the United States 1997*, Washington, DC: U.S. Dept. of Commerce, Bureau of the Census, p. 452).

29. *Statistical Abstract of the United States*. Figures are for 1963 and 1993.

30. *Statistical Abstract*, 1997.

31. It is important to note that the fruits of this enormous growth in our Gross National Product have not accrued equally to all segments of the population. The relative percentage of wealth and income going to the upper fifth, and especially the upper one or two percent, have increased very substantailly, while that going to those at the bottom of the distribution has declined. Despite the enormous increase in overall production, real wages for working men and women have scarcely changed over several decades. This maldistribution is a serious problem, and it is part of the reason there is so much opposition to taxes or programs to aid the most disadvantaged. What should be clear, however, from the figures I have cited is that the problem is not a result of "hard times" economically or of an absence of economic growth. The growth has been enormous, but inequitable. More reliance on the market rather than on social spending and government regulation—the currently most fashionable solution to the sense of deprivation that persists in the face of a magnitude of production so enormous it threatens the very ecology that sustains life on our planet—will not bring the desired sense of affluence. Such a course takes us, rather, further along the path that has generated sour discontent even as our stocks of goods keep doubling. See *The Poverty of Affluence* for a detailed discussion of why this is the case.

Chapter Thirteen

1. See, for example, R. McKey, L. Condelli, H. Ganson, B. Barrett, C. McConkey, & M. Plantz, *The Impact of Head Start on Children, Families, and Communities*, Washington, DC: U.S. Govt. Printing Office, 1985; V. Lee, J. Brooks-Gunn, & E. Schnur, Does Head Start work?: A one-year follow-up comparison of disadvantaged children attending Head Start, no preschool, and other preschool programs, *Developmental Psychology*, 1988, 24, 210–222; J. Currie & D. Thomas, Does Head Start make a difference?, *American Economic Review*, 1995, 85, 341–364.

2. See Chapter Five for a discussion of why IQ scores are a misleading criterion for judging the effects of intervention programs.

3. R. McKey et al, op. cit.; T. Gamble, & E. Zigler, The Head Start Synthesis project: A critique, *Journal of Applied Developmental Psychology*, 1989, 10, 267–274; L. Schweinhart, & D. Weikart, What do we know so far? A review of the Head Start

Synthesis Project, *Young Children*, 1986, 41, 49–55; V. Lee, J. Brooks-Gunn, J. Schnur, & F. Liaw, Are Head Start effects sustained?: A longitudinal follow-up comparison of disadvantaged children attending Head Start, no preschool, and other preschool programs, *Child Development*, 1990, 61, 495–507.

4. Lawrence J. Schweinhart and David P. Weikart, High/Scope perry preschool programs at age 27, in J. Crane (Ed.), *Social Programs That Really Work*, Sacramento, CA: Sage, in press. For discussion of research documenting other successful early intervention programs as well, along with further consideration of the factors that lead to results being more or less enduring and substantial, see Craig T. Ramey & Sharon Landesman Ramey, Early intervention and early experience, *American Psychologist*, 1998, 53, 109–120.

5. See, for example, William Celism, III, Study suggests Head Start helps beyond school, *New York Times*, April 20, 1993, A23.

6. There are some who might contend that such a conclusion makes sense in principle, but that we simply cannot afford such an investment. I have discussed this issue in the previous chapter.

7. It should be noted, however, that Head Start does make some useful contribution to changing the children's environment more permanently, in that it often provides employment opportunities for the *parents* of the Head Start youngsters. This is an important positive feature of well-conducted Head Start programs, and is consistent with the more integrated, multifaceted approach to breaking the cycle of inequity and deprivation that is advocated in this chapter.

8. See, for example, Edward Zigler and Susan Muenchow, *Head Start: The Inside Story of America's Most Successful Educational Experiment*, New York: Basic Books, 1992.

9. Project Follow Through, designed as its name implies to follow through on the gains attained by Head Start, never received anywhere near the level of funding that Head Start did; the once-and-for-all "magic bullet" fantasy prevailed. Thus, as the children grew older and encountered the full panoply of forces set loose in neighborhoods of despair, there was little to sustain them. For details on the limited funding for Project Follow Through, see Carol Doernberger & Edward Zigler, Project Follow Through: Intent and reality, in Edward Zigler & Sally J. Styfco (Eds.), *Head Start and Beyond*, New Haven: Yale University Press, 1993, pp. 43–72. For a discussion of the circumstances Head Start graduates encounter after their participation is terminated, and of the role those circumstances play in the dwindling of the gains achieved, see V. Lee and S. Loeb, Where do Head Start attendees end up? One reason why preschool effects fade out, *Educational Evaluation and Policy Analysis*, 1995, 17, 62–82.

10. See, for example, Ramey & Ramey, op. cit.; F. A. Campbell & C. T. Ramey, Cognitive and school outcomes for high-risk students at middle adolescence: Positive effects of early intervention, *American Educational Research Journal*, 1995, 32, 743–772; J. Royce, R. Darlington, & H. Murray, Pooled analyses: Findings across studies, in consortium for longitudinal studies, *As the Twig Is Bent: Lasting Effects of Preschool Programs*, Hillsdale, NJ: Erlbaum, 1983, pp. 411–459.

11. The enduring changes achieved in the Perry program do not necessarily imply that the ongoing environmental contingencies are unimportant. It is very likely that what occurred is that the changes were of sufficient magnitude that the participating children elicited different responses from teachers and others (at least at school) than their nonparticipating peers, essentially creating a different later environment

for them than for the control group. Psychological development is characterized by complex, interactive feedback loops, and at times small changes can have large consequences. See in this connection, Ramey & Ramey, op. cit., pp. 118–119.

12. Jonathan Kozol, *Savage Inequalities: Children in America's Schools*, New York: Crown, 1991.

13. *New York Times*, December 10, 1988.

14. Kozol, op. cit., p. 198.

15. Ibid., p. 57. Inflation has no doubt changed somewhat the figures Kozol cites here, but not the essential reality he describes.

16. Ibid., pp. 58–59.

17. See Kozol, pp. 133–134.

18. See, for example, James Comer, et al, *Rallying the Whole Village: The Comer Process for Reforming Education*, New York: Teachers College Press, 1996.

19. Robert Rosenthal and Lenore Jacobson, *Pygmalion in the Classroom*, New York: Holt, Rinehart and Winston, 1968. See also, 1992 revised and enlarged edition, New York: Irvington Press.

20. See, for example, T. X. Barber & M. Silver, Fact, fiction, and the experimenter bias effect, *Psychological Bulletin Monograph Supplement*, 70, No. 6, part 2, 1968, 1–29; J. Elashoff & R. Snow *Pygmalion Reconsidered*, Belmont, CA: Wadsworth, 1971; R. Thorndike, review of *Pygmalion in the Classroom*, *American Educational Research Journal*, 1968, 82, 637–645; S. Wineburg, The self-fulfillment of the self-fulfilling prophecy, *Educational Researcher*, 1987, 16, 28–44; J. Brophy, Teacher-student interaction, in J. Dusek (Ed.), *Teacher Expectancies*, Hillsdale, NJ: Erlbaum, 1985, pp. 303–328; J. Brophy, Research on the self-fulfilling prophecy and teacher expectations, *Journal of Educational Psychology*, 1983, 75, 631–661. But see also, Elisha Babad, "Pygmalion—25 years after interpersonal expectation in the classroom, in Peter D. Blanck (Ed.), *Interpersonal Expectations: Theory, Research, and Applications*, New York: Cambridge University Press, pp. 125–153, as well as references cited in the following note.

21. See, for example, Robert Rosenthal & Donald. B. Rubin, Interpersonal expectancy effects: The first 345 studies, *The Behavioral and Brain Sciences*, 1978, 3, 377–386; R. Rosenthal, From unconscious experimenter bias to teacher expectancy effects, in J. Dusek (Ed.), *Teacher Expectancies*, Hillsdale, NJ: Erlbaum, 1985, pp. 37–65; M. Smith, Teacher expectations, *Evaluation in Education*, 1980, 4, 53–55; M. Harris and R. Rosenthal, Mediation of interpersonal expectancy effects: 31 Meta-analyses, *Psychological Bulletin*, 1985, 97, 363–386; M. Harris, Personality moderators of interpersonal expectancy effects: Replication of Harris and Rosenthal, *Journal of Research in Personality*, 1989, 23, 381–397.

22. See R. M. Baron, D. Y. Tom, and H. M. Cooper, Social class, race, and teacher expectations, in J. B. Dusek (Ed.), *Teacher Expectancies*, Hillsdale, NJ: Erlbaum, 1985, pp. 251–269; Marylee C. Taylor, Expectancies and the perpetuation of racial inequity, in P. Blanck (Ed.), *Interpersonal Expectations: Theory, Research, and Applications*, New York: Cambridge University Press, 1992, pp. 88–124.

23. I put it in this way, rather than "experiences the teacher has had with children from the same racial or ethnic group," because there is really no *logical* reason to assume that race or ethnicity are the basis for forming expectations. One could as readily shape one's expectations by whether the child is a girl or a boy (and teachers, of course, often do); by whether the child comes from a single-parent family or a two-

parent family; by whether the child's parents are academics, corporate executives, carpenters, or janitors; even by whether the child is tall or short, loud or quiet, shy or outgoing. Any of these (or other) dimensions could be the basis for expecting the child to perform in the manner others "like him" have performed. But in our society, there is much reason to think that one of the most salient dimensions along which teachers generalize from past experiences with children of "the same group" is that of race.

24. For a good summary of the arguments related to how realistic teachers' expectations are, see Lee Jussim, Jacquelynne Eccles, & Stephanie Madon, Social perception, social stereotypes, and teacher expectations: Accuracy and the quest for the powerful self-fulfilling prophecy, in Mark P. Zanna (Ed.), *Advances in Experimental Social Psychology*, Vol. 28, San Diego, CA: Academic Press, 1996, pp. 281–388.

25. Regarding disidentification with school, see again the discussion in Chapter Five of the work of Claude Steele and of John Ogbu.

26. See, for example, Jussim, Eccles, & Madon, 1996, pp. 302–314.

27. Measures of teacher expectation alone, studied in isolation from all the other factors that can impede the intellectual development of inner-city children account for only a small part of the observed differences in grades and test performance (see Jussim, Eccles, & Madon). They are but one part of an interlocking *set* of influences. But they are a part, nonetheless, and in contributing to the maintenance of all the other contributing factors, they are part of the glue that holds the whole pattern together.

28. For a review of the prevalence and impact of the range of influences just noted, see Vonnie C. McLoyd, Socioeconomic disadvantage and child development, *American Psychologist*, 1998, 53, 185–204; and G. Duncan and J. Brooks-Gunn, *The Consequences of Growing Up Poor*, New York: Russell Sage Foundation, 1997.

29. See, for example, Laurence Steinberg, op. cit.; Osborne, op. cit.; Ogbu, op. cit.

30. See Betty Hart and Todd Risley, American parenting of language-learning children: Persisting differences in family-child interactions observed in natural home environments, *Developmental Psychology*, 1992, 28, 1096–1105; Dale Walker, Charles Greenwood, Betty Hart, and Judith Carter, Prediction of school outcomes based on early language production and socioeconomic factors, *Child Development*, 1994, 65, 606–621; Betty Hart and Todd Risley, *Meaningful Differences in the Everyday Experience of Young American Children*, Baltimore, MD: Paul H. Brookes, 1995.

31. Sandra Blakeslee, Studies show talking with infants shapes basis of ability to think, *New York Times*, April 17, 1997, p. D21.

32. Jerome Kagan, Resilience and continuity in psychological development, in A. M. Clarke & A. D. B. Clarke (Eds.), *Early Experience: Myth and Evidence*, New York: Free Press, 1976, pp. 97–121; J. Kagan,& R. E. Klein, Cross-cultural perspective on early development, *American Psychologist*, 1973, 28, 947–961.

Chapter Fourteen

1. In a New Jersey court case challenging the enormous disparities in funding between rich and poor districts in the state, the lawyers *defending* the disparities used this very phrase, contending that the children in the poorer districts "simply cannot now benefit from the kind of vastly superior course offerings found in the richer districts." See Kozol, op. cit., p. 170.

2. Vonnie C. McLoyd, The impact of economic hardship on black families and chil-

dren: Psychological distress, parenting, and socioemotional development, *Child Development*, 1990, 61, 311–346.

3. Schorr, *Within Our Reach.* See also Ramey & Ramey, op. cit., pp. 116–117.

4. See, for example, James Comer, et al, *Rallying the Whole Village: The Comer Process for Reforming Education*, New York: Teachers College Press, 1996; and Deborah Meier, *The Power of Their Ideas: Lessons for America from a Small School in Harlem*, Boston: Beacon, 1995.

5. See, for example, Jonathan Crane, The epidemic theory of ghettos, *American Journal of Sociology*, 1991, 96, 1226–1259.

6. Jonathan Crane, The epidemic theory of ghettoes and its policy implications, *Policy Forum*, 1992, Vol. 5, No. 3; Optimal resource allocation policies for reducing the incidence of contagious social problems, *Journal of Socioeconomics*, 1996, 25, 245–269.

7. See Malcolm Gladwell, The tipping point, *The New Yorker*, June 3, 1996, pp. 32–38.

8. Jennifer L. Hochschild, *Facing Up to the American Dream: Race, Class, and the Soul of the Nation*, Princeton, NJ: Princeton University Press, 1995. See also Ellis Cose (*The Rage of a Privileged Class*, pp. 6–8).

9. See, for example, Orlando Patterson, *The Ordeal of Integration*, Washington, DC: Civitas/Counterpoint, 1997, especially pages 68–77; Ashley Montagu, *The Concept of Race*, New York: Free Press, 1964; M. Mead, T. Dobzhansky, E. Tobach, and R. Light, *Science and the Concept of Race*, New York: Columbia University Press, 1968; Marvin Harris, *Our Kind*, New York: Harper, 1989; Jared Diamond, Race Without Color, *Discover*, November 1994; Pat Shipman, *The Evolution of Racism: Human Differences and the Use and Abuse of Science*, New York: Simon & Schuster, 1994.

10. Patterson, op. cit.

Index